Avenues

Alfredo Schifini
Deborah J. Short
Josefina Villamil Tinajero

Erminda García
Eugene E. García
Else Hamayan
Lada Kratky

HAMPTON-BROWN

Grades 3–5 Curriculum Reviewers

Fran Alcántara
Bilingual Support Teacher
Cicero Public Schools District 99
Cicero, Illinois

Santina Y. Buffone, Ed.D.
Coordinator
Bilingual/Compensatory Education
Dearborn Public Schools
Dearborn, Michigan

Anastasia Colón
Bilingual Teacher
Buhrer Elementary
Cleveland Municipal School District
Cleveland, Ohio

Kelley E. Crockett
Team Leader, Language Center
Meadowbrook Elementar
Fort Worth Independent School
   District
Fort Worth, Texas

Marian Evans
Teacher
Ault Elementary
Cypress-Fairbanks Independent
   School District
Houston, Texas

David Garcia
Bilingual/ESL Teacher
Winston Elementary
Edgewood Independent School
   District
San Antonio, Texas

Sue Goldstein
*Bilingual Education Coordinator
   and Program Teacher*
Regional Multicultural Magnet School
New London, Connecticut

Sandra Guerra
Assistant Principal
Chapa Elementary
La Joya Independent School District
La Joya, Texas

Ruth Henrichs
ESL Teacher
Fleetwood Elementary
East Ramapo Central School District
Spring Valley, New York

Linda Hoste, M.Ed.
ESL Specialist
Birdville Independent School District
Fort Worth, Texas

Virginia Jama
ESL Coordinator, K–12
New York City Board of Education
Brooklyn, New York

Liliana Jaurrieta
Teacher
Lujan-Chavez Elementary
Socorro Independent School District
El Paso, Texas

Clara Levy
Teacher
Mesita Elementary
El Paso Independent School District
El Paso, Texas

Dr. Mark R. O'Shea
Professor of Education
Institute for Field-Based Teacher
   Education
California State University,
   Monterey Bay
Monterey, California

Lily Pham Dam
Former Administrator
Dallas Independent School District
Dallas, Texas

Raul Ramirez, Jr.
Bilingual/GT Teacher
Royalgate Elementary
South San Antonio
   Independent School District
San Antonio, Texas

Christa A. Wallis
*Elementary Program Specialist
   English Learners*
San Bernardino City Unified School
   District
San Bernardino, California

Acknowledgments

Every effort has been made to secure permission, but if any omissions have been made, please let us know. We gratefully acknowledge the following permissions:

Cover Design and Art Direction: Pronk&Associates.

Cover Illustration: David Diaz.

Cincinnati Arts Museum: *"A Picture of Freedom"* cover for Detail from the Underground Railroad (#3 request). Courtesy of the Cincinnati Arts Museum, Subscription Fund Purchase.

Acknowledgments continue on page 508.

Hampton-Brown
P.O. Box 223220
Carmel, California 93922
800-333-3510
www.hampton-brown.com

Printed in the United States of America

ISBN 0-7362-1745-2

03 04 05 06 07 08 09 10 11 12 9 8 7 6 5 4 3 2 1

Avenues Go Everywhere

Unit 2

EARTH
THE INSIDE STORY

Science
- Earth's History
- Earth Systems

Unit 5

Social Studies
□ Landforms
Science
□ Earth Systems

Nonfiction
Geography Article

Greetings from America **260**
by Elizabeth C. Sengel

Fiction
Tall Tale

The Bunyans **286**
by Audrey Wood

Unit 6

It's Electrifying!

Going Places
with Patricia McKissack

Social Studies
☐ Civil Rights Era

FAMILY ALBUM

Make a Family Collage

1. Draw a picture of your family.
2. Add colors, patterns, and other things that remind you of your family.
3. Tell about your family collage.

Social Studies Words

Generations

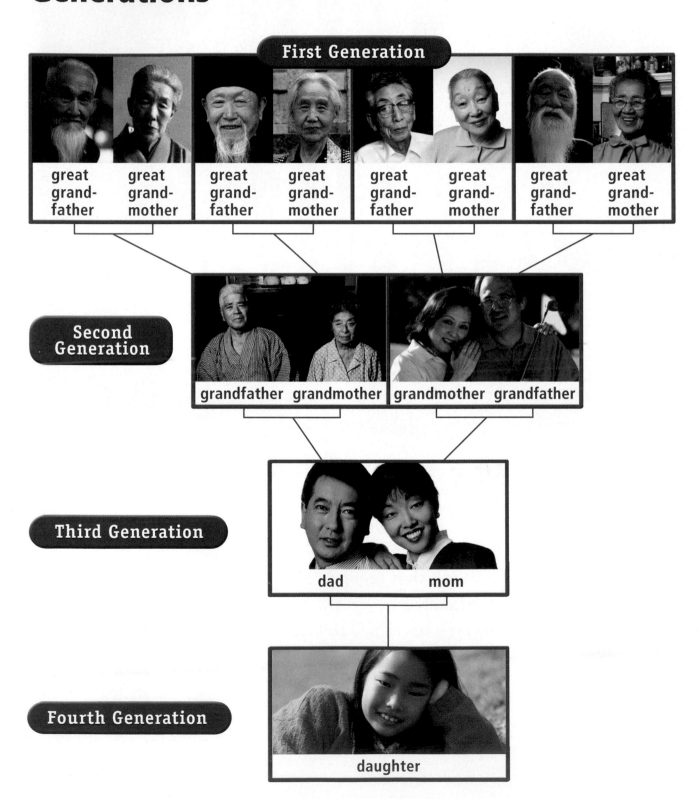

First Generation

great grand-father   great grand-mother   great grand-father   great grand-mother   great grand-father   great grand-mother   great grand-father   great grand-mother

Second Generation

grandfather   grandmother   grandmother   grandfather

Third Generation

dad   mom

Fourth Generation

daughter

What Ancestors Pass Down

Traditions

▲ Japanese Tea Ceremony

▲ Hanukkah Celebration

Values

▲ hard work

▲ education

Traits

▲ eye color

▲ hair color

Talents

▲ art

▲ music

Vocabulary

CARIBBEAN BAND

I have some **records**

That my grandpa loved to **play**.

I found them in the

cellar **packed** away.

I love the **album**

with the Caribbean **band**.

You can feel the sun,

the ocean, and the sand.

The music makes me

want to dance.

It **captures** the warmth

of this land.

—*Maria Del Rey*

Tune: "El manisero" (The Peanut Vendor)

16

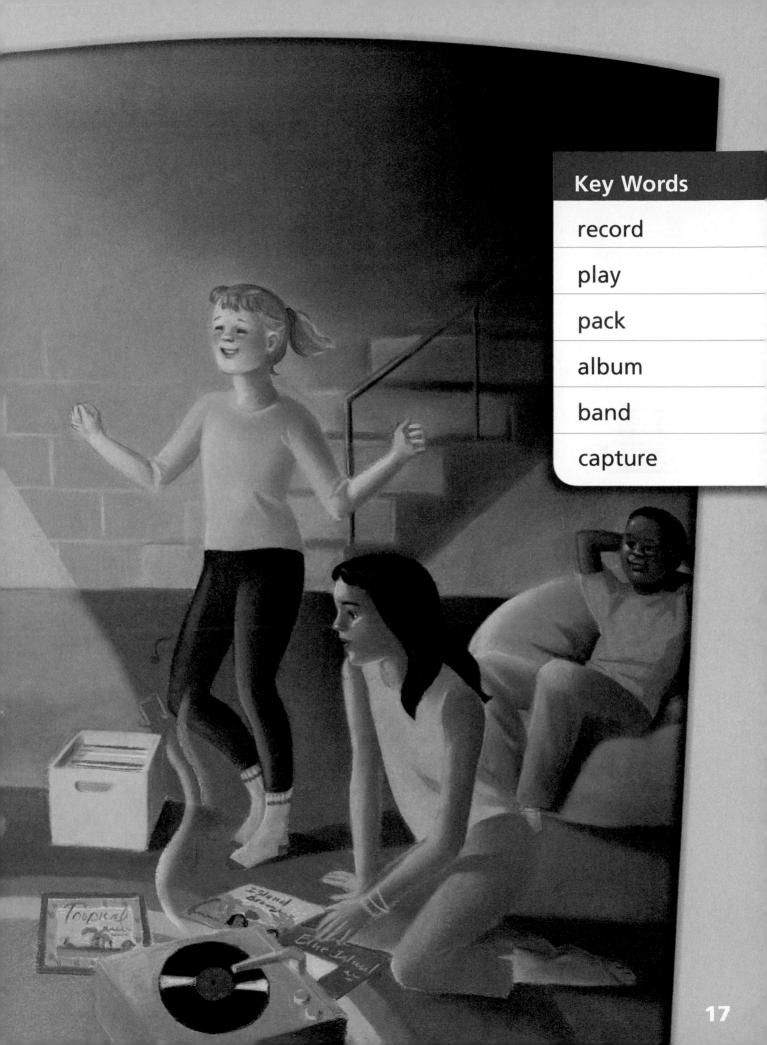

Grandma's Records

by Eric Velasquez

Read a Story

Genre

A **realistic fiction** story tells about characters who could be real and events that could really happen. This story tells about a boy and what he learns from his grandmother.

Characters

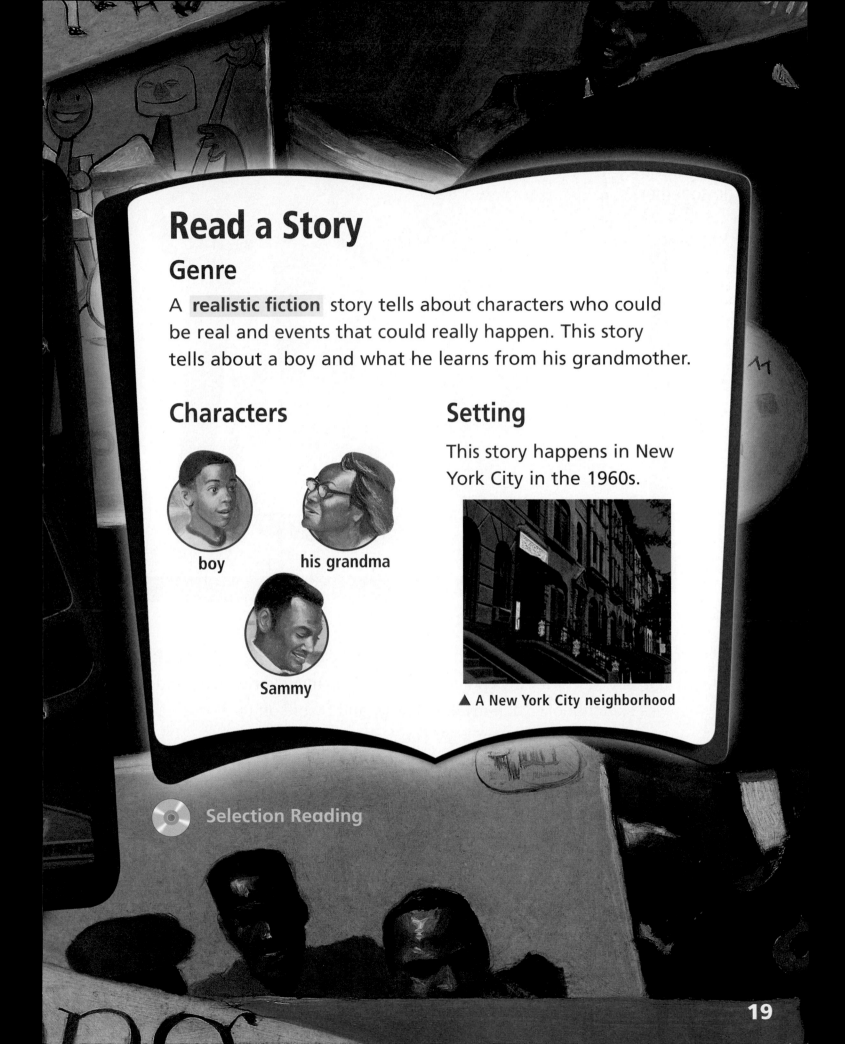

boy

his grandma

Sammy

Setting

This story happens in New York City in the 1960s.

▲ A New York City neighborhood

Selection Reading

A boy lives with his grandma each summer. What will they do together?

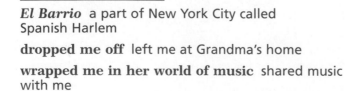

Every year, right after the last day of school, I'd **pack** a suitcase with my cool summer clothes, my favorite toys, and a sketchbook. Then my dog, Daisy, and I were off to Grandma's apartment in *El Barrio*. Because my parents worked, Grandma's apartment was my summer home.

From the time my parents **dropped me off**, until the day they picked me up, Grandma **wrapped me in her world of music**.

El Barrio a part of New York City called Spanish Harlem

dropped me off left me at Grandma's home

wrapped me in her world of music shared music with me

Sometimes when she **played** a **record**, we would dance together. Other times, she would dance alone and tell me her stories about growing up **in Puerto Rico**.

When Grandma played a **merengue** from the Dominican Republic, her hips would sway from side to side. As her favorite **salsa** record played, she'd say, "Just listen to that conga," while she played an imaginary drum.

Grandma liked all types of music. But one record was very special to her. Whenever she played it, she would put her hand over her heart and close her eyes as she sang along. When it was over, Grandma would sometimes sit quietly, thinking about Grandpa and the old days in Santurce, her hometown.

---

in Puerto Rico on an island in the Caribbean Sea
merengue kind of dance music
salsa Caribbean music

"Sometimes," Grandma said, "a song can say everything that **is in your heart** as if it were written just for you."

My favorite days were the ones when Grandma would tell me, "You pick the records today." No matter what I would choose, Grandma would always say, "*Siempre me gusta tu selección.*" (I always like your selection.)

Sometimes I would **sneak in** Grandma's special song just to watch her put her hand over her heart and sing.

Then she'd always ask, "*¿Cómo tú sabes?*" (How did you know?)

―――――――――

is in your heart you feel
sneak in surprise Grandma and play

If it was too hot to go outside, I'd spend hours looking through all of Grandma's **album** covers. I'd pick out my favorites and make sketches of the art. As I drew, I could see the **record covers coming to life** and the **bands performing** right there in Grandma's living room.

---

record covers coming to life characters on the covers moving as if they were alive

bands performing bands playing music

Before You Move On

1. **Conclusion** How does the boy feel about visits to Grandma? How do you know?

2. **Motive** Why does Grandma want her grandson to listen to her records?

23

2

Find out what happens when Grandma's nephew comes to visit.

Grandma never went to any **nightclubs** to see her favorite bands perform. She was happy just to stay home with me and listen to her scratchy records. But Santurce was home to hundreds of musicians, and she knew a lot of the people who played on the records.

Grandma's nephew Sammy played **percussion** in Rafael Cortijo's band, the best band in Puerto Rico. One day when the band was **in town**, Sammy brought over Cortijo and the band's lead singer, Ismael Rivera, for a surprise visit.

---

nightclubs places open at night for music and dancing

percussion the drums

in town in New York City

Home-cooked meals were **hard to come by on the road**, and they couldn't pass up the chance to taste Grandma's famous *arroz con gandules* (rice and pigeon peas).

While eating dessert, Sammy had another surprise for Grandma: two tickets to the band's first New York concert, and their brand-new record, which wasn't even in the stores yet. I raced over to the record player, **thrilled** to be the first New Yorker to hear their **latest** music.

The next day, Grandma and I spent all day shopping for clothes to wear to the show.

She even made me get a haircut.

---

hard to come by on the road not easy to get when they were traveling

thrilled happy, excited

latest newest

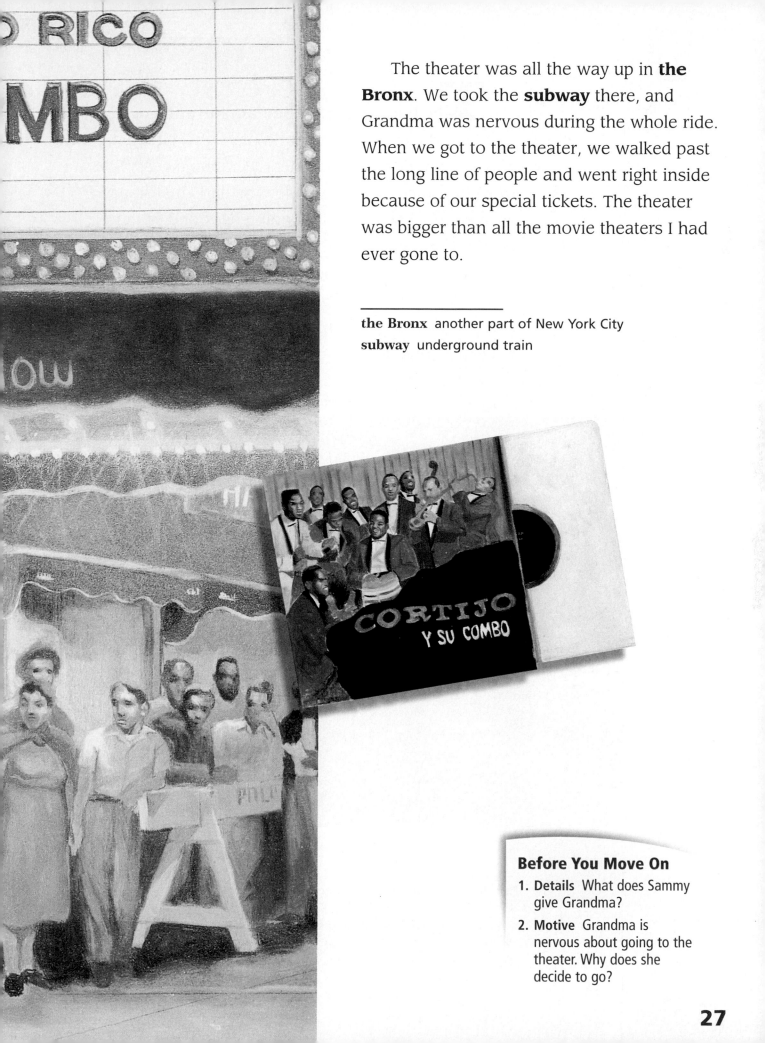

The theater was all the way up in **the Bronx**. We took the **subway** there, and Grandma was nervous during the whole ride. When we got to the theater, we walked past the long line of people and went right inside because of our special tickets. The theater was bigger than all the movie theaters I had ever gone to.

―――――――――

the Bronx another part of New York City
subway underground train

Before You Move On

1. **Details** What does Sammy give Grandma?

2. **Motive** Grandma is nervous about going to the theater. Why does she decide to go?

27

3

Find out what happens at the concert.

The band **made a spectacular entrance**. Suddenly the theater went dark, tiny lights glittered, and a loud **siren** filled the air. I heard Grandma gasp. She thought something was wrong. The darkened stage seemed to fill with people running back and forth **in confusion**. Next, everything went dark again, and a loud and steady conga beat began BOOM BAK BOOM BAK BOOM BAK. Then the lights came on with a loud BOOM, and the band began to play the song *"El Bombón de Elena"* ("Elena's Candy").

---

made a spectacular entrance came onto the stage in a very exciting way

siren sound like the warning sound from a police car

in confusion as if they didn't know what they were doing

Grandma and I were surprised at how different the music **sounded live**. The musicians made familiar songs sound **fresh** by adding new musical phrases and words.

Before the last song began, Ismael said, "This one goes out to Carmen," and he pointed to Grandma as he sang her special song. I looked at her as she put her hand over her heart, raised the other hand, closed her eyes, and began to sing along. Ismael was singing to my grandma! Then I looked around and **realized** that everyone in the theater had their hands over their hearts, too.

---

sounded live seemed when you could hear it in person

fresh new and different

realized saw

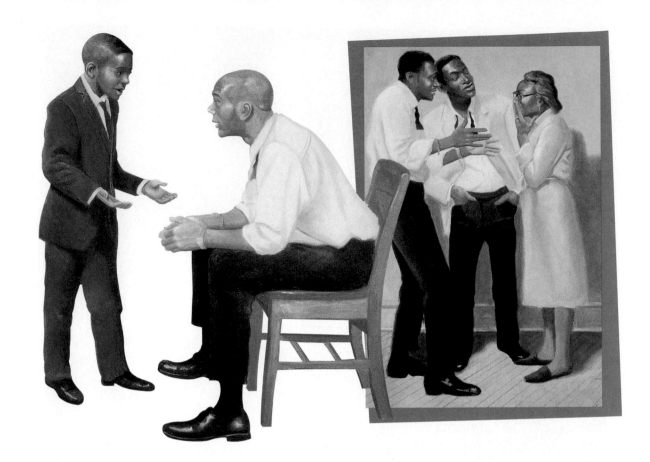

After the show we went **backstage**. I asked Ismael how he knew about Grandma's song. He explained that the song was about coming to a new country and having to leave those you love behind. People put their hands over their hearts to show that **their hearts remain in Puerto Rico** even though they may be far away. Now I understood why Grandma's song was special to so many people.

Over the next days and weeks, Grandma and I put on our own shows **imitating** Cortijo's band. Grandma wished such a special night had been **captured** in a recording so that she could listen to it again and again. Even then I knew that a concert is so special because it leaves you with the memory of a **magical moment in time**.

---

backstage behind the stage

their hearts remain in Puerto Rico they still love Puerto Rico and the people there

imitating acting like we were

magical moment in time special time that you'll never forget

As I got older, I started bringing over my records to play for Grandma. I brought Brazilian music, **jazz**, even **rap**. She loved listening to it all.

Even now, when I'm playing CDs in my studio, I imagine I'm back in Grandma's living room and she turns to me and says, "You be the **DJ** today. *Siempre me gusta tu selección.*" (I always like your selection.) And as I work, Grandma's special song surrounds me.

---

jazz a kind of American music
rap music with people talking to the rhythm
DJ disc jockey; person who plays recorded music

Before You Move On

1. **Details** What does the boy discover about Grandma's song?

2. **Motive** What does the boy do when he gets older? Why?

Grandma's Special Song

"In My Old San Juan"

original Spanish version by Noel Estrada

In my old San Juan I grew up with so many dreams.
My first **illusion and anxieties** about love
Are all **soulful memories**.
One evening I left for this foreign land.
It was **destiny's will**,
But my heart remained by the seashore of my old San Juan.

Chorus

Good-bye, beloved Borinquen.
Good-bye my pearl of the sea.

I'm leaving, but someday I will return, to look for my love,
To dream once again, in my old San Juan.

But time passed, and **destiny eased my homesickness**;
And I could not return to the San Juan that I loved,
Little piece of my native land.
My hair has turned white as **my life slowly fades**.
Death seems to call, and I don't want to die
Separated from you, Puerto Rico of my soul.

Chorus

---

illusion and anxieties dreams and fears

soulful memories memories that mean a lot to me

destiny's will something I had to do

destiny eased my homesickness I got busy and missed San Juan less

my life slowly fades I get old

Meet the Author and Illustrator

Eric Velasquez

Eric Velasquez grew up in a neighborhood in New York City where many Puerto Rican families live. As he worked on his art, he listened to all kinds of music. "I have always felt a strong connection between the art I create and the music that I listen to," says Mr. Velasquez.

Grandma's Records is a very personal story for Mr. Velasquez. He wanted to write a book that honored his Grandma and the musicians who were family friends. Writing *Grandma's Records* helped Mr. Velasquez better understand and rediscover his Puerto Rican heritage.

Think and Respond

Strategy: Analyze Story Elements

Make a story map for "Grandma's Records."
Show all the parts of the story.

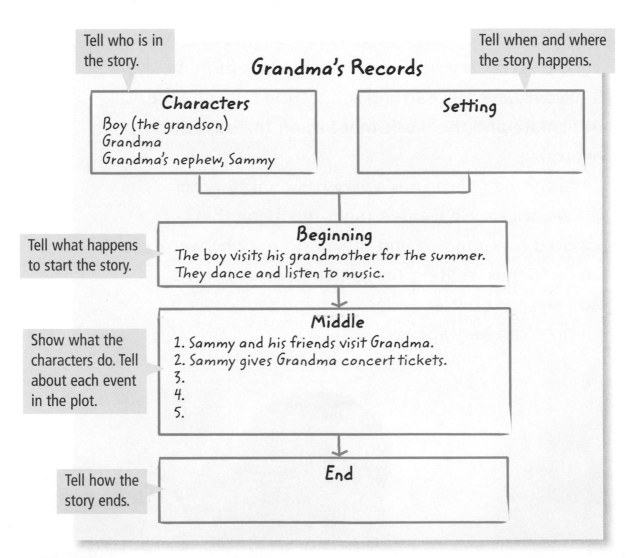

Tell who is in the story.

Grandma's Records

Tell when and where the story happens.

Characters
Boy (the grandson)
Grandma
Grandma's nephew, Sammy

Setting

Tell what happens to start the story.

Beginning
The boy visits his grandmother for the summer.
They dance and listen to music.

Show what the characters do. Tell about each event in the plot.

Middle
1. Sammy and his friends visit Grandma.
2. Sammy gives Grandma concert tickets.
3.
4.
5.

Tell how the story ends.

End

Retell the Story

Retell the story to a partner. How are your retellings
the same? How are they different? Talk about it.

Talk It Over

1 **Personal Response** Does this story make you think of music you like? Tell a friend about it.

2 **Judgment** Is music the best way to keep memories alive? Why or why not?

3 **Author's Purpose** Why do you think Eric Velasquez wrote this story?

4 **Speculate** Why do you think some people leave a place they love to come to America?

Compare Genres

Compare the story and Grandma's special song. How does each make you feel?

35

Content Connections

LISTENING/ SPEAKING

Teach a Dance

small group

What dance do you know how to do? Did you learn it from your relatives or ancestors? Teach a dance you know. Choose the music. Practice giving directions for the dance to a partner. Then teach the dance to your group.

SOCIAL STUDIES

Make an Album Cover

partners

Internet

Research one kind of music. Where does it come from? Who plays it? When? Take notes and collect examples of the music. Then make an album cover. Play the music for the class. Use your album cover to help you tell more about it.

Japanese Folk Music

Japan

samisen

A musician plays the samisen during puppet shows.

Hold a Sound Fair

small group

Our ears let us hear music and other sounds. What do you want to know about sound?

- Brainstorm topics and choose one.
- Write questions about your topic. Do research to find the answers.
- Display the facts.

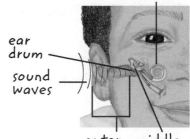

How the Ear Hears Sound

inner ear

ear drum

sound waves

outer ear

middle ear

Sound waves enter through the outer ear.

WRITING

Write to Express Your Feelings

on your own

Think about a relative or ancestor. Write something to say thank you to that person Choose a form to express your feelings:

- a letter
- a poem or song
- a story

Choose words that fit your audience.

Dear Grandfather,
Thank you for teaching me the meaning of Aikido.

Draw Conclusions

When you read and **draw conclusions**, you figure out things on your own. To draw a conclusion:

✔ Read carefully.
✔ Think about the details the author gives you.
✔ Combine the details with what you already know.

Try the strategy.

from **Grandma's Records**

Every year, right after the last day of school, I'd pack a suitcase with my cool summer clothes, my favorite toys, and a sketchbook. Then my dog, Daisy, and I were off to Grandma's apartment in *El Barrio*. Because my parents worked, Grandma's apartment was my summer home.

> I read that the narrator takes a sketchbook to Grandma's. I know that a sketchbook has drawing paper. The narrator must like to draw.

Practice

Take this test and **draw conclusions** about "Grandma's Records."

Read each item. Choose the best answer.

1 Look at the diagram.

Detail: Grandma would think about the old days in Santurce, her hometown.	+	Detail: When the band from Santurce was traveling, Grandma made them a home-cooked meal.	=	Conclusion:

What is the best conclusion you can draw?

    A   Grandma is a good cook.

    B   Grandma likes live music better than records.

    C   Grandma feels homesick for her old life in Santurce.

    D   Grandma travels to Santurce to see different bands.

2 Which detail helps you draw the conclusion that Grandma likes music with a good beat? • • • • • • •

    A   One record was very special to her.

    B   Ismael was singing to my Grandma.

    C   Grandma wrapped me in her world of music.

    D   When Grandma played a merengue, her hips would sway from side to side.

> ✔ **Test Strategy**
>
> Read parts of the article or story again. Then choose your answer.

3 At the end of the story, what conclusion can you draw about the narrator, Eric Velasquez?

    A   He lives in Brazil.

    B   He writes songs for Grandma.

    C   He like many kinds of music.

    D   He teaches in New York City.

My Family Album

This is one of my **ancestors**, great-grandfather Juan. Because he loved **adventure**, he came to America by himself when he was 16. He had a lot of **courage**.

This is my grandmother Elena. She is dancing the salsa. The dance is part of our **heritage**.

Key Words

ancestor

adventure

courage

heritage

proud

presence

comfort

trust

Here is Ana, my favorite aunt in Cuba. She is **proud** of her congrí, a rice dish she cooks. I miss her. When I look at her picture, I feel like she's here with me. I feel her **presence**.

These are my parents. They always **comfort** me when I'm sad. They'll always help me if I have a problem. I **trust** them a lot!

41

Read an Art Essay

An **art essay** is nonfiction. It uses art and text to give information.

✔ Study the **paintings** or **drawings**. They show details about a topic.

painting

✔ Read the **text** to find out more about the art and what it shows.

Selection Reading

42

WE HONOR
Our Ancestors

by **Carl Angel**, **Hung Liu**, **JoeSam.**, and **Patssi Valdez**

Set Your Purpose

Use the art and the text to find out how the artists feel about their ancestors.

IF YOU DREAM AT NIGHT OF FRESH FISH YOU'LL BE PROSPEROUS THE NEXT DAY

IF YOU HAVE LONG TOES, YOU'LL BE RICH

IF YOU KEEP DROPPING SILVERWARE, SOMEONE IS COMING TO VISIT

CLEAN YOUR PLATE SO YOUR BROTHER WILL GET MARRIED

MY MOTHER AND FATHER
Trinidad Angel and Carlos Angel
by **Carl Angel**

About the Artist

Carl Angel is a painter and illustrator. He was born in Maryland and raised in Hawaii. He now lives in Oakland, California.

My parents' stories are like hot cocoa on a cold night. They warm me up and **comfort** me. Mom tells me stories about her dreams. I remember her story of Bangus, the milkfish. If he swims into your dreams, it means good **fortune** the next day.

Dad tells me stories of real-life **adventure**. I'd imagine him as a boy during World War II **dodging** enemy bombs in the Philippines, or later on, as a sailor in the U.S. Navy, traveling to strange new places.

That's Dad in the Sun and Mom in the Moon, and me in between, riding the milkfish. The words are from my Mom's stories.

Mom's stories helped her believe in her dreams. Dad's stories helped him **trust his adventurous spirit**. Through their stories, I've grown to believe in both. When I paint, their worlds of dreams and adventure flow through me, and my own colorful story begins!

fortune luck
dodging staying away from
trust his adventurous spirit do brave things

Before You Move On
1. **Inference** Where does Carl Angel get his ideas for his paintings?
2. **Viewing** Describe your favorite part of Carl Angel's painting.

MY GRANDMOTHER
Wang Ju-shou

by **Hung Liu**

Many years ago in China, my grandmother made shoes for our family. Her shoes were very comfortable. They were cool in summer, warm in winter.

I used to love to watch my grandmother make shoes. She would gather pieces of old clothes and **used fabric**, paint them with a creamy flour paste, and then **layer them** on a flat wooden board to dry. The changing colors and patterns of the fabric were beautiful to watch. Soon, the fabric became a strong, **sturdy** sheet, and she would cut pieces of it to form the shoes. Sometimes she would even let me be her little helper!

I was amazed by every cut and snip and fold. Watching her was like watching a master artist. She made all her decisions **on the spot**. I was **proud** of my grandmother because she used faded old clothes to make colorful new shoes.

About the Artist

Hung Liu is a painter. She was born in China. She now lives in Oakland, California, where she teaches art at Mills College.

---

used fabric cloth that had been used before
layer them put the pieces on top of one another
sturdy hard to tear; firm
on the spot quickly; without thinking about them for too long

Before You Move On

1. **Steps in a Process** What steps did the grandmother follow to make shoes?

2. **Conclusion** How does Hung Liu feel about her grandmother's work?

MY THREE AUNTS
Edna, Viney, and Grace Mannings

by **JoeSam.**

About the Artist

JoeSam. is a sculptor and a painter. He was born in Harlem, New York, and now lives in San Francisco, California.

When I think about my **ancestors**, I think of the three aunts who raised me in Harlem during the 1940s. Edna, Viney, and Grace were maids who worked in the white neighborhoods of Manhattan. Originally from Trinidad, they hated the hard, gray landscape of New York City, especially during the cold winters.

My aunts **draped themselves in** the most colorful clothing they could find. Even in winter they would wear bright **turbans** or decorate their hats with colorful scraps. They brought the warmth of Africa and the West Indies to Harlem.

My aunts' bright clothing created a ring of light around them; that's why I show them against a background of deep, golden yellow. Each portrait uses a different medium: watercolor, pastel crayon, and collage. The collage above them **evokes the mood** of Africa and the Caribbean, and shows how Edna, Viney, and Grace carried their **heritage** with them wherever they went.

---

draped themselves in wore

turbans scarves on their heads

evokes the mood gives you the feeling

a sculptor an artist who makes things from material like clay, stone, or wood

Before You Move On

1. **Cause/Effect** Why did JoeSam. paint a portrait of his three aunts?

2. **Viewing** How did JoeSam. show his aunts' pride in their heritage?

MY MOTHER
Jovita Martinez
by **Patssi Valdez**

About the Artist

Patssi Valdez is a painter and a **set and costume designer** for theater, film, and television. She lives in Los Angeles, California.

Every morning I used to watch my mom get ready for her workday. I watched her put on makeup, lipstick, and her favorite **cologne**. She always made sure she looked her best. She would leave when it was still dark outside and walk to the bus stop to go to work at a big store.

We lived on Record Street in East Los Angeles. My mom worked hard to care for me and my sister. Sometimes I felt sad because she had to leave us alone. But if she hadn't gone to work, we wouldn't have had a place to live.

Years later, my mom **put herself through school** and started her own business. She gave me the **courage** to be independent, hardworking, and honest.

This is a painting of my mom's room, but I didn't put her in the picture. Instead, I painted her things and her shadow in the mirror. I wanted to show how I felt her **presence** in the room even when she wasn't there.

---

cologne perfume

put herself through school worked so she could go to school

set and costume designer person who decorates the stage and makes actors' clothing

Before You Move On
1. **Inference** Why do you think the artist chose to paint her mom's bedroom?
2. **Viewing** What does the painting tell you about the artist?

Pride

Proud of my family
proud of my language
proud of my culture
proud of my people
proud of being who I am.

—*Alma Flor Ada*

Meet the Poet

Alma Flor Ada was born in Cuba and speaks both Spanish and English. She shares her love for the two languages by publishing most of her books in both Spanish and English with help from her daughter, Rosalma.

Before You Move On

Comparison How is the poem like "We Honor Our Ancestors"?

53

Think and Respond

Strategy: Draw Conclusions

Review each art essay. How do the artists feel
about their ancestors?

✔ Think about what the artist tells you.
✔ Think about what you know.

Record your conclusions in a chart.

We Honor Our Ancestors

Artist	Ancestors	How the Artist Feels and Why
Carl Angel	mother and father	He loves his parents. Their stories make him feel good and give him ideas for his paintings.
Hung Liu		
JoeSam.		
Patssi Valdez		

Relate to Personal Experience

The artists knew what their ancestors cared about
by watching their ancestors' actions. Tell a partner
about one of your ancestors and what he or she did.
Tell what you think your ancestor cared about.

Talk It Over

1 **Personal Response** Which painting do you like best? Why?

2 **Comparison** How are the artists' descriptions of their ancestors the same? How are they different?

3 **Generalization** Why is it important to know about our ancestors?

4 **Opinion** Is a painting a good way to honor ancestors? Why or why not?

Compare Ideas

What ideas in "We Honor Our Ancestors" are the same as in "Grandma's Records"?

In both selections, a child remembers and honors a grandma.

Content Connections

Interview an Artist

large group

Invite an artist to class. What do you want to learn from the artist? Before the visit, write your questions. During the visit, ask questions if you don't understand something or if you want to know more. Remember to thank the artist for coming.

Where do you get ideas for your paintings?

MATH

2×5

Count Ancestors

partners

How many great-great-grandparents do you have? Figure it out with a partner. In your math journal, show how you got your answer. Then share your answer with a group. Did everyone get the same answer?

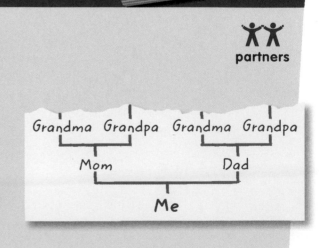

Grandma Grandpa Grandma Grandpa

Mom   Dad

Me

Experiment with Art

Internet

1. Study art styles.

2. Experiment with art materials.

3. Describe a picture. Tell how the artist uses colors, shapes, or lines to give a message.

Write a Description

Create a portrait of an ancestor you honor. Then describe the person. Tell what the person is like and what the person does that makes him or her special. Share your work with the class. Tell how you feel about the person and why.

My Great Aunt Daphne
Aunt Daphne was a nurse when she was young. She taught me which flowers and plants are used in medicines.

Subjects and Verbs

Listen and sing.

Song

MY AUNT VERA

Aunt Vera comes from Málaga.
She wears a shawl so bright.
It is red, and it is gold,
and it is quite a sight!

We are always glad
  to see her when she swishes by.
She waves her hand.
  She calls our names.
Aunt Vera, you are fine!

—Jane Zion Brauer

Tune: "Al ánimo"

How Language Works

The **verb** always goes with the **subject** of the sentence.

Action Verbs	The Verb *be*
■ Add **-s** to the verb if the subject is **he**, **she**, or **it**. Examples: He **plays** the piano. She **plays** the piano. ■ Do not add **-s** to the verb if the subject is **I**, **you**, **we**, or **they**. Examples: They **love** music. We **listen** to it all day.	■ Use **is** if the subject is **he**, **she**, or **it**. Examples: He **is** in a band. She **is** in the band, too. ■ Use **are** if the subject is **you**, **we**, or **they**. Examples: They **are** great singers. **Are** you proud of them? ■ Use **am** if the subject is **I**. Example: I **am** proud of them.

Practice with a Partner

Choose the correct verb. Say the sentences.

is / are	**1.** In my family, we _____ all artists.
paint / paints	**2.** Dad _____ with watercolors.
draw / draws	**3.** Mom _____ pictures for books.
is / are	**4.** I make collages. They _____ colorful.
is / are	**5.** My brother _____ a collage artist, too!

Put It in Writing

Think about the special things that people in your family can do. Write about them. When you edit your work, make sure each verb goes with its subject.

My brother sings in a band. He dances, too.

Show What You Know

Talk About Ancestors

In this unit, you read a story and an art essay about people's ancestors. Look back at the unit. Show a picture of the most interesting person. Tell what you like about the person.

Make a Mind Map

Work with a partner. Make a mind map to show what people can learn from their ancestors.

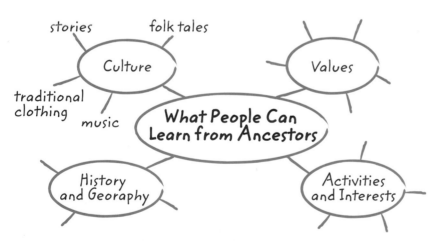

Think and Write

What would you like to write about your ancestors? Write your thoughts. Add this writing to your portfolio. Include work from this unit that shows what you learned about ancestors.

Read and Learn More

Leveled Books

An Old Family Recipe
by Refugio Paz

Ayu and the Perfect Moon
by David Cox

Theme Library

Honoring Our Ancestors
edited by Harriet Rohmer

Grandfather Counts
by Andrea Cheng

Internet

Go to: www.hbavenues.com

Art Appreciation

Sound

Ancestors

EARTH

THE INSIDE STORY

Make an Earth Model

1. Roll yellow clay into a ball the size of a round lemon.
2. First cover the ball with orange clay. Then cover it with red clay and green clay.
3. Now make the outside of the ball look like Earth.
4. Cut your model in half. Talk about the layers with a partner.

Earth's Natural Resources

Resources	Products
▲ Wind	▲ Electricity
▲ Water	▲ Electricity
▲ Coal	▲ Electricity
▲ Trees	▲ Newspaper
▲ Oil	▲ Plastics

Earth Changes

Volcanoes Erupt

▲ Mount St. Helens, May 16, 1980

▲ Mount St. Helens, September 10, 1980

Earthquakes Shake the Earth

▲ Before an earthquake

▲ After an earthquake

Vocabulary

THE QUILTING CONTEST

I have a **task**
For you to do
A piece of work
For a kid like you.

3rd Very good

Your **clever** hands,
The **stitching** they do,
Will show the **beauty**
in your **handiwork**,
The beauty in your handiwork.

—Evelyn Stone

Tune: "The Green Grass Grew All Around"

Quilting Contest Award Winners

2nd Excellent

1st Superior

Key Words

task

clever

stitching

beauty

handiwork

contest

superior

material

material

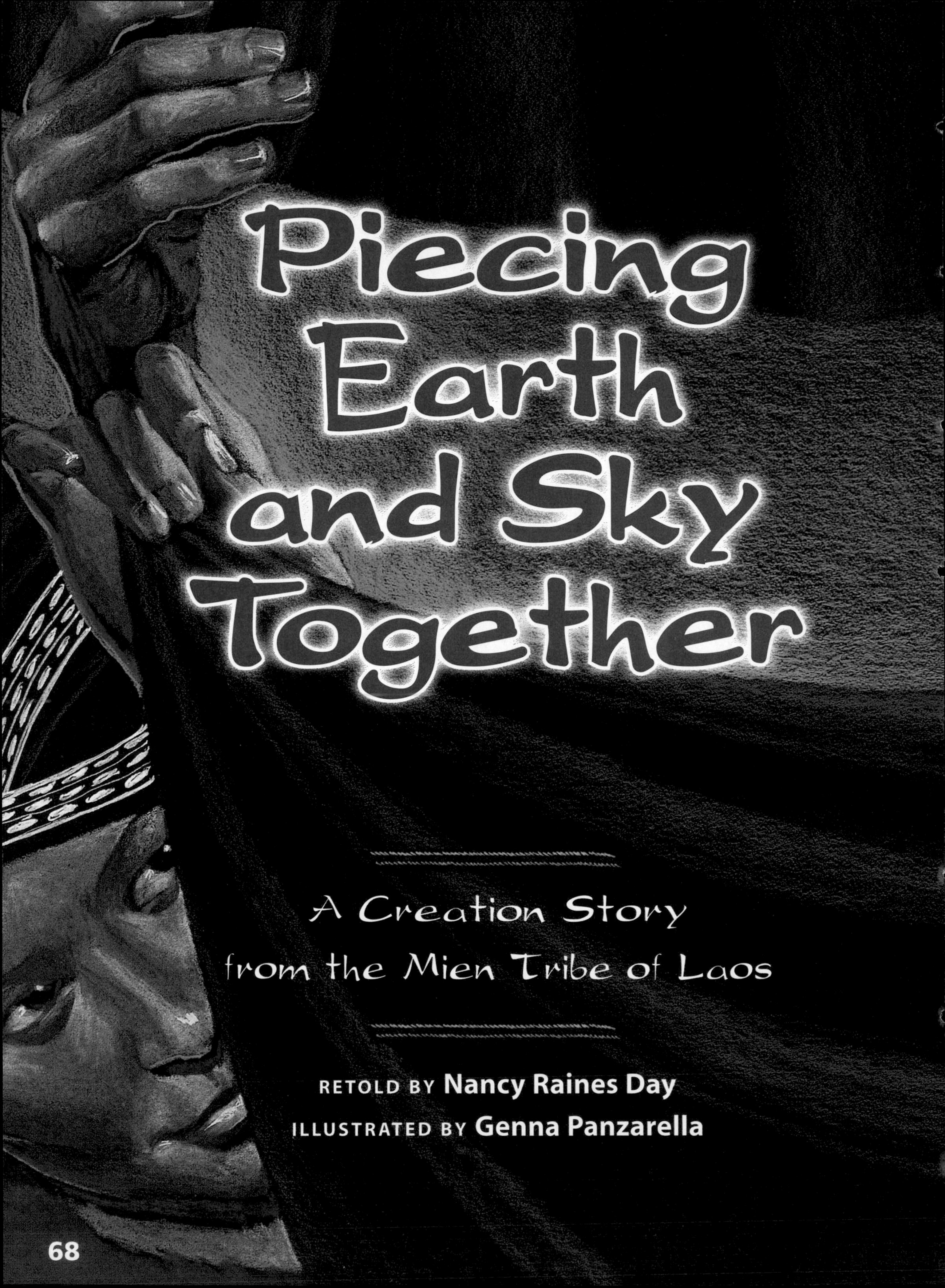

Piecing Earth and Sky Together

A Creation Story
from the Mien Tribe of Laos

RETOLD BY **Nancy Raines Day**

ILLUSTRATED BY **Genna Panzarella**

Read a Myth

Genre

A **myth** is a very old story. It often tells how something in the world came to be. This one tells how a sister and brother created the earth and sky.

Characters

Grandmother

Mei Yoon

Faam Koh

Faam Toh

Grandmother tells the myth to Mei Yoon.

The characters in the myth are Faam Koh and Faam Toh.

 Selection Reading

1

What does Grandmother want Mei Yoon to learn?

Mei Yoon **pricked** her finger with the needle. "**Embroidery** is so hard, Grandmother." She dropped her work onto her lap. "And it takes so long. I'll never learn it."

Grandmother looked up from her **stitching**. "Today is New Year's, the first day of the whole year. We must make a good beginning."

"Couldn't I start by painting words like my brothers?" Mei Yoon asked.

"Someday it will be your task to make your family's clothes beautiful in the **Mien way**," the old woman said. "The job is hard and long, but when you're finished . . ."

---

pricked hurt; made a tiny hole in

Embroidery This kind of sewing

Mien way way our people from the country of Laos do

Grandmother held up the **panel** she had just completed.

"Oh!" the girl **gasped**. "I could never make anything that fine."

"The harder you work, the better it gets." Grandmother's **wrinkled face softened**. "That reminds me of a story you might like to hear while we work."

Mei Yoon clapped her hands. "A story? What is it about?"

"A woman whose task was much bigger than yours or mine!" With that, Grandmother **switched to** her storytelling voice.

---

panel square piece of cloth

gasped said

wrinkled face softened old face looked kind and gentle

switched to began to speak with

Before You Move On

1. **Details** Why should Mei Yoon learn embroidery?

2. **Character** Does Mei Yoon like sewing? How do you know?

Find out how Koh and Toh do their work.

In the beginning, a helper from heaven named Faam Koh came down to make the sky. His sister, Faam Toh, came down to make the earth.

"My sky will be a thing of  beauty ," Koh daydreamed out loud. "I will use fine, **shimmering material** and the darkest **indigo dye**."

"My earth will be made to last," Toh **snorted**. "I will use strong material and put in many stitches, patterns, and colors."

shimmering material shiny cloth
indigo dye blue color for the cloth
snorted said

"But that's too much work," her brother pointed out. "I will finish long before you!"

"What does that matter?" the sister said. "My handiwork will be far superior to yours."

Koh **drew himself up tall**. "If this is to be a contest," he told her, "I will work **in secret**."

"I will work in secret as well," Toh said.

drew himself up tall stood up straight

in secret by myself so no one can see what I do

His back to his sister, Koh created the sky. Then he **fashioned** the moon and stars to light it by night, and the sun to light it by day. He **glanced** over his shoulder. "Do not look," he **cautioned**.

"Why would I want to?" Toh sniffed. "I am busy making the earth." **Masterfully, she blended** rock and soil into a quilt of textures.

fashioned made
glanced looked quickly
cautioned warned
Masterfully, she blended With great skill, she mixed

Soon, Koh gathered up his work. He tapped Toh's back.

"I am done," he **crowed**. "Are you?"

"The best things take time," she said. "Mine will be worth the wait."

So Koh sat down to wait. He **drummed his fingers**. He waited. He sighed. He waited some more. Finally, he lay down and fell fast asleep.

crowed said proudly
drummed his fingers tapped his fingers again and again

Before You Move On

1. **Goal** What do Koh and Toh want to do?

2. **Comparison** Who works more slowly? Why?

3

What problem do Toh and Koh have?

At long last, Toh shook his shoulder. "Wake up, brother. I am done with my work. But let me see yours first."

Koh showed off his sky.

His sister **nodded**. "Your sky <u>is</u> lovely to look at."

"Let me see your earth," Koh **urged**.

So Toh unrolled and unrolled her handiwork.

At long last After a long time; Finally
nodded moved her head up and down
urged asked

"Your work is **fine indeed**," her brother **observed**.
"It looks like a good match."

But when she held up her earth and he held up his
sky, they did not fit together.

"Your earth is too big for my sky!" Koh shouted.

"Your sky is too small for my earth!" his sister
shouted back.

fine indeed really good
observed said

"Fine, then," said Koh. "I will make the sky bigger."
While his sister held one end, he pulled and tugged
at the other with all his **might**. It stretched a little bit,
and a little bit more.

Then it tore! **Its white, fluffy stuffing** showed through the **rips**. These pieces of stuffing were the first clouds.

"Now see what you made me do!" Koh howled.

"Never mind," said his sister. "I have a plan."

Its white, fluffy stuffing The soft white part inside of the cloth

rips places in the cloth where it tore apart

Before You Move On

1. **Cause/Effect** Why don't the earth and sky fit together?

2. **Sequence** How do Koh and Toh try to fix the problem? What happens?

79

4

Find out if Toh can fit the pieces together.

80

Out of her sewing basket, Toh pulled a needle and thread. The needle flew, up and down, in and out of the earth. Then she pulled the threads, making **pleats and gathers**. She pushed **jagged** mountains and rolling hills up out of plains and tucked rushing rivers and streams into **gorges and valleys**.

pleats and gathers folds in the cloth

jagged rough and uneven

gorges and valleys narrow spaces between high, rocky areas

Beside the water, trees and vines with blossoms **sprang up**. Tigers, pigs, and other animals came to drink the water, and water bugs **skated** on top.

---

sprang up grew
skated moved smoothly

Kon gasped. "Your earth is **wondrous**, truly a work of art!" he cried.

Toh **beamed**. "Let us see if it fits your sky now," she said. The sister held up the earth, and the brother, the sky. This time, they fit together exactly right.

wondrous beautiful
beamed smiled with joy

Mei Yoon stopped her stitching and looked up with shining eyes. "I like the way Toh figured out what to do."

Grandmother nodded. "She's **clever** with her head and hands. And takes the time to do it right."

"See what I finished, Grandmother!"

Mei Yoon held up a **sash**, her very first handiwork.

The old woman's face **crinkled into a smile**. "A very good beginning," she said.

---

sash long, narrow strip of cloth
crinkled into a smile formed wrinkles as she smiled

Before You Move On

1. **Outcome** How does Toh make the earth and sky fit together?

2. **Conclusion** What do you think Mei Yoon learns from this myth?

Meet the Illustrator

Genna Panzarella

When **Genna Panzarella** was a little girl, people asked her what she wanted to be when she grew up. She answered with the biggest word she knew. "An illustrator!"

Today, Ms. Panzarella's dream has come true. *Piecing Earth and Sky Together* is one of her first picture books. "The hardest part was drawing the stitching patterns," she remembers. "The best part was working with a brother and sister from the Mien culture. They came in costume to my house to pose for me."

Think and Respond

Strategy: Goal and Outcome

Some stories tell how characters reach a goal. Look for the goal, the actions, the obstacle, and the outcome.

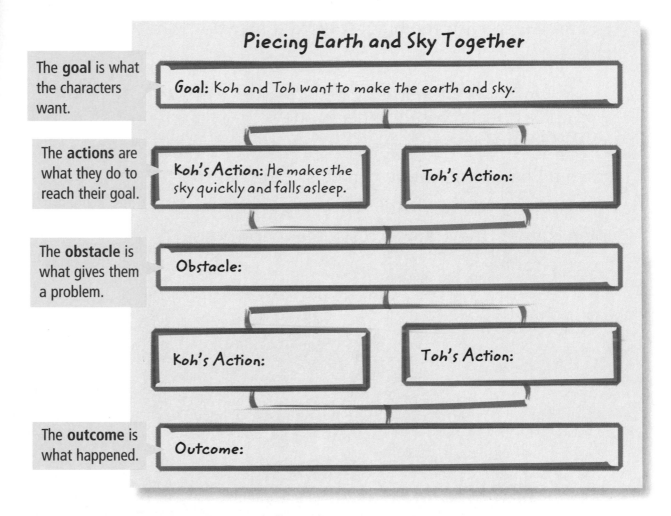

Piecing Earth and Sky Together

The **goal** is what the characters want.

Goal: Koh and Toh want to make the earth and sky.

The **actions** are what they do to reach their goal.

Koh's Action: He makes the sky quickly and falls asleep.

Toh's Action:

The **obstacle** is what gives them a problem.

Obstacle:

Koh's Action:

Toh's Action:

The **outcome** is what happened.

Outcome:

Make a story map. Show Koh and Toh's goal, their actions, the obstacle, and the outcome.

Retell the Story

Use your story map to retell the myth to a partner.
Does your retelling match your partner's? Talk about it.

Talk It Over

1 **Personal Response** Do you think you are more like Toh or Koh? Explain.

2 **Problem/Solution** What could Koh and Toh have done to keep their problem from happening?

3 **Inference** Why did Grandmother tell Mei Yoon the myth?

4 **Personal Experience** Did you ever do something that seemed too hard at first? Tell how you did it.

Compare Ideas

Think of a story about how things were created. How is it like this myth? How is it different?

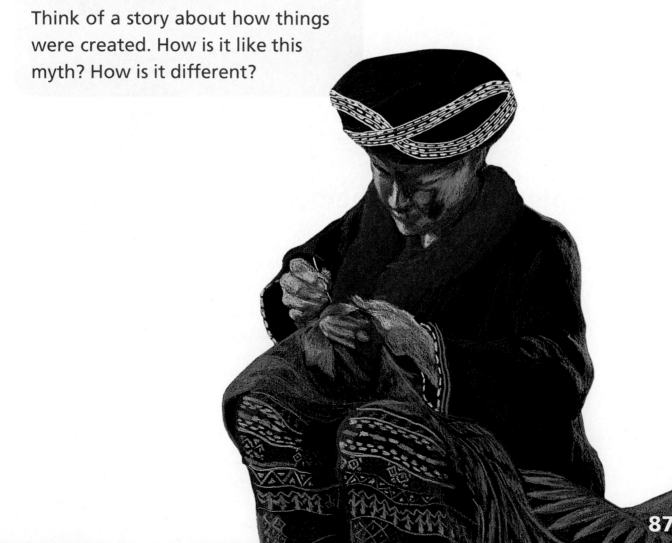

Content Connections

Guess the Picture

Who is in the picture?

partners

Choose a favorite picture from the story. Have your partner ask questions about it. Answer each one until your partner guesses which picture you chose. Then tell why you like the picture. Talk about the lines, colors, and shapes.

Compare Story Themes

large group

Read two more myths. Compare them to "Piecing Earth and Sky Together." Add your ideas to a class chart. What other myths do you know about?

Title and Culture	Characters	Theme
"Piecing Earth and Sky Together" Mien tribe of Laos	Koh and Toh are brother and sister. Koh works fast. Toh works carefully.	You can solve a problem if you are clever and you don't give up.

Research an Animal

Internet

Research an animal from Laos. Take notes. Use them to make a page for a class book. What other questions do you have about the animals or Laos? Do research to add more pages to the book.

Animal and Scientific Name:
tiger (panthera tigris)
Habitat: forest, swamp, grassland

partners

WRITING

Write to Entertain

Write to tell how something in nature was created. Use your imagination! Choose the best form to entertain your audience:

- a poem
- a song
- a myth

Choose specific nouns to describe the creation.

on your own

The First Mountain
    Long ago, there were no mountains, valleys, or hills. Earth was flat. The tiger and the bear decided to have a contest.

Identify Main Idea and Details

The **main idea** is the most important idea of a story or article. **Supporting details** give more information about the main idea. To identify the main idea and supporting details:

✔ Read carefully.
✔ Think about the most important idea.
✔ Look for details that tell more about the main idea.

Try the strategy.

The Earth's Surface

The Earth's surface is covered by continents, which are large land masses, and oceans. Seven continents cover about 29% of the Earth's surface. The continents are Asia, Africa, Europe, North America, South America, Antarctica, and Australia. Oceans cover the rest of the Earth. The three major oceans are the Atlantic Ocean, the Pacific Ocean, and the Indian Ocean.

> The main idea is continents and oceans cover the Earth's surface. One supporting detail is that seven continents cover about 29% of the surface.

Practice

Take this test and **identify the main idea and supporting details**.

Read the article. Then read each item. Choose the best answer.

Oceans are an important resource. They hold about 97% of the Earth's water supply and are an important source of food, too.

Oceans help balance the Earth's temperature. They absorb heat energy from the Sun. Then strong ocean currents move this heat energy around the globe. This helps to heat and cool the land and air.

1 **What is the main idea of paragraph 1?**

    A   Oceans are a source of food.

    B   Oceans are an important resource.

    C   Oceans hold about 97% of the Earth's water supply.

 Test Strategy

Try to answer the question without reading the answer choices. Then compare your answer to the choices

2 **Which detail belongs in the box?**

Main Idea–Paragraph 2: Oceans help balance the Earth's temperature.		
Detail:	**Detail:** Ocean currents move heat energy.	**Detail:** The heat energy heats and cools the Earth.

    A   Oceans absorb the Sun's heat energy.

    B   The oceans have strong currents.

    C   The land on Earth is cooler than the air.

Our EARTH SCIENCE Notebook

by Claudia Gutiérrez & Anna Rashid

one plate

another plate

San Andreas fault

An Earthquake Fault

This is the San Andreas **fault**. It is a long crack in the Earth between two **plates**, or pieces of Earth's **crust**. **Earthquakes** happen here when the two plates rub against each other. Luckily, **gravity** keeps us on the ground during earthquakes!

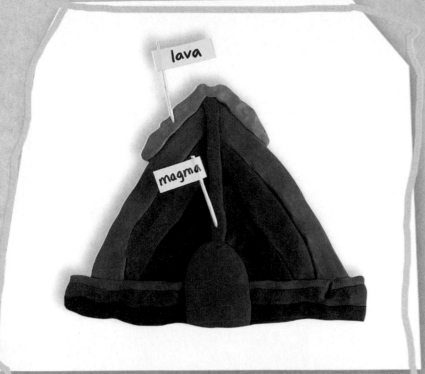

lava

magma

Our Volcano Model

Key Words

fault
plate
crust
earthquake
gravity
volcano
mantle
core

Sometimes a **volcano** appears where two plates crash into each other. The red clay at the bottom of our model is magma, or hot melted rock. It comes from the **mantle**, the layer around Earth's **core**.

When magma spills out the top of a volcano, it is called lava.

Read a Science Article

A **science article** is nonfiction. This article tells how things in nature work.

✔ Look for **diagrams**. They show the parts of something or how something works.

diagram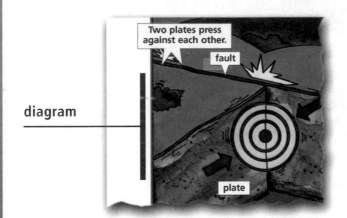

Two plates press against each other.

fault

plate

✔ Look at **photographs**. Read their **captions** to learn more facts.

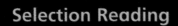 Selection Reading

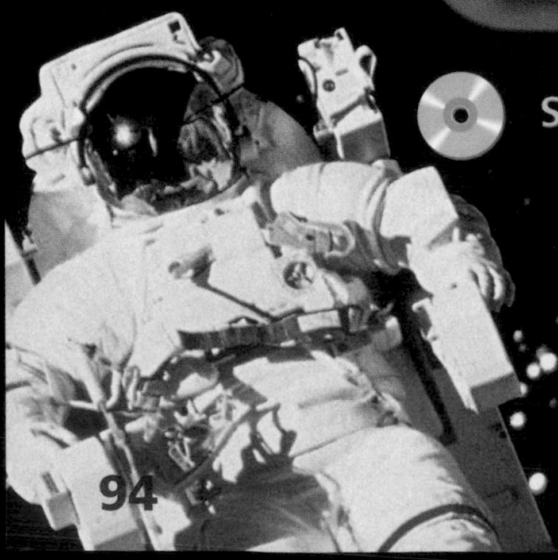

Planet Earth/ Inside Out

by Gail Gibbons

Earth's Formation

Earth is the third planet from the Sun. It is the only planet we know of that has **just the right environment** for plants and animals to live in.

———————————

just the right environment enough air, water, and sunlight

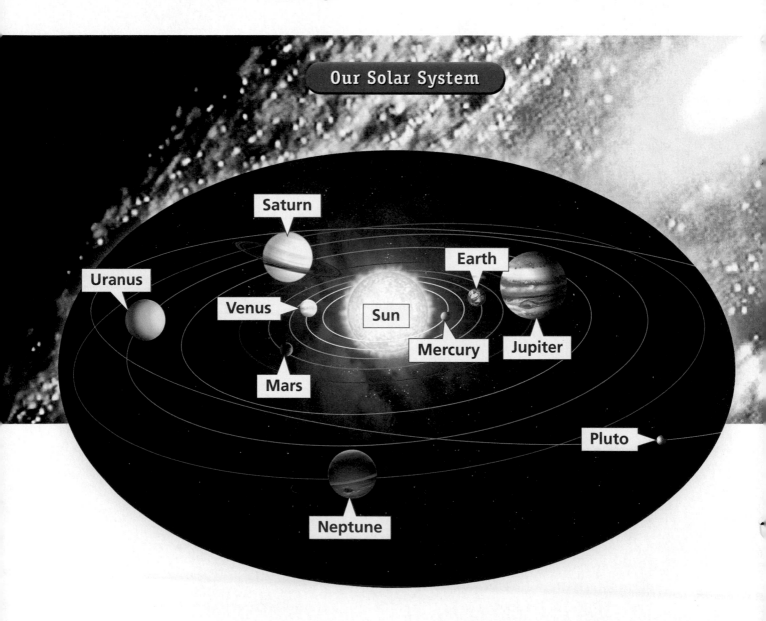

Our Solar System

Saturn

Earth

Uranus

Venus

Sun

Mercury

Jupiter

Mars

Pluto

Neptune

96

Scientists believe planet Earth was formed about 4.6 billion years ago. They think this happened when a cloud of gases and dust was pulled together by a force called **gravity** . As the cloud spun around, small **particles** began sticking together. Slowly Earth became **denser** and bigger. The heaviest materials, like iron and nickel, sank to the center.

---

particles pieces
denser thicker and heavier

Earth begins to form.

gases and dust

▲ **Earth formed when gravity pulled gases and dust together into a tight ball.**

At first Earth was very hot. As it cooled down, it became hard on the outside. Steam rose from the **planet's surface** and fell back as rain. Over a long period of time, most of Earth became covered with the oceans.

The surface that remained above water became land. Some scientists think that at one time on Earth there was a single **massive** piece of land, which they call Pangaea. These scientists believe that about 250 million years ago, Pangaea slowly split apart into seven smaller land **masses.** Between them, the oceans created their own shapes.

planet's surface ground
massive very, very big
masses sections

▼ **Most of Earth became covered with oceans.**

250 million years ago

There was once one piece of land called Pangaea.

50 million years ago

The land slowly split apart.

Today

ASIA

AFRICA

Now there are smaller land masses, called continents.

Before You Move On

1. **Details** How old is Earth?
2. **Paraphrase** Tell how the land called Pangaea changed over millions of years.

99

Earth's Layers

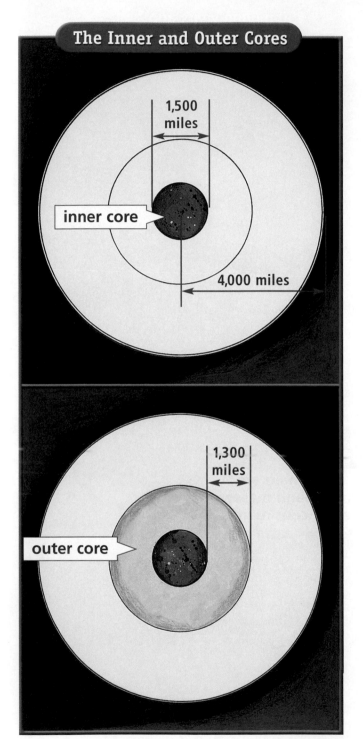

The Inner and Outer Cores

1,500 miles

inner core

4,000 miles

1,300 miles

outer core

Planet Earth looks different on the inside. It has four layers. The distance to its center from the planet's surface is about 4,000 miles. At its center is the inner **core**. Scientists believe the inner core is a hot ball of **solid** iron and nickel, about 1,500 miles across, with temperatures reaching 11,000°F. That's about fifty times as hot as boiling water! It is thought that the inner core is solid because of the huge weight of the rest of Earth pressing all around it.

Outside the inner core is the outer core. The outer core is about 1,300 miles thick. That's about how far it is from New York City to Miami, Florida. Scientists believe that the outer core is made up of very hot liquid iron and nickel. At its deepest level it can get to be about 9,000°F. The outer core moves around the inner core very slowly.

solid tightly packed

Around the outer core is the **mantle**. It is about 1,800 miles thick and can be as hot as 6,700°F. Most of the mantle surrounding the outer core is solid. But some of the outer mantle is made up of partially molten, or melted, rock that moves slowly.

Outside the mantle is the Earth's **crust**. It is very thin compared to the other layers. Earth's crust is made up of rock and soil. If Earth were the size of a peach, its crust would be about as thin as a peach's skin.

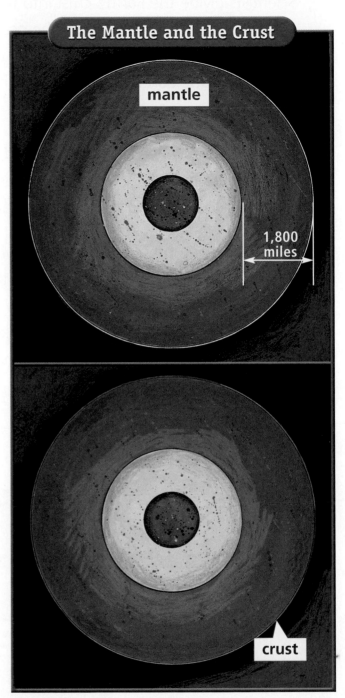

The Mantle and the Crust

mantle

1,800 miles

crust

peach

thin skin

Before You Move On

1. **Paraphrase** Tell a partner what the inner core of Earth is like.

2. **Graphic Aids** Which layer of Earth is the thinnest?

A Planet in Motion

Scientists divide the Earth's crust into two parts, the oceanic crust and the continental crust. The oceanic crust lies below the oceans. It forms the ocean floor. Some oceanic crust runs underneath the continental crust, which forms the land above **sea level**.

The crust is not one solid piece. Instead, it is split into seven major pieces and many other smaller pieces, called **plates**. Each plate curves to fit the shape of planet Earth.

Plates are made up of a thin **portion** of crust and a thicker portion of outer mantle that lies beneath them. These plates slowly move, because they float on top of partially molten rock. Earth's plates are about forty miles thick under the oceans and about sixty miles thick under the continents.

Earth's Crust

sea level

continental crust

oceanic crust

outer mantle

---

sea level the height of the ocean's surface

portion part

Plates Move

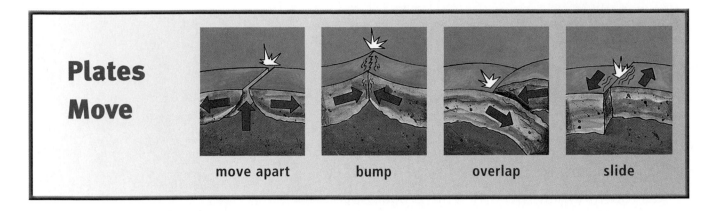

move apart　　bump　　overlap　　slide

When the plates move apart, bump together, overlap, and slide against one another, the surface of Earth changes. The surface usually moves very slowly. The plates **drift** at rates of about one to four inches each year.

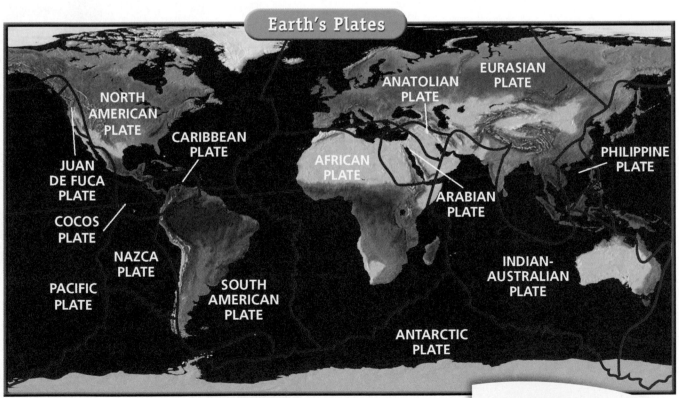

Earth's Plates

NORTH AMERICAN PLATE

JUAN DE FUCA PLATE

COCOS PLATE

PACIFIC PLATE

NAZCA PLATE

CARIBBEAN PLATE

SOUTH AMERICAN PLATE

AFRICAN PLATE

ANTARCTIC PLATE

ANATOLIAN PLATE

EURASIAN PLATE

ARABIAN PLATE

INDIAN-AUSTRALIAN PLATE

PHILIPPINE PLATE

▲ The seven major plates and the other smaller plates of Earth are always moving.

_____

drift move

Before You Move On

1. **Comparison** What are the two parts of Earth's crust? How are they different?

2. **Cause/Effect** Why are Earth's plates always moving?

Sudden Movements of the Earth

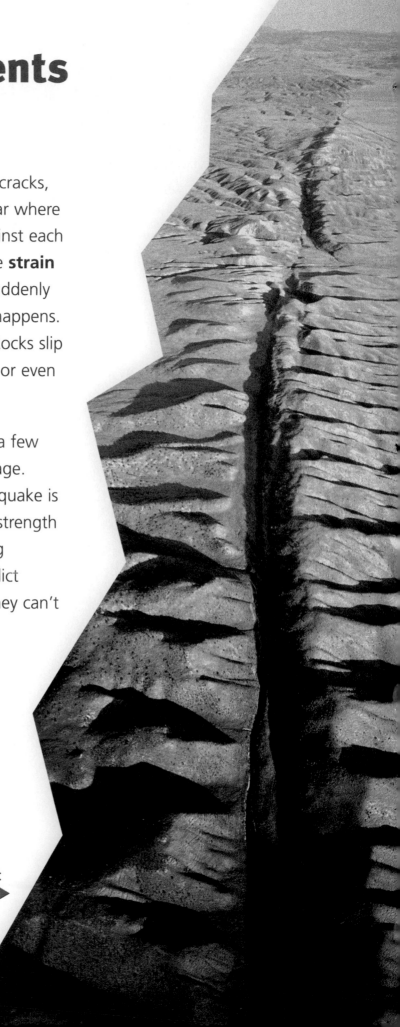

Throughout Earth's crust there are many cracks, called **faults** . Major faults are found near where plates touch. When two plates press against each other, pressure begins to build. When the **strain** becomes too great, the ground moves suddenly along these faults and an **earthquake** happens. **Vibrations move through the Earth**. Rocks slip and slide. Sometimes the Earth **buckles**, or even breaks open.

An earthquake can last from seconds to a few minutes. Sometimes it causes great damage. Scientists can tell how powerful an earthquake is by using **instruments** that measure the strength of the vibrations, or shock waves, moving through the ground. Often they can predict where earthquakes might happen, but they can't tell when.

---

strain force, pressure
Vibrations move through the Earth
The Earth shakes
buckles folds up
instruments scientific tools

The San Andreas fault is about 600 miles long and goes from northwest California to the Gulf of California. ▶

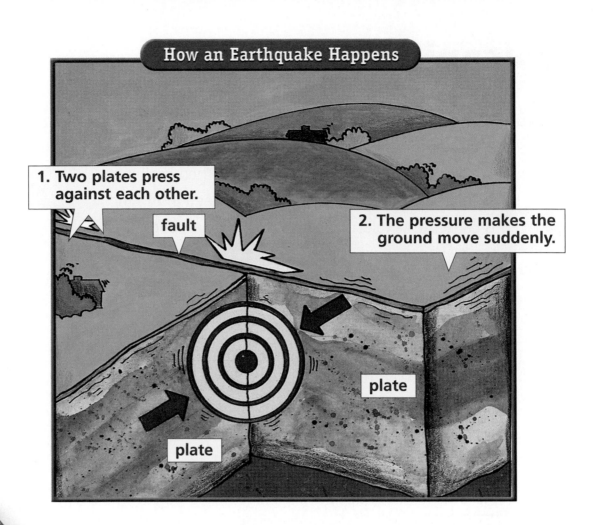

How an Earthquake Happens

1. Two plates press against each other.

fault

2. The pressure makes the ground move suddenly.

plate

plate

A major earthquake can destroy buildings. ▶

Before You Move On

1. **Graphic Aids** Tell how an earthquake happens.

2. **Cause/Effect** What can a major earthquake do to Earth and to buildings? Why?

Volcanic Eruptions

Volcanoes, like most earthquakes, usually form near where the edges of plates **collide**. Pressure builds up below the surface, causing cracks or holes to appear in the crust. Then molten rock, called magma, and gases push up from deep inside the Earth. This causes an explosion called a volcanic eruption.

Magma shoots out of the volcano's opening, called the crater. Volcanic ash darkens the sky. The magma flows in streams called lava. Ash and lava can destroy life for miles around. When the lava cools, it can harden into layers that form steep-sided cone-shaped hills or mountains. Or it can harden into much flatter layers. Active volcanoes erupt often. Dormant volcanoes rest for a long time between eruptions. Extinct volcanoes will never erupt again.

---

collide crash into each other

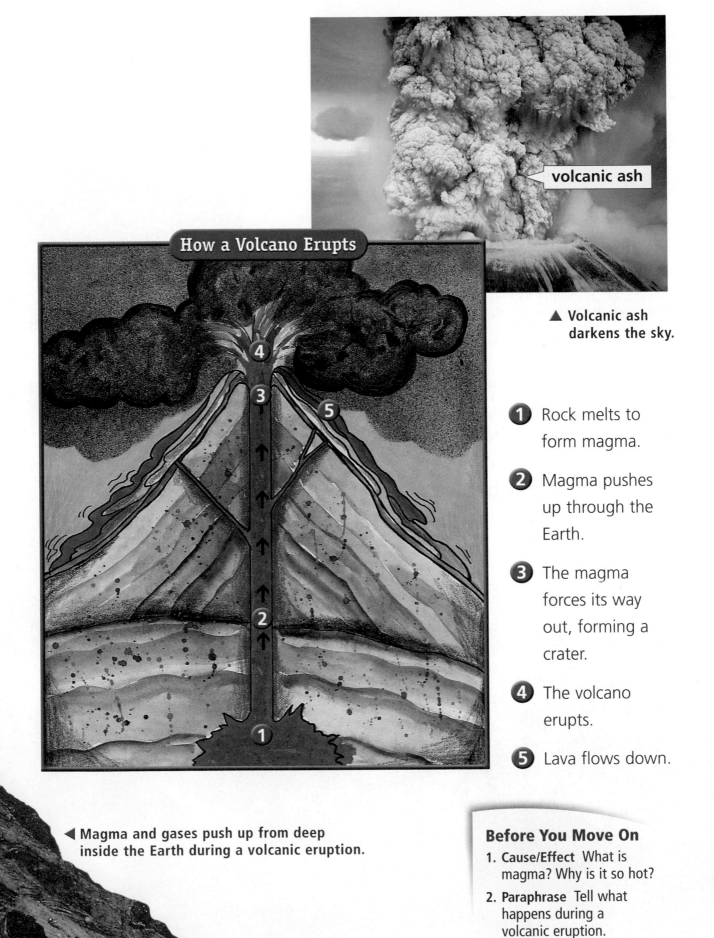

volcanic ash

▲ Volcanic ash darkens the sky.

How a Volcano Erupts

1 Rock melts to form magma.

2 Magma pushes up through the Earth.

3 The magma forces its way out, forming a crater.

4 The volcano erupts.

5 Lava flows down.

◄ Magma and gases push up from deep inside the Earth during a volcanic eruption.

Before You Move On

1. **Cause/Effect** What is magma? Why is it so hot?

2. **Paraphrase** Tell what happens during a volcanic eruption.

107

Changes to Earth's Surface

The shape of the land has formed over millions of years. Great forces have worked to make this happen. When plates crashed into one another, they made the layers of continental crust fold and buckle to form mountain ranges. And when plates pulled apart, they formed **depressions** in the continental crust called rift valleys.

Vast ice sheets, called glaciers, also changed the Earth's surface. They pushed down over the land, shaping and forming it into valleys, **plains**, and hills. Most of these changes happen too slowly for people to see.

---

depressions low areas
Vast Large
plains flat lands

Mountain Range

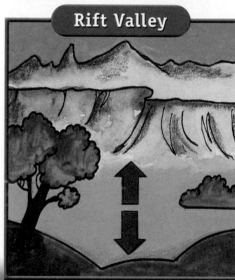

Rift Valley

glacier

▲ Some of Earth's environment has been damaged by **pollution**.

Humans have changed planet Earth the most. Many of these changes have been harmful. People have **abused Earth's natural resources**, and some of Earth's environment has been damaged. Now many people are working to protect Earth and its resources for a better future.

◄ Glaciers can be many miles long. Moving slowly, they carve out valleys.

---

pollution trash, dirty air, and other things that hurt the Earth

abused Earth's natural resources not always used things from the Earth wisely

Every place on Earth should be special to the people who live there. It is our beautiful, living, and ever-changing Earth, inside and out.

People can recycle many things. This helps protect Earth's resources.

Before You Move On

1. **Cause/Effect** How do glaciers change the Earth's surface?

2. **Details** How do people change the Earth? What can they do to protect it?

Meet the Author and Illustrator
Gail Gibbons

AWARD WINNER

As a child, **Gail Gibbons** tried to understand everything about a subject. Just knowing the time wasn't enough for her. She had to know how the clock worked! That's probably why Ms. Gibbons writes nonfiction books today!

Ms. Gibbons decided to make her books, like *Planet Earth/Inside Out*, bright and alive. "I love working with bright, bold, beautiful colors," says Ms. Gibbons. She also loves to see how kids react to her books. "A lot of times I get ideas from them," she says.

Think and Respond

Strategy: Main Idea and Details

Make a chart. For each section of the article, write the most important details. Then write a sentence that tells the main idea.

Section	Important Details	Main Idea
Earth's Formation	• Gases and dust pulled together 4.6 billion years ago. • The planet became hard on the outside. • Most of Earth became covered with water. • Pangaea began to split apart into continents 250 million years ago.	Scientists think Earth was formed over millions of years.
Earth's Layers		
A Planet in Motion		

Share Information

Work with a group. One of you tells a main idea from your chart. Then the others tell details from their charts that go with the main idea. Take turns telling the main idea.

Talk It Over

1 **Personal Response** What surprises you the most about the Earth? Are there more things you want to know? What are they?

2 **Graphic Aids** Which diagram helped you understand the most about how Earth moves? Explain.

3 **Comparison** How are earthquakes like volcanic eruptions? How are they different? Give examples from the article.

4 **Judgment** Is it important for scientists to study the Earth? Why or why not?

Compare Genres

How is "Piecing Earth and Sky Together" similar to "Planet Earth/Inside Out"? How is it different?

They both show what Earth looks like, but the science article gives facts.

Content Connections

Make an Earth Quilt
Internet

large group

Find three facts about a place on Earth. Make a quilt square to show the place. Tell your facts as you add your square to a class quilt. What does your class want to teach about Earth? Write a border to persuade others.

Take care of the ocean. It is home to many animals.

Make a Seismograph

small group

An earthquake makes seismic waves, or vibrations in the ground. A seismograph records the waves. The width of the waves shows how strong an earthquake is. Make a seismograph and put it on a table. Shake the table. Look at the waves. Which group's earthquake is strongest?

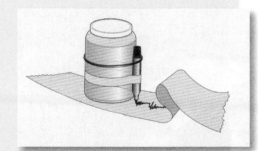

partners

Recycle It!

What products do people in your area recycle? Make a survey form. With a partner, survey at least five people. Show the results on a class graph. Discuss how recycling affects our natural resources.

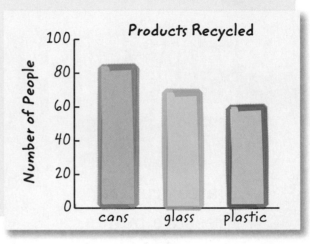

WRITING

on your own

Write a Poem

A diamante is a poem that looks like a diamond. It is seven lines long. It can tell about things that are opposites or show how one thing changes into another. Write a diamante about two things in nature.

Mountain to Valley

mountain
lofty, white,
snowing, blowing, melting,
brook, creek, river, grass, flowers, buds,
sprouting, growing, blooming
sunny, emerald
valley

Plural Nouns

Listen and chant.

Chant

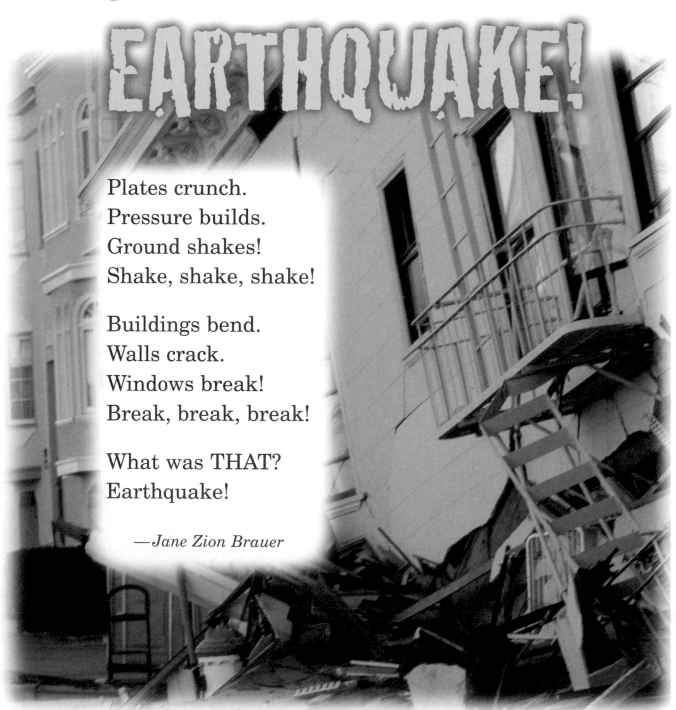

EARTHQUAKE!

Plates crunch.
Pressure builds.
Ground shakes!
Shake, shake, shake!

Buildings bend.
Walls crack.
Windows break!
Break, break, break!

What was THAT?
Earthquake!

—*Jane Zion Brauer*

How Language Works

You can count most **nouns**. They have a singular and a plural form.

How to Make Nouns Plural		Examples:	
1.	To make most nouns plural, add –**s**.	planet	planet**s**
2.	If the noun ends in **x**, **ch**, **sh**, **s**, or **z**, add -**es**.	stitch	stitch**es**
3.	For most nouns that end in **y**, change the **y** to **i** and add –**es**.	sk**y**	sk**ies**
4.	Some nouns cannot be counted. They have only one form.	gravity	magma
		lava	air

Practice with a Partner

Use the correct form of each red noun. Say the sentence.

hour

magma

lava

town

family

1. The volcano erupted for several _____ .
2. Gas and _____ shot into the air.
3. A lot of _____ flowed down the mountain.
4. It raced toward the three _____ below.
5. Many _____ ran from their homes.

Put It in Writing

Pretend that you are in a huge earthquake or see a volcano erupt. Write about what happens.

Lava covered the ground.
Many trees were destroyed.

Show What You Know

Talk About Earth

In this unit, you read a myth and a science article about Earth. Look back at the unit. Find a picture that shows how Earth changes. Use the picture to tell a partner about the changes.

Make a Mind Map

Work with a partner. Make a mind map to show what you learned about how Earth changes.

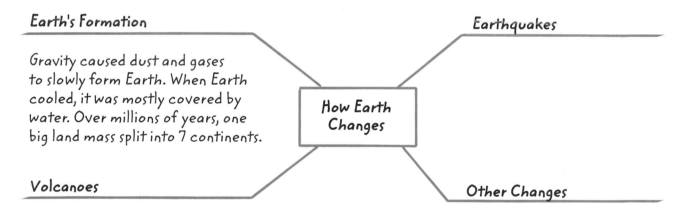

Earth's Formation

Gravity caused dust and gases to slowly form Earth. When Earth cooled, it was mostly covered by water. Over millions of years, one big land mass split into 7 continents.

Earthquakes

How Earth Changes

Volcanoes

Other Changes

Think and Write

What questions do you still have about Earth? Make a list. Add the list to your portfolio. Include work that shows what you learned about Earth.

Read and Learn More

Leveled Books

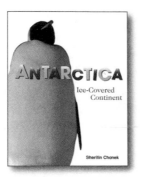

The Birth of an Island
by Michael Jedrzejczak

Antarctica
by Sherilin Chanek

Theme Library

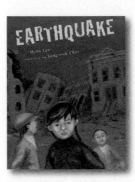

Mountain Dance
by Thomas Locker

Earthquake
by Milly Lee

Internet

Go to: www.hbavenues.com

Earthquakes

Wildlife in Laos

Volcano Facts

BODIES
IN MOTION

Play Charades

1. Look at pictures of people playing sports.
2. Pretend to play the sport. Have a partner guess the sport. If the guess is correct, give your partner the picture.
3. Take turns until all the pictures are gone.

hoop

ball

basketball

ball

soccer

Body Systems

Respiratory

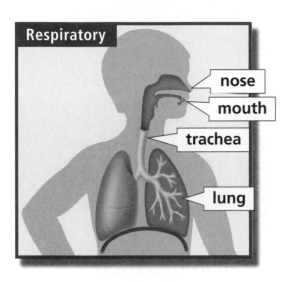

nose

mouth

trachea

lung

Skeletal

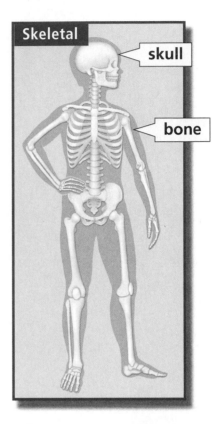

skull

bone

Muscular

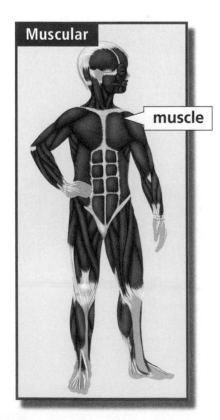

muscle

Circulatory System

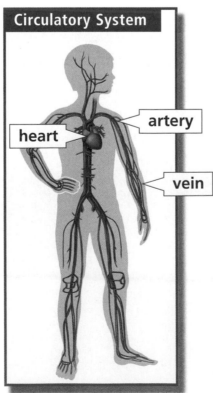

artery

heart

vein

Nervous System

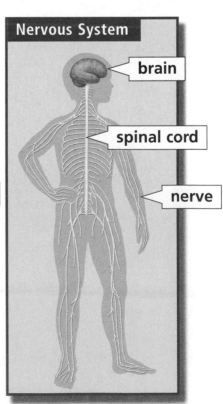

brain

spinal cord

nerve

Medical Technology

Medical Images

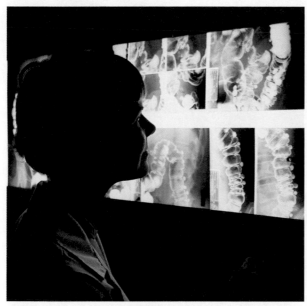

▲ An X ray helps doctors see inside a person's body.

Antibiotics

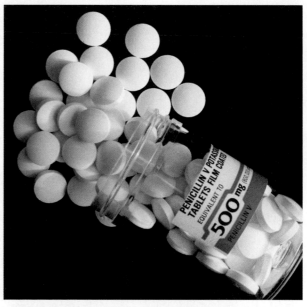

▲ Antibiotics like penicillin help sick people get well.

Immunization

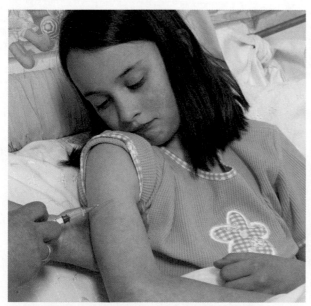

▲ Immunizations keep people from becoming sick.

Prosthetics

▲ People without a body part use prosthetic limbs to do more things.

ON STAGE!

Act out the scene.

> Look at that dancer! It takes a lot of **energy** to jump that high.

> The dancers really show **expression** in their faces and bodies.

audience

Key Words

energy

expression

audience

movement

performance

improve

Their **movements** sure go with the music.

I love this **performance**! It is better than last year. They worked hard to **improve**.

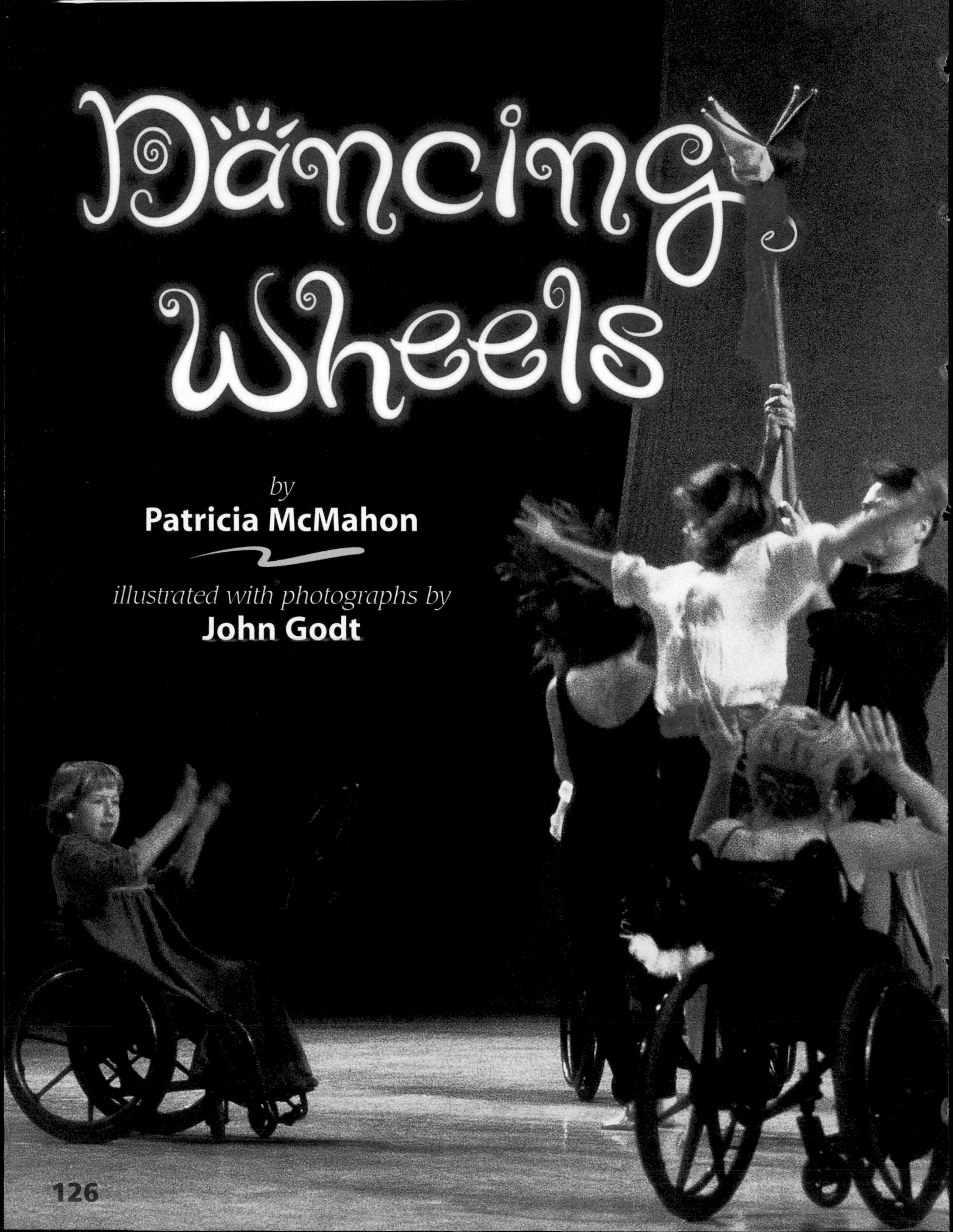

Dancing Wheels

by
Patricia McMahon

illustrated with photographs by
John Godt

Read a Photo-Essay

Genre

A **photo-essay** is nonfiction. It uses words and photographs to tell a true story. This photo-essay tells how a woman started a children's dance group.

Dancers

Mary

Jenny and Devin

Barbara

Sabatino

Setting

Most of this photo-essay takes place in a dance studio in Cleveland, Ohio.

 Selection Reading

1

Find out how dancers get ready for a performance.

"On stage, on stage now. Four minutes **to curtain!**" Barbara Verlezza, the **rehearsal director**, hurries through the backstage area of the theater on this autumn afternoon. Clapping her hands for attention, she calls again, "Everyone to center stage!"

Dancers finish their makeup and rush onto the stage in their costumes, scurrying, wheeling to join the others before the **performance** begins. They gather in a circle. On the other side of the **massive** curtain, the **audience** waits, **fidgeting as the lights dim**.

"Dancers always believe that all would be well if there were just one more day for rehearsal," Barbara reminds everyone. "But there never is just one more day. We've got to be ready now." The dancers grab one another's hands, reaching down, reaching up. Without words, they wish one another well.

---

to curtain until the show begins

rehearsal director person who gets everyone ready to perform

massive very large

fidgeting as the lights dim moving in their seats as the room gets dark

▼ A dancer wears makeup so her face can be seen from the back of the theater.

▲ Dancers gather before the performance to wish one another good luck.

Moments later, when everyone is **offstage**, the curtain goes up, the spotlight comes on. The stand-up dancers walk on; the sit-down dancers wheel on. **They pause**, **pose**. The loud, rhythmic sounds of an ancient Italian song fill the air. The dancers move to the music, with the music.

Dancing Wheels **takes the stage**.

---

offstage off of the stage

They pause, pose They stop and stand still in a special position

takes the stage begins a performance

▲ The dancers perform together onstage.

Before You Move On

1. **Sequence** What do the dancers do before the performance starts?

2. **Viewing** Why is the group called "Dancing Wheels"?

2

Find out
who starts
Dancing Wheels
and why.

In the center of the whirling and the twirling, Sabatino Verlezza and Mary Verdi-Fletcher dance together. They are the leaders of the **company**. Sabatino, a stand-up dancer and **choreographer**, creates the dances for the group. And Mary? Mary Verdi-Fletcher is the reason everyone is here today, the reason for the dancing. Because for years Mary had a dream, an idea everyone thought was **crazy**.

Mary Verdi-Fletcher was born with spina bifida, a **spinal cord problem** that occurs before birth, while a baby is growing. Spina bifida creates a weakness in the legs and spine and often prevents feeling or muscle control in the lower portion of the body.

---

company group of dancers

choreographer person who plans the dance

crazy impossible

spinal cord problem problem inside the backbone, or spine

◀ Sabatino and Mary lead the company. They are also dancing partners.

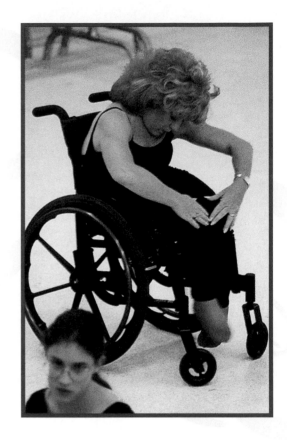

When Mary was born in the 1950s, a baby with her condition was not expected to live long or to have a normal life. But the doctors who made that prediction had not understood Mary's family. The doctors were so very wrong about Mary's life.

Mary's parents did not leave her in the hospital; they took her home. They had **braces** made for her legs to help her walk. Mary was not **shut out of their world**; she was part of it. When her cousins and friends danced and played around the house, Mary found her own way to join in. Mary's parents told her not to think of what she couldn't do, but of what she could do.

---

braces metal frames

shut out of their world stopped from doing the same things they did

◀ As a little girl, Mary wanted to be a dancer. Now she shows others how to dance.

When she was small, Mary was always hurrying to **catch up**. And she did. When she was older and everyone began **disco dancing**, so did Mary. She and a friend entered a dance contest. They won first prize along with everyone's cheers. Mary knew for sure that this was what she wanted to do, this was what she wanted to be: a dancer.

Mary entered more contests, and won more prizes. She looked for dancers to teach her. She studied and worked hard. She did not listen to people who said, "You cannot dance if you are in a wheelchair." She did not listen to people who said, "If you dance in a chair, it is not really dancing." She did not listen when people said, "Wheelchair dancers should only dance with others in wheelchairs."

---

catch up do the things the other kids were doing
disco dancing dancing to a certain kind of music

▲ Barbara, Mary, and Sabatino show students
that everyone can dance.

Mary formed her own company, Dancing Wheels.
The company has two kinds of dancers: stand-up dancers who
use their legs, arms, backs, necks, and faces for **expression** ;
and sit-down dancers who use their legs, arms, backs, necks,
and faces for expression—along with their wheelchairs.

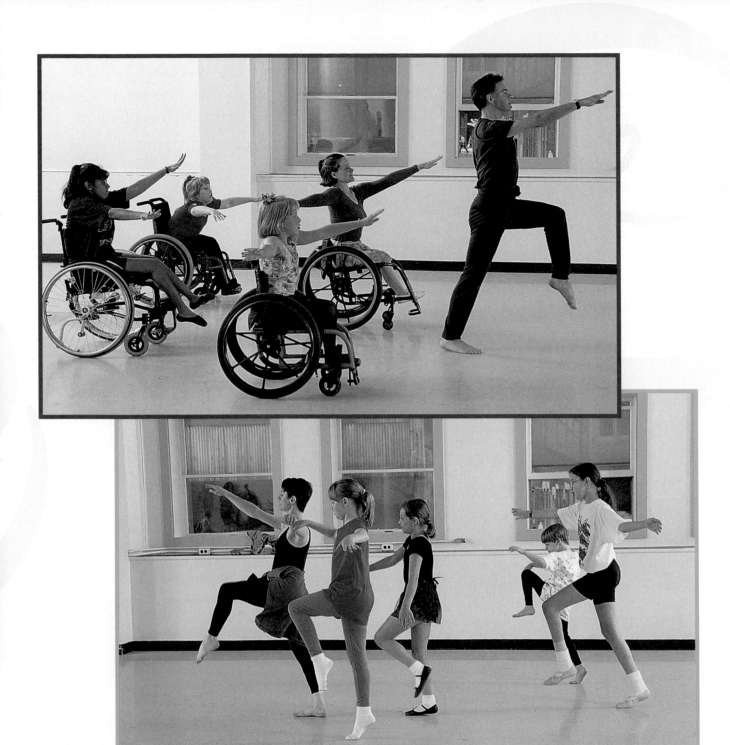

▲ Sabatino and Barbara lead the dancers. They remind them, "Your **movements** must be big!"

Before You Move On

1. **Cause/Effect** What did Mary's parents tell her? How did that help her?

2. **Sequence** What did Mary do after she won her first dance contest?

3

Devin and Jenny are dance partners. Find out what they are like.

Mary watches the young dancers rush offstage. Devin and Jenny hurry to change their costumes. They have lead roles in the main dance on today's program. Jenny almost barrels into three people, calling out "Sorry! Sorry!" as she **whips by**. Devin complains again about wearing **tights** today. Little Sabatino **hitches a ride** on a sit-down dancer's chair.

Young Sabatino came to live in Cleveland when Mary invited his parents to work with her and the Dancing Wheels company. She thought they were the right people to keep her crazy idea going. So the Verlezzas came.

Mary and the grown-up Sabatino run Dancing Wheels together, and they dance together as partners. Barbara **oversees rehearsals**, and she dances with the company as well.

▲ Barbara and Sabatino encourage the students, "Come on, you can do this."

---

whips by rolls quickly by

tights thin, stretchy pants

hitches a ride rides

oversees rehearsals makes sure the dancers practice enough

▲ **Devin and Jenny have fun together whether they are dancing or not.**

Devin and Jenny are the partners who open the main dance. They rush out of the **dressing rooms** to wait **in the wings** by Mary. Jenny fidgets in her wheelchair. "No more time to worry," she thinks. "Time to begin dancing." Devin tries to loosen up, moving his legs, reminding himself of his opening moves. He wonders if Jenny is **running through the dance in her mind**, the way he does. The dance is a long one, but Devin feels ready. He has done this dance before. And he and Jenny worked hard this summer, getting ready for performances like this.

---

dressing rooms places where performers put on costumes and makeup

in the wings on a side of the stage the audience cannot see

running through the dance in her mind thinking about the dance step by step

▲ Dancing requires a lot of **energy** . Dancers build their strength and **flexibility** with exercise.

The dancers form lines and face the mirrors. Devin and Jenny are in different lines. The sit-downs take their places behind the stand-ups; then the stand-ups sit down on the floor. "We're going to work those muscles now," Sabatino warns them. He calls out directions, his words a song.

> **Flex** your hands; flex your feet.
> Fold like a book. Open like a book.
> You are the book. This is your story.

The experienced dancers move along with him. The dancers who are new **frown with concentration**, following as well as they can.

---

flexibility ability to move easily
Flex Bend
frown with concentration think hard

Bodies **fold**, open again.

"This is about what you <u>can</u> do, not what you cannot," Sabatino says to encourage them. Mary, opening and folding with everyone else, hears the same words her parents said, the words that led her to be here this morning in the studio.

"Do it as best you can," Sabatino says. Wanting them to sit tall, he tells everyone, "Imagine you are sitting in a pool of water up to your nose. Now rise out of the water. Come on, Devin, you are going under."

Devin pulls himself up.

"Good", Sabatino urges. "But," he adds, "can you stay like that all day?"

Devin works hard to **hold the position**, trying not to join in the laughter around him.

▲ Devin holds a position.

---

fold bend

hold the position stay in the same position; not move

141

Dancing is Devin's great joy. Having begun dancing with The School of the Cleveland Ballet, Devin and his sister Kristen started to study with Dancing Wheels after their mother heard about the group. Like the sit-down dancers, their mother uses a wheelchair to **get around**. Devin plans on becoming a ballet dancer. But unlike so many of the dancers, who are proud to have everyone know about their work, Devin sometimes feels he has to be quiet, to keep his plans to himself. Some of the boys his age make fun of dancing. They make fun of dancers, especially male dancers. And they make fun of Devin. But here in the studio it doesn't matter. Here in the studio Devin has no problems with dancing, unless he doesn't work hard enough.

▲ Devin's shirt says it all.

get around move

▲ Devin wants to be a ballet dancer when he grows up. It takes a lot of hard work, but it's also a lot of fun!

143

Jenny loves to be silly and is happy to be so **at the slightest invitation**. When Sabatino gives her the stop-being-too-silly look, Jenny takes a breath and picks up the movement. Jenny loves to be at the Dancing Wheels studio as much as she loves to be goofy. Jenny's parents first brought her to a dance class there after seeing Mary dance. Jenny was four years old, the same age Mary was when she first told someone she wanted to be a dancer. Like Mary, Jenny was born with spina bifida.

As she watches Devin **warming up**, Jenny knows she is lucky. She doesn't have to worry about kids making fun of her because she dances. A lot of kids in her school think it's great that Jenny gets her picture in the newspaper or is interviewed by reporters.

▲ Jenny leads the group as the wheelers turn sharp on the count of six.

---

at the slightest invitation whenever there is an opportunity

warming up getting his muscles ready

Jenny knows, though, that some kids say mean things about her being in a wheelchair. At the studio, it doesn't matter what anyone else thinks. Here dancers dance, whether or not some people say boys shouldn't dance or girls in wheelchairs can't.

▼ **Jenny loves being silly, but she can be serious when she has to be.**

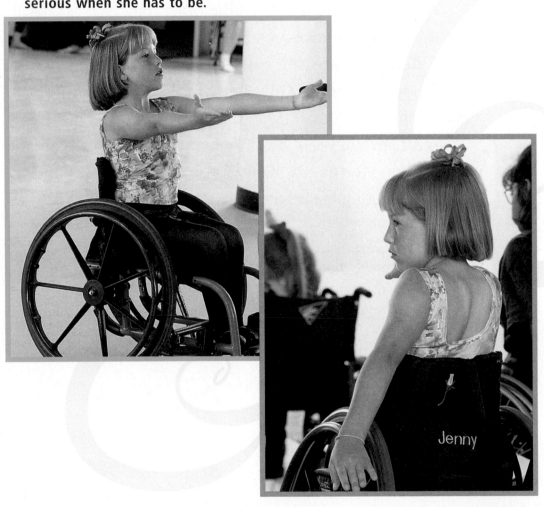

Before You Move On

1. **Details** How do Barbara and Sabatino help the dancers practice?

2. **Comparison** How are Devin and Jenny alike? How are they different?

The dancers practice a lot. What will the performance be like?

All afternoon, the dancers work and practice together. "It is **essential** to be able to dance well with someone," Sabatino tells them. "Dance cannot always be done alone."

"Try to think of it as a series of questions and answers," Mary suggests. "One dancer's movement asks a question; the other's movement answers the question. Learn to trust the other dancer."

Barbara takes a student named Katie to **demonstrate** and she leans back against her. Katie does not let her fall. Katie **breaks into a smile**. Jenny and Devin try it, too. They have been partners for several years now. Jenny thinks they have been asking the question, "Will you be my friend?" and answering each other, "Yes!"

---

essential very, very important
demonstrate show others how to dance together
breaks into a smile smiles

▼ Barbara and Katie practice together so they can be dance partners.

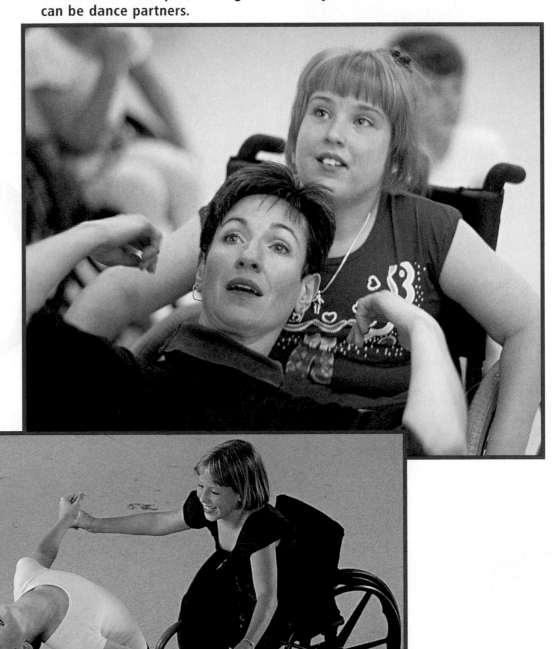

▲ Devin and Jenny work well together as partners.

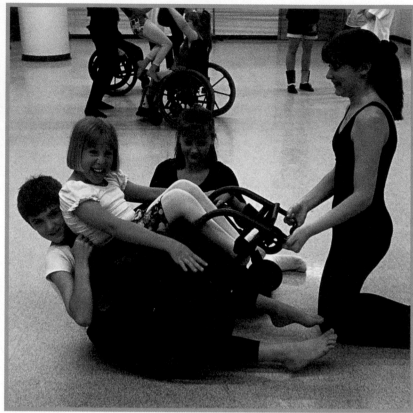

▲ When they aren't rehearsing, Jenny, Devin, Kristen, and Jessica use their energy to **goof around**.

And so it goes each day of the workshop. Long mornings and afternoons of work. The new dancers learn different ways to think of their bodies and their movements. The others practice the steps they know and try to **improve**.

"Make it bigger," Barbara calls out to them. "Remember the audience in the back row."

In their fall performance, Devin plays "The Brother Who Cannot See," and Jenny plays "The Sister Who Cannot Walk."

---

goof around play

In the **opening scene**, Devin must carry his friend onto the stage. And she must help him to see. They have to trust each other to be able to make their journey, just as two dancers must trust each other.

On the day of the performance, Sabatino takes his place on stage. The lighting, the costumes, the music are all **in place**. The practice has been worth it, for the performance **comes off without a hitch**. Devin forgets about who might be in the audience. He does what he loves to do, and what he does so well. Jenny manages to **keep a straight face**, count her beats, and dance her best.

▲ Devin carries Jenny in the opening scene of the fall performance.

opening scene first part of the show

in place ready

comes off without a hitch takes place without any mistakes

keep a straight face be serious; not laugh

▲ Lights! Costumes! Music! Dancers! Everything and
everyone work together to make the show a success.

For much of the performance, Mary sits in the wings,
watching the dance **unfurl** like magic. All of this is
happening today because she didn't listen to what people
said she could or couldn't do. She didn't worry about what
people would think. She just had a crazy idea . . .
she wanted to dance.

Before You Move On

1. **Conclusion** Do Devin and
   Jenny trust each other?
   How do you know?

2. **Inference** How does
   Mary feel about the
   fall performance?

---

unfurl happen

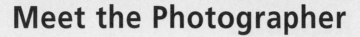

Meet the Photographer

John Godt

AWARD WINNER

John Godt started taking photographs when he was eleven years old. He says, "My grandfather gave me a camera for my birthday. My father had a friend who was a professional photographer. He set up a darkroom for me in our third-floor bathroom."

Today, Mr. Godt works full-time as a photographer. *Dancing Wheels* is his second book for kids. The kids in Dancing Wheels inspired Mr. Godt. "Dancing gives them hope. It was my job to help readers see the beauty of their movements and feel the freedom of their dance."

Think and Respond

Strategy: Sequence

The events in a photo-essay can be in time order, or sequence. To understand the sequence, look for:

✔ dates like "in the 1950s"
✔ time order phrases like "when she was small," "all afternoon," and "this summer."

Make a sequence chain about Mary's life.

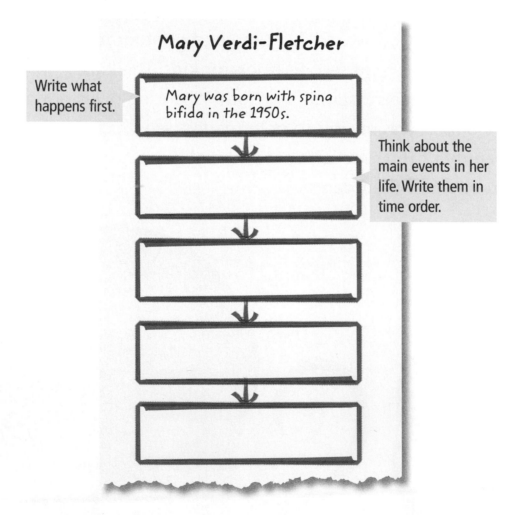

Mary Verdi-Fletcher

Write what happens first. → Mary was born with spina bifida in the 1950s.

Think about the main events in her life. Write them in time order.

Give Information

Tell a partner about Mary's life. Include details that tell what she is like.

Talk It Over

1 **Personal Response** How did you feel about people in wheelchairs before reading this photo-essay? Have your feelings changed since reading it? How?

2 **Cause/Effect** How has Mary affected the lives of others?

3 **Inference** "Think about what you <u>can</u> do and not about what you can't." What does this mean?

4 **Author's Purpose** Why do you think the author wrote "Dancing Wheels"? Do you think she accomplished this purpose?

Compare Characters

How is Mary like the parents and grandparents in "We Honor Our Ancestors"?

They all show that wonderful things <u>can</u> be done.

Content Connections

partners

Give a Review

Watch a dance performance. Then tell what it was like.

- Tell your partner about it.
- Tell your teacher and the class.

Did you change the way you gave the review? Talk about how the two reviews were different.

Hey, Pablo! On Saturday I saw a great show by a group called Dancing Wheels.

2×5 MATH

Plan a Budget

small group

How much does it cost to have a dance performance? Talk about what you'll need. Add the costs. If you sell tickets for $10 each, how many must you sell to make a 10% profit? Record your calculations.

Performance Budget
Daily Costs:

theater rental = $100

5 performers × $25 each = $125

director = $35

Invent a Simple Machine

Internet

small group

Find out about simple machines. Take notes. Make or draw a diagram of an invention that uses one or more simple machines. Then "sell" your invention. Tell why people should buy it.

screws

pulleys

knock knock

lever

Write to Express Your Feelings

on your own

Mary Verdi-Fletcher is Jenny's role model. Write something to tell about a person you admire or want to be like. Choose the best form:

- a poem

- a journal entry

- instructions for how to be a role model.

Does your writing sound like you?

November 10

I love my Dad. He was very tired after work, but he still came to watch me play basketball tonight.

155

Use Context Clues

Context clues can help you figure out the meaning of new words. Context clues are the other words and sentences in the story or article. To **use context clues**:

✔ Read the sentence again.
✔ Look for clues, or hints, about the word's meaning.
✔ Reread the sentences that come before and after to find more clues.
✔ Use the clues to guess a meaning for the word.
✔ Try the meaning in the sentence.

Try the strategy.

from Dancing Wheels

In the center of the whirling and the twirling, Sabatino Verlezza and Mary Verdi-Fletcher dance together. They are the leaders of the company. Sabatino, a stand-up dancer and choreographer, creates the dances for the group.

When I reread the last sentence, I saw the words "creates the dances." A choreographer must be a person who makes dances.

Practice

Take this test and **use context clues** to understand words in "Dancing Wheels."

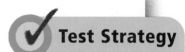
Read each item. Choose the best answer.

1 Read these sentences.

The <u>experienced</u> dancers move along with Sabatino. The dancers who are new frown. It is hard to learn the movements.

What does <u>experienced</u> mean?

A strong and flexible

B in an unhappy way

C the opposite of new

D with a lot of concentration

2 Read the meanings of the word <u>company</u>. Then read the sentence.

> **company** (**kum**-pu-nē) *noun*
>
> **1.** a group of people who work or share an activity together **2.** friendship or companionship **3.** guests in someone's home

Sabatino Verlezza and Mary Verdi-Fletcher are the leaders of the <u>company</u>.

Which meaning best fits the way <u>company</u> is used in the sentence?

A Meaning 1

B Meaning 2

C Meaning 3

Vocabulary

Chant

Your Busy Body

Your **skeleton** helps you
stand upright.

Your **heart** pumps blood
all day and night.

Your lungs breathe **oxygen**
out and in.

Your **muscles** let you
turn and spin.

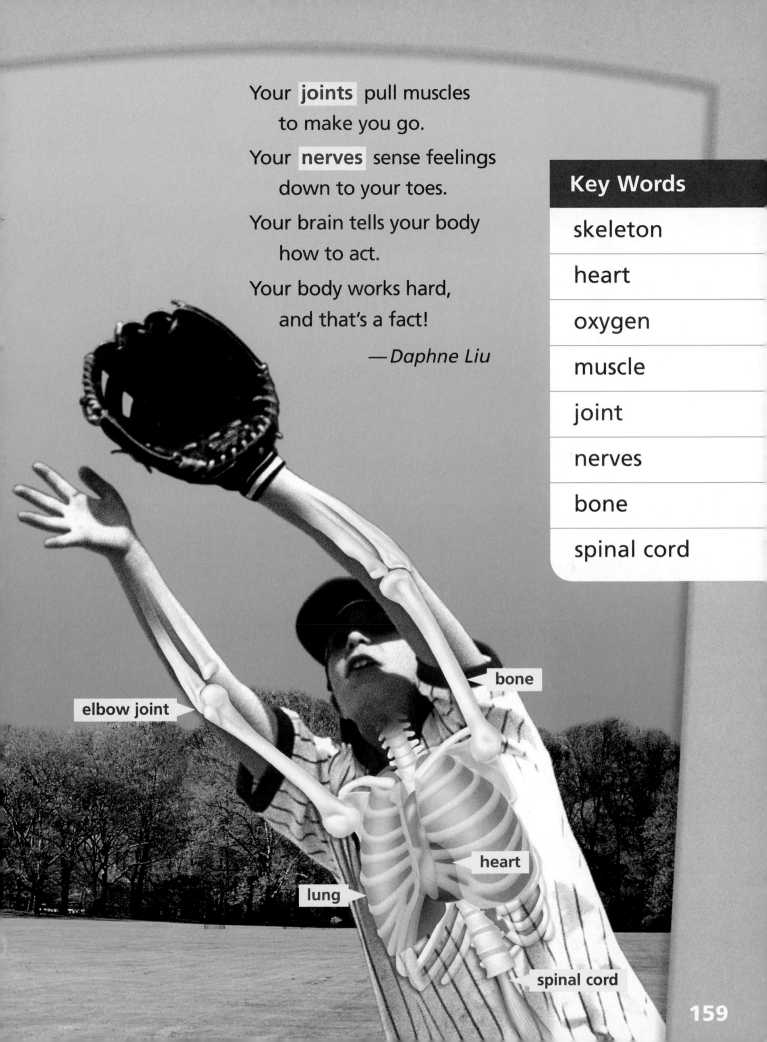

Your **joints** pull muscles
to make you go.
Your **nerves** sense feelings
down to your toes.
Your brain tells your body
how to act.
Your body works hard,
and that's a fact!

—*Daphne Liu*

Key Words

skeleton

heart

oxygen

muscle

joint

nerves

bone

spinal cord

elbow joint

bone

heart

lung

spinal cord

159

Read a Science Article

A **science article** is nonfiction. It can describe the parts of something and how things work.

✔ Look for **illustrations** with **labels** and **captions**. They show the parts of something.

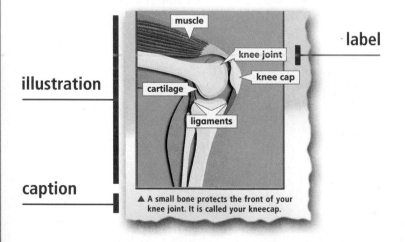

illustration

caption

label

muscle

knee joint

knee cap

cartilage

ligaments

▲ A small bone protects the front of your knee joint. It is called your kneecap.

✔ Study the **photographs** and **diagrams** to find out more.

 Selection Reading

Moving

by **Anita Ganeri**

What Happens When You Move?

What happens to your body when you move? Your brain, **nerves**, **muscles**, and **bones** all work together to make you walk, run, or jump. You can also make smaller movements, such as a smile or a frown. You are always moving, even when you are asleep. Your **heart** and lungs move inside you to keep you alive.

The Heart and Lungs

heart

lungs

▲ Exercise makes your heart and lungs work harder.

162

What Is a Skeleton?

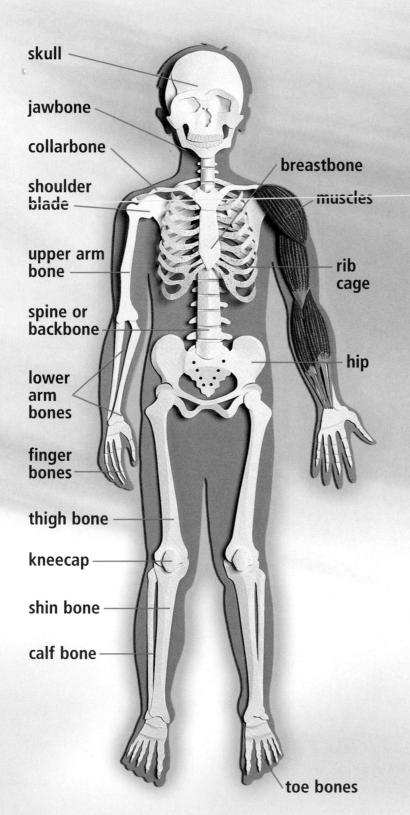

skull

jawbone

collarbone

shoulder blade

upper arm bone

spine or backbone

lower arm bones

finger bones

thigh bone

kneecap

shin bone

calf bone

breastbone

muscles

rib cage

hip

toe bones

There is a strong, hard framework of bones inside your body. This framework is called your **skeleton**. It holds your body up and keeps it from **collapsing in a heap**.

Your skeleton also helps you to move. There are muscles attached to the bones. They pull on different parts of your body to move them. Your skeleton also protects **delicate parts of your body**.

---

collapsing in a heap falling down
delicate parts of your body parts of your body that can be easily hurt

Before You Move On
1. **Details** What happens when you exercise?
2. **Paraphrase** What does your skeleton do for your body?

What's Inside Your Bones?

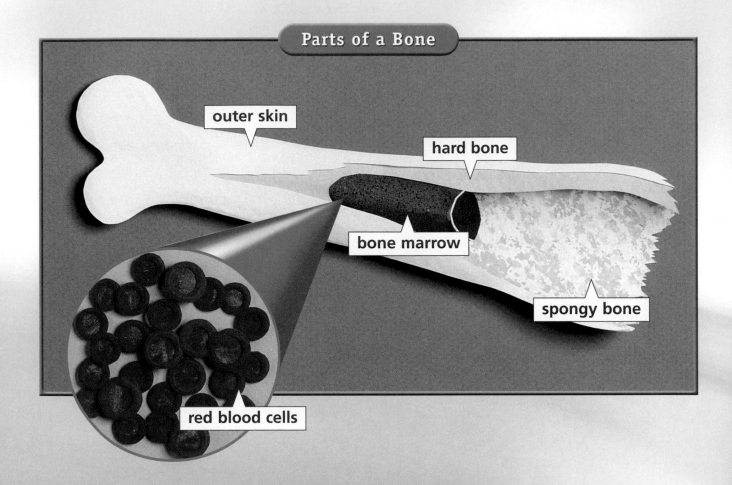

Parts of a Bone

outer skin

hard bone

bone marrow

spongy bone

red blood cells

Bones are made of water and hard **minerals**, such as **calcium**. The outside of a bone is stiff and tough. However, the inside is spongy and soft. This makes bones very strong but **very light.**

Bones are covered in a special type of skin. If a bone breaks, the skin helps to make new bone to repair the crack. Some bones also contain jelly-like bone marrow. Red bone marrow makes new **red blood cells**.

---

minerals nonliving material found in nature

calcium material needed for strong bones

very light not heavy

red blood cells tiny parts of the blood that carry oxygen to all parts of the body

164

What's the Purpose of the Skull?

Your skull is a hollow case of bones on top of your neck. One of its main jobs is to protect your brain. The bones in your skull are joined together like a **jigsaw puzzle** to make your skull stronger.

When you are born, some patches of your skull are soft and squishy. These **knit** together into hard bone as you grow older. Your skull is made up of a total of 22 bones by the time you are about 20. Most of these bones do not move.

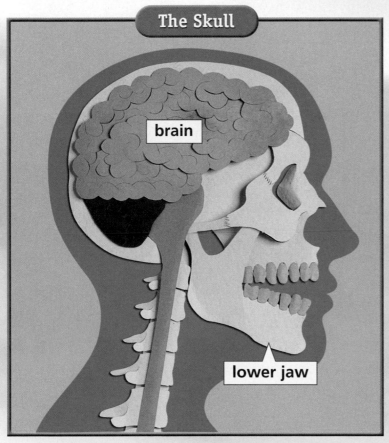

The Skull

brain

lower jaw

◄ **Your brain controls everything you do. The skull protects the brain. The lower jaw is the only bone in your skull that moves. It moves up and down when you chew.**

---

jigsaw puzzle puzzle with connecting pieces
knit grow

Before You Move On
1. **Comparison** How is the outside of a bone different from the inside?
2. **Main Idea/Details** How does the skull protect the brain?

165

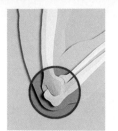

hinge-and-pivot

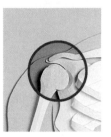

ball-and-socket

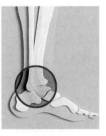

gliding

How Do Joints Work?

Your elbows, knees, shoulders, and hips are called movable **joints**. These are places where two bones meet but do not usually touch each other. Your movable joints allow you to bend, turn, and twist your body. Without them, you would have to stand straight and stiff all the time.

There are different types of joints. Each type moves in a different way. Your elbow is a hinge-and-pivot joint. It opens and closes like a door. It also **rotates**, or pivots, at one end. The shoulder is a ball-and-socket joint. It lets your arm swing around. Lots of small bones make up the gliding joint in your ankle.

▲ **Joints allow people to bend, turn, and twist.**

---

rotates turns

Inside a Joint

Most bones inside a joint are held in place by strong, stretchy straps. These are called ligaments. The ends of some bones are covered in rubbery **gristle**, which is called cartilage. It keeps the bones from **grinding** together and wearing out. A special liquid keeps movable joints slippery and well-oiled so that they work smoothly.

knee

▲ Your knee joint is the biggest joint in your body. It is a hinge joint.

The Knee

muscle

knee joint

knee cap

cartilage

ligaments

▲ A small bone protects the front of your knee joint. It is called your kneecap.

gristle strong material
grinding rubbing

Before You Move On

1. **Main Idea** What do movable joints let you do?

2. **Details** What holds most bones in place inside a joint?

What Is the Backbone?

A long chain of bones runs down your back. This is your backbone, or spine. It has 33 separate bones, called vertebrae. Your spine is very strong, but it can bend, so you can move.

Spine is straight.

Spine is curved.

▲ Your spine can be straight or slightly curved. Your spine can bend because it is made of 33 separate bones.

Your backbone supports your body and protects your **spinal cord**. The spinal cord is a thick bundle of nerves running from your brain to other parts of your body. If your spinal cord is damaged, you can **be paralyzed**.

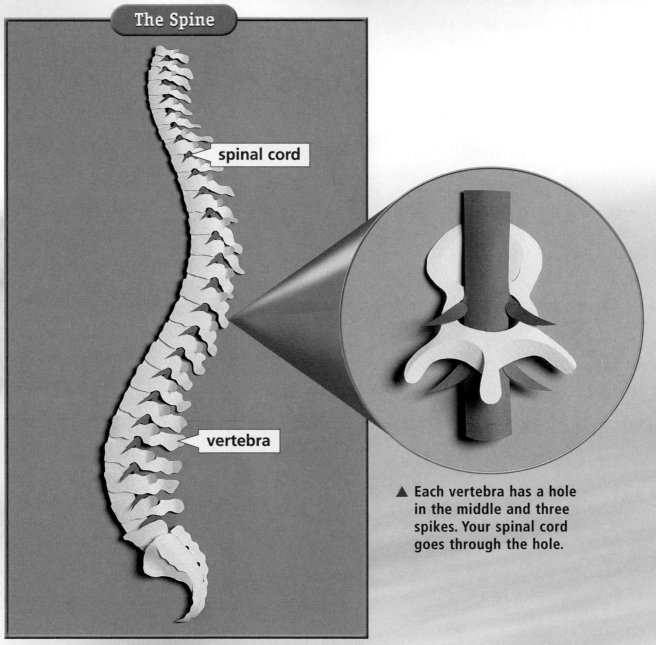

The Spine

spinal cord

vertebra

▲ The spinal cord is protected inside the backbone. Cartilage keeps the bones from rubbing together.

▲ Each vertebra has a hole in the middle and three spikes. Your spinal cord goes through the hole.

Before You Move On

1. **Graphic Aids** How does cartilage protect vertebrae?

2. **Summary** Why is the spine such an important part of your body?

_____

be paralyzed become unable to move your body

How Do Your Muscles Work?

Hundreds of muscles lie under your skin. They work with your bones to help you move. The muscles are attached to your bones by bands, called tendons. **Clench your fist and pull it up** toward your shoulder. Can you feel the muscles in your upper arm?

Some muscles are big and powerful. Others are tiny and used for **fine** movements. There are muscles deep inside your body. They keep your heart beating and your lungs working.

Large Muscle Movements

Your muscles pull on your bones to make you move. When you want to move your arm, your brain tells your arm muscles to get shorter, or contract. This pulls on your arm and makes it move. Muscles cannot push. They can only pull, so they often work in pairs. One muscle contracts to bend your arm. Then it relaxes, and its partner contracts to straighten the arm.

Clench your fist and pull it up
Make a fist and bend your arm

fine small

◄ **This athlete uses powerful arm muscles to make the cycle's wheels go fast.**

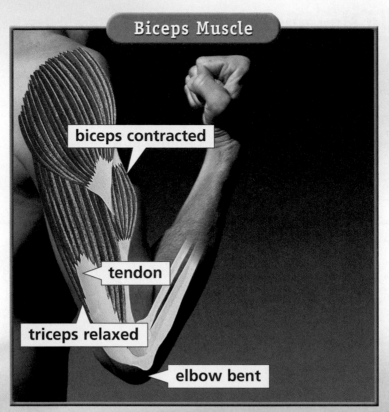

Biceps Muscle

biceps contracted

tendon

triceps relaxed

elbow bent

▲ Your biceps muscle contracts to bend your arm.

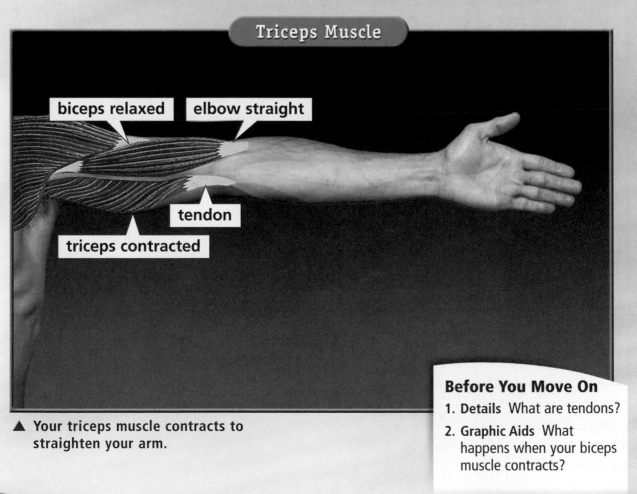

Triceps Muscle

biceps relaxed   elbow straight

tendon

triceps contracted

▲ Your triceps muscle contracts to straighten your arm.

Before You Move On

1. **Details** What are tendons?
2. **Graphic Aids** What happens when your biceps muscle contracts?

Small Muscle Movements

Each time you **make a face**, you use a lot of different muscles.
The muscles in your face do not pull on bones. They pull on your
skin to make it move. There are more than 30 muscles in your face.
You can show people how you are feeling by the **expression** on
your face.

Facial Muscles

▲ Muscles at the corners of your mouth let you smile.

▲ Muscles in your forehead help you frown.

▲ Muscles let you close your eyes and wrinkle your nose.

▲ Muscles near your eyes and nose help you make faces.

---

make a face let a feeling show on your face
expression look

Fuel for Muscles

Your muscles need energy to make them work. They get this energy from the food you eat and the air you breathe. Your blood carries nutrients from your food and **oxygen** from the air to your muscle cells. Then the cells use the oxygen to release energy from the food. The harder your muscles have to work, the more energy they need.

How Blood Flows

Your blood carries nutrients and oxygen to your muscles. Nutrients are vitamins and other things your body needs. When you work hard, you need more nutrients and more oxygen. ▶

Now you know what happens when you move your body. Even as you read this science article, your brain, nerves, muscles, and bones are working together. You use large muscles in your arms to lift the book. You use tiny muscles in your eyes to read. Think about your bones and muscles as you walk around school. Even when you are asleep, muscles in your heart and lungs are working to keep you alive!

Before You Move On

1. **Cause/Effect** How do muscles change the expression on your face?

2. **Paraphrase** Tell how your blood helps get energy to your muscles.

Think and Respond

Strategy: Classify Details

Work with a group. Make a word map for one part of the body: skeleton, joint, backbone, or muscle.

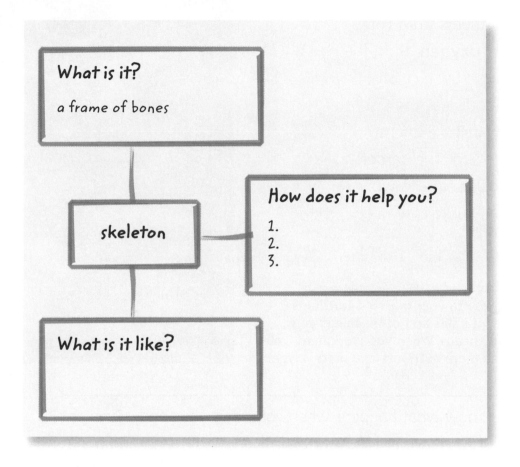

What is it?

a frame of bones

skeleton

How does it help you?

1.
2.
3.

What is it like?

Give an Oral Report

Use your word map to give an oral report. Show pictures to help you explain. Remember to use new vocabulary and speak slowly and loudly enough for everyone to hear you.

Talk It Over

1 **Personal Response** What's the most surprising thing you learned about the human body?

2 **Conclusion** What body parts do you use to jump? Explain how they work together.

3 **Main Idea** Think of another good title for this article.

4 **Conclusion** What can you do to keep your body healthy? Why is this important?

Compare Nonfiction

Both "Dancing Wheels" and "Moving" are nonfiction. How are they different? How are they the same?

Both "Dancing Wheels" and "Moving" use photographs to show things.

Content Connections

Learn Exercises

large group

What exercises are good for different muscles?
Invite a physical education teacher to show you.
Ask questions and
take notes. What main
ideas did you learn
from the speaker?

Main Ideas	Details
Push-ups work your triceps muscle.	After push-ups, my triceps muscle feels warm.
	Athletes do push-ups for stronger triceps muscles.

SCIENCE

Make a Diagram

on your own

1. Draw a skeleton inside the shape of the human body.

2. Turn the paper over. Trace the body shape.

3. Draw and label the organs.

4. Hold your diagram up to the light.

5. Discuss what the skeleton is and how it protects the organs.

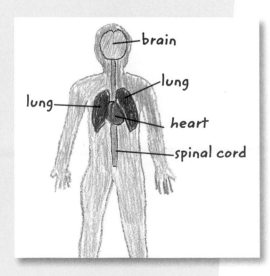

Research Medical Advances

Internet

Choose an important medical discovery or invention and write research questions. Find out when it was invented, what problem it solved, and how people's lives changed because of it. Give a report.

This medicine helps people control their blood pressure so they can live normal lives.

Write to Inform

Explain how people can keep their bodies healthy. Choose the best form to give the information:

- instructions
- a report
- a review of a book or an article

Be sure you include only important details.

In his book, *10 Steps to a Healthier You*, Mr. Dulay says it is important to get enough sleep every night. He says if you exercise a lot, you may need even more sleep!

Pronouns

Listen and sing.

Song

CAN YOU DANCE WITH ME?

Can you dance with me?
Can we kick a foot up high?
Let us raise our hands.
Let our fingers touch the sky.

Let us whirl and twirl around.
Let me lift you off the ground.
Can you dance with me?

—*Jane Zion Brauer*

Tune: "Turkey in the Straw"

How Language Works

A **pronoun** take the place of a noun.

<table>
<tr><td colspan="2">■ Use these pronouns in the subject of a sentence.</td></tr>
</table>

One	More than One
I	we
you	you
he, she, it	they

Example: Nan dances.

➡

She dances.

■ Use these **pronouns** after a verb or a preposition like *to, with* or *for*.

One	More than One
me	us
you	you
him, her, it	them

Example: Al dances with **Nan**.

➡

Al dances with **her**.

Practice with a Partner

Choose the correct red pronoun. Then say the sentence.

I / Me   1. _____ go to ballet class every Monday.

I / me   2. Judy takes the class with _____ .

She / Her   3. _____ is a great dancer.

We / Us   4. _____ work very hard in class.

we / us   5. Our teacher makes _____ practice a lot.

Put It in Writing

Think about dancers you have seen on television or in the movies. Write about the way dancers move. When you edit your work, make sure your pronouns are correct.

He twirls her. She loves to dance with him.

Show What You Know

Talk About the Human Body

In this unit, you read a photo essay and a science article about the human body. Look back at the unit. Find your favorite photo or diagram. Tell your group why you like it. Use it to tell what you learned about the human body.

Make a Mind Map

Work with a partner. Make a mind map to show what you learned about the human body.

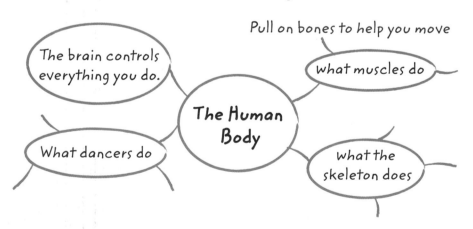

Pull on bones to help you move

The brain controls everything you do.

what muscles do

The Human Body

What dancers do

what the skeleton does

Think and Write

Would you like to try dancing or a new sport? Why or why not? Write about it. Add the writing to your portfolio. Include work that shows what you learned about the human body.

Read and Learn More

Leveled Books

Hoop with Swoopes
by Susan Kuklin

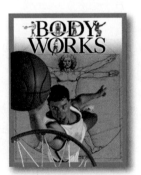

Body Works
by Janine Wheeler

Theme Library

Dem Bones
by Bob Barner

**The Best Part
of Me**
edited by Wendy Ewald

Internet

Go to: www.hbavenues.com

Simple Machines

The Human Body

Medicine Through Time

Freedom's Trail

In CONGRESS, July 4, 1776.

The unanimous Declaration of the thirteen united States of America.

Make a Freedom Trail

Show what "freedom" means to you.

1. Draw a picture or write some words about freedom. Use paper cut-outs that look like your footprints.
2. Put your footprints together on the floor.
3. Follow the "freedom trail." Does freedom mean the same thing to everyone?

Freedom means you can say what you want!

The British Colonies

▲ King George III of England ruled the colonies.

New England

New Hampshire

Massachusetts

Middle Colonies

New York

Rhode Island
Connecticut
New Jersey
Delaware
Maryland

Pennsylvania

Southern Colonies

Virginia

North Carolina

South Carolina

Georgia

Life in the Colonies

▲ making candles

▲ growing crops

▲ protecting their towns

▲ cooking

▲ spinning yarn

▲ making furniture

184

A Time Line of the American Revolution

1773
Patriots dump tea at the Boston Tea Party.

1775
Colonists fight the British at Concord and Lexington.

1776
The Declaration of Independence is signed.

1781
The Continental Army defeats the British at Yorktown.

1787
Delegates sign the Constitution.

1789
George Washington becomes the first president.

From Colonies to a Country

The 13 Original Colonies

In 1773, there was no United States. People lived in **colonies**. The king of Great Britain, King George III, ruled the colonies.

Many colonists did not like King George's **politics**, or the way he ruled the colonies. They felt it was unfair to pay **taxes** when they bought things.

GREAT BRITAIN

ATLANTIC OCEAN

The king called the colonists who didn't follow his rules **traitors**. However, they called themsleves **patriots**.

These patriots formed an army of **soldiers** to fight for their freedom from Great Britain. The patriots won the Revolutionary War. The colonies became the United States of America.

Key Words

colony

politics

tax

traitor

patriot

soldier

representative

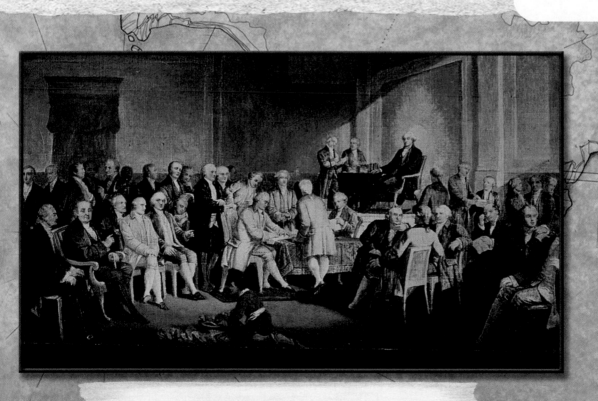

▲ **Representatives** from the new states wrote a plan for the new government.

Joining the
Boston Tea Party

by Diane Stanley
illustrated by Holly Berry

Read a Story

Genre

Some stories contain **fantasy**, or events that could never happen in real life. In this fantasy, a boy and a girl travel into the past to learn about events that <u>really</u> happened in 1773.

Characters

the twins

Grandma

Ben Reed

Setting

This story takes place today and in 1773 in Boston, Massachusetts.

▲ Old South Meeting House today

Selection Reading

The twins and Grandma travel into the past. Who do they meet there?

It was summer and time to visit Grandma. We were so excited! Our parents think we like to go there because we take walks in the woods and make homemade ice cream and pick berries and watch the stars. We do all those things, of course, but there's something else we do with Grandma.

We do something pretty **amazing**. We travel back in time! It's a thing she does with her magic hat. You'll see.

We could hardly wait to have another adventure. First we had to pick one of our ancestors to visit, and change our clothes.

---

amazing wonderful, surprising

It's my turn! I pick him!

Ah, yes. That's Ben Reed. He was your grandfather's great-great-great-grandfather.

When we were ready, Grandma put on her traveling hat. We all held hands and closed our eyes.

Is everybody ready for Boston? Next stop, 1773! Close your eyes.

Go back to England, you dogs, and leave us alone!

Traitor! How dare you insult His Majesty's soldiers!

---

insult His Majesty's soldiers say something bad about the King's soldiers

We opened our eyes, and there we were, standing on a Boston street. There were no cars, no **fast food**, and let's just say you could tell that the horses had been there. Just then a snowball flew past our heads! It hit the brick wall of a butcher shop, barely missing a soldier in a red coat. The soldier was really mad.

Hey, is that **George Washington**?

No, dear. Lots of men wear **powdered wigs** like that. It's the latest fashion.

---

fast food restaurants with food such as hamburgers and french fries

George Washington the man who became the first President of the United States

powdered wigs false hair covered with white powder

193

The boy who threw the snowball **dashed** around the corner. Grandma told us to hurry up and follow him. She said it was Ben Reed, and if we ran fast enough, we could catch up with him. We did, and he seemed glad to meet some "**long-lost relatives**." He even invited us to stay at his family's house.

dashed ran

long-lost relatives family members that he had not met before

our dropping in like this that we are coming to
visit without being invited

complained about them said they did not like
the taxes

King George the Third The King of England from
1760 to 1820

Ben's mother **invited us in**. A lot of her friends were there, **chatting** and drinking out of pretty **china cups**. She poured us each something from her silver teapot. Only it wasn't tea. It was hot chocolate. She said her club was called the Daughters of Liberty, and they wouldn't drink any more tea until England stopped making them pay taxes on it.

Doesn't everybody have to pay taxes?

---

invited us in asked us to come into her house
chatting talking
china cups tea cups

Sure. **Our elected officials** collect taxes right here in Massachusetts. The money is used to **pave the streets** and pay the police. These things make our lives better.

And if we don't like the way they're spending our money, we can vote them out of office!

But it's not fair for the English to tax us, too. There aren't any **representatives** from Massachusetts in the **Parliament of England**. We **don't have any say at all on** how much tax we have to pay or how the money is spent, either.

Our elected officials The leaders we voted for

pave the streets make the streets smooth

Parliament of England group that makes the laws for England

don't have any say at all on can't tell the Parliament how we feel about

Before You Move On

1. **Setting** Where do Grandma and the twins go? What is it like there?

2. **Problem** Why are the colonists angry?

197

2

The colonists make a plan. What do the twins do?

That night at supper we met the rest of the family. They mostly talked about **politics** . Mr. Reed told us that for the last six years the British Parliament had been trying to raise money by taxing the American **colonies** . The colonists had **pitched a fit over** it. They stopped going to stores that sold **English goods**. They wrote **complaining letters** and held lots of meetings. There were even **riots**.

---

pitched a fit over become very angry about

English goods cloth, tea, and other things from England

complaining letters letters explaining what they didn't like

riots angry crowds of people gathered in the streets

Finally, Parliament **gave up on** the taxes, except the one on tea. They kept that one just to **make the point** that England had the right to tax the colonies.

I heard there are three English ships down at the harbor, all full of tea. The Sons of Liberty aren't going to let them unload any of it, though.

Who are the Sons of Liberty?

A group of good citizens who are **determined** to make the British treat us right.

Some of us are ordinary **tradesmen**, like the silversmith Paul Revere. Others are important men, like John Hancock, the richest man in Boston. Then there's my friend and **fellow lawyer** John Adams, and his cousin Sam, who is really our leader.

---

gave up on stopped
make the point prove
determined working hard
tradesmen workers
fellow lawyer lawyer like me

The next morning, Ben said that Sam Adams had a big surprise planned. Ben wouldn't tell us what it was. We'd find out later, he said. We could even be a part of it if we wanted.

Ben was right. The night of December 16 was **something**! Thousands of people had gathered at a church called the Old South Meeting House. They were **riled up**, too. We couldn't get close enough to hear all the speeches, but we did hear one man ask the **governor**, Thomas Hutchinson, to send the tea back to England. But he wouldn't do it. Then Sam Adams ended the meeting with one short sentence. Ben said it was a **signal**.

something a big surprise

riled up angry

governor leader of Massachusetts

signal secret way to tell the Sons of Liberty to go ahead with their surprise

We ran back to Ben's house, where he told us what was about to happen. Some **patriots** were going to **disguise themselves as Mohawk Indians** and **board** the three ships in the harbor. Then they were going to throw all the tea **overboard**. We wanted to go too, so he helped us with our disguises. He told us to blacken our faces with soot from the fireplace and gave us feathers for our hair. It was a very bad costume.

disguise themselves as Mohawk Indians pretend to be
Native Americans

board get onto

overboard off the ship and into the water

even remotely like a Mohawk like a Native American at all

recognizing us knowing who we are

be considered treason make people think that we are fighting

put us to death have us killed

YIKES! Oh, no!

Before You Move On

1. **Solution** How did the colonists get the English Parliament to stop most of the taxes?

2. **Cause/Effect** Why do the colonists wear costumes?

3

Find out what happens when the twins join the colonists in their plan.

When we got to the **waterfront**, a group of "Mohawks" was already there. They looked as silly as we did, but we didn't recognize any of them either, so I guess the disguises worked. One of the men divided us into three groups and picked a leader for each one.

I don't see any tea.

It's down in the **hold**. See that man over there? That's the captain of the ship. He's giving the keys to unlock the hold to Sam . . . er, I mean, our Mohawk leader.

Isn't the captain upset that we're about to throw all **his cargo** into the water?

Sure, but he's not going to fight this crowd. He and the crew are going **down below** until it's all over.

---

waterfront part of the city that is next to the ocean
hold lower part of the ship
his cargo the tea on the ship
down below in the rooms under the ship's deck

We were **assigned** to the ship "Dartmouth." By the time we boarded, a crowd had gathered at the wharf to cheer us on.

_____
assigned told to go

The **tea chests** were heavy. We **hacked** them open with axes and dumped the tea over the side. Soon the whole ship smelled spicy and sweet.

tea chests wooden boxes of tea
hacked broke, chopped

After a couple of hours our job was finished. The captain got his keys back, and we even swept the tea and **wood splinters** off the deck. Then we marched off the ship in a double line, our axes over our shoulders, while someone played a tune on a **fife**. Everybody was **in a jolly mood**, and the crowd **treated us like heroes**.

---

wood splinters tiny pieces of wood

fife musical instrument like a flute

in a jolly mood happy

treated us like heroes acted as if we had done something brave or great

We thought Grandma would be **furious** when she found out where we'd been, but she wasn't. She said she'd read her history and knew that only one man, a carpenter named John Crane, was hurt at the Boston Tea Party. He was knocked in the head by a **winch**, but he soon **recovered** and walked home.

---

furious very angry
winch machine on the ship
recovered felt better; got well

Cool!

Grandma said she thought we'd had enough excitement for one visit. Maybe it was time to **head home**. So Grandma got out her traveling hat. When we were finally alone, we all held hands and closed our eyes and waited.

Cool! Good!
head home go back to Grandma's house

Suddenly we were at Grandma's house on a perfect summer day.

Before You Move On

1. **Paraphrase** Tell what happens during the Boston Tea Party.

2. **Details** How do the twins get back to Grandma's house?

210

Diane Stanley

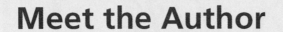

AWARD WINNER

Diane Stanley says, "Books are written by ordinary people who like words and are willing to work hard." Ms. Stanley's mother, Fay Stanley, was also a writer. She loved reading, words, and adventure, too. Her mother encouraged Diane to become a children's book author and illustrator. Now she travels all over the world with her own family to research story ideas.

A TAX on TEA

FAIR or UNFAIR?

If you were a colonist, what would you say about the British tax on tea?
Read what these two colonists have to say about it.

UNFAIR:

"The tax on tea is unfair! American colonists do not have any representatives in the Parliament in England. We cannot even vote for them, but England says we must pay taxes. Why should they decide how our money is spent?

Here in the colonies, we elect our own representatives. Let <u>them</u> tax us, not the British! If we don't like how our representatives spend our money, we can vote for someone else! We get to decide. We must make King George understand that we have the right to vote on taxes and other things for our own colonies.

We said "No!" to King George's taxes once before, and what happened? He sent soldiers here to control us. Send the **bullies** back, I say! No taxation without representation!"

bullies mean and bossy people

FAIR:

"What's wrong with us? Parliament has **repealed** every tax except one. We should be happy. Instead, we complain. We are acting like **spoiled children**!

Have you forgotten how many taxes we had before? Now we have only one small tax: a tax on tea. I think it's a small price to pay for our safety.

English soldiers have fought for us. They protect our towns. They protect our children. Someone has to pay these soldiers. Should people living in England pay to keep us safe? No. They should not!

There's an old saying, "Don't bite the hand that feeds you." Well, I say, "Don't bite the hand that protects you!" King George has been like a father to us. Let him have his tax!"

---

repealed stopped

spoiled children children who always get what they want

Before You Move On

1. **Main Idea** Why did one speaker think the tea tax was unfair?

2. **Fact and Opinion** What words in the speeches signal opinion?

Content Connections

Communicate a Message

small group

Imagine you are either a patriot or a colonist who supports the king. Give your group a message. Give some of the information without speaking. Listen and watch the other speakers. What do they want you to do?

We must support our king.

MATH

Calculate Taxes

partners

If you buy a book that costs $1.00 and the tax is 8 percent, your total cost is $1.08. What is the total cost for each of these?

sandwich:	$ 5.00
football:	$11.00
shoes:	$47.00
CD player:	$95.00

Item Cost	Tax	Total Cost
$1	$.08	$1.08

Give a Demonstration

Internet

small group

What things did the colonists make themselves? Find out about one product or craft. Make the product. Then demonstrate the steps to your class.

To make candles, you need wax or fat, wicks, and a pot.

WRITING

Write to Persuade

on your own

Imagine you are a colonist. What do you feel strongly about? Write something to persuade others to agree with your opinion. Choose the best form:

- a political cartoon

- a protest song or poem

- a letter to the editor.

Be sure to give reasons for your opinion.

October 31, 1773

Dear Editor:
We should all drink cofee, not tea! The tax on tea is unfair. Let's not send our hard-earned money to Britain! We don't have any say in how our money is used.

Identify Fact and Opinion

A **fact** is a statement you can check to be sure it's true. An **opinion** is a statement that tells what someone thinks, feels, or believes. To tell a fact from an opinion:

✔ Look to see if you can prove the statement. It is probably a **fact**.

✔ If you can't prove it, the statement is probably an **opinion**. *Think, should,* and *must* are some clues that the writer is giving an opinion.

Try the strategy.

Too Many Taxes

Great Britain called for new taxes on the American colonies in the late 1700s. I think the Sugar Act of 1764 was really unfair. It forced colonists to pay taxes on sugar and coffee. The colonists also had to pay taxes on stamps, glass, paints, paper, and tea. I feel sorry for the colonists.

The first statement is a fact. I can check it in a book. The writer says the Sugar Act was unfair. That is an opinion. It tells what the writer thinks.

Practice

Take this test and **identify facts and opinions**.

Read the speeches on pages 212–213. Then read each item. Choose the best answer.

Read the speeches on pages 212–213.

✓ Test Strategy

Read the directions carefully. Make sure you understand what to do.

1 **Which sentence is a fact?**

A   We should be happy.

B   The tax on tea is unfair!

C   Send the bullies back, I say!

D   American colonists do not have any representatives in the Parliament in England.

2 **Which sentence is an opinion?**

A   English soldiers have fought for us.

B   Someone has to pay these soldiers.

C   I think it's a small price to pay for our safety.

D   Parliament has repealed every tax except one.

3 **Complete this sentence with a fact.**
The tax on tea —

A   is fair

B   is unfair

C   should be changed

D   helps pay for the British soldiers

Song

Come to the Convention

We need a U.S. **Constitution**.

Let's decide what we should do.

Let's **declare** an **independent**
government:

A President and **Congress**, too.

Delegates come to the sessions

From the sea to the new **frontier**.

The Constitutional Convention

Is happening right here!

—*Joyce McGreevy*

Tune: "I've Been Working on the Railroad"

Key Words

Constitution

declare

independent

government

Congress

delegate

frontier

Read a Biography

A **biography** is the story of someone's life written by another person.

✔ Study the **illustrations** to learn about the time and place.

✔ Look for **dates** and words like *then*, *at last*, and *later* to find out when things happened.

date ——— George was born in 1732. He grew up in Virginia not far from the Potomac River. ▶

💿 **Selection Reading**

GEORGE WASHINGTON

by
James Cross Giblin
illustrated by
Michael Dooling

Set Your Purpose

Learn why George Washington is called "The Father of Our Country."

George Washington grew up in a big family. His father had been married before, and George had two older **half brothers**, Lawrence and Augustine. He also had three younger brothers, Samuel, John, and Charles, and a younger sister, Elizabeth. They all lived and played on a farm in Virginia called Ferry Farm.

George was an **athletic** boy, and tall for his age. His father gave him a pony and taught him how to ride.

Mr. Washington sent George's half brothers to the same school he had gone to in England, but George went to school near home. There a **minister** taught him how to read and write and do **sums**. George had a hard time with spelling. Was it *coff* or *cough*?

George was born in 1732. He grew up in Virginia not far from the Potomac River. ▶

---

half brothers brothers with the same father but a different mother

athletic active and healthy

minister person who works for a church

sums math

Nothing really bad happened to George until he was eleven. That was when his father died. Now George **looked to** his half brother, Lawrence, for **guidance**.

Later, Lawrence married and moved to a farm called Mount Vernon. His house stood on a hill that sloped down to the Potomac River. George often visited his brother at Mount Vernon, and he came to love the place. Some days, he and Lawrence went fishing in the river.

▲ In the 1740s, young George enjoyed visits at his brother's farm in Virginia. The farm was called Mount Vernon.

---

looked to depended on, turned to
guidance help in growing up

Key Places in Washington's Life

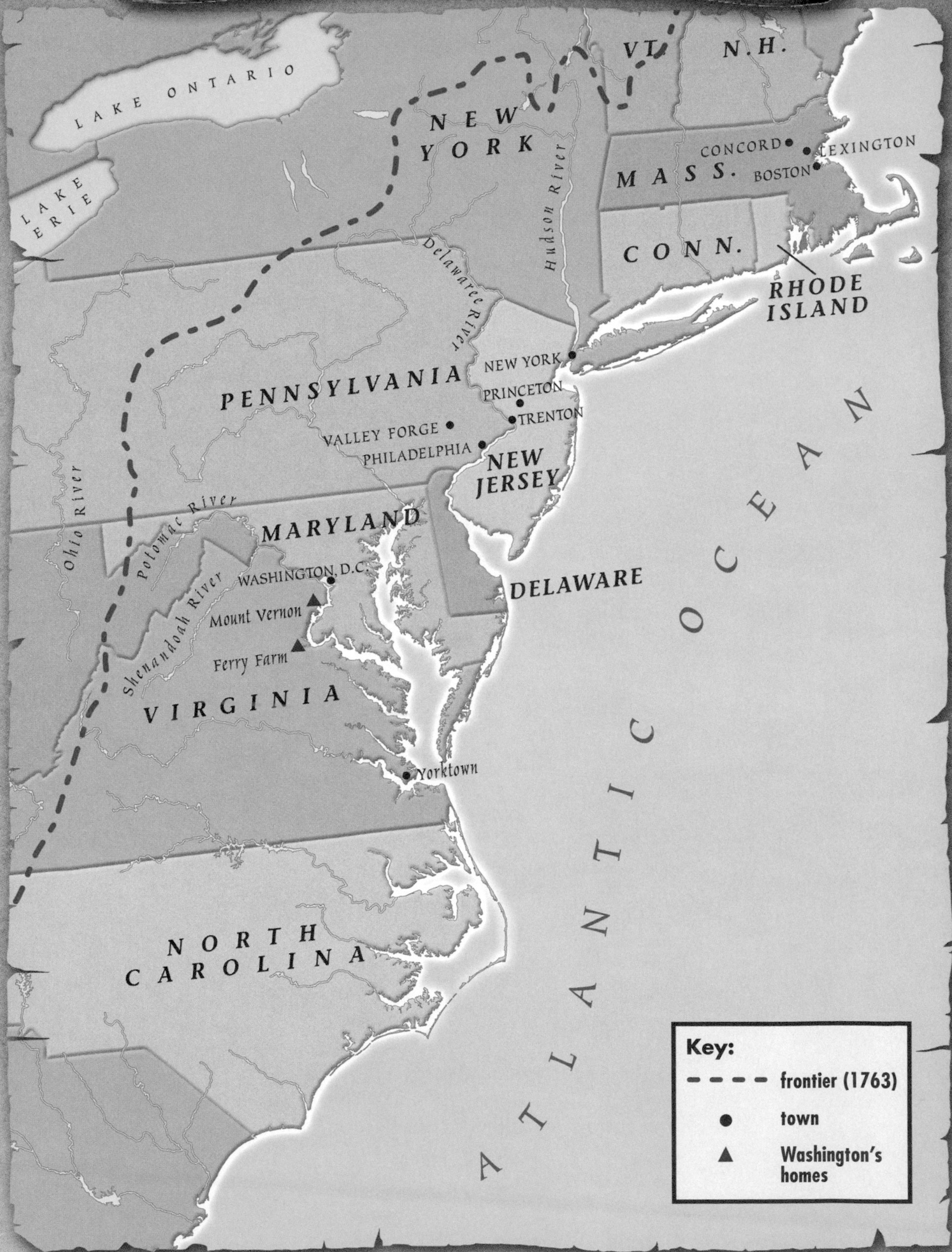

LAKE ONTARIO

LAKE ERIE

VT.   N.H.

NEW YORK

MASS.

CONCORD • • LEXINGTON
BOSTON •

CONN.

RHODE ISLAND

Hudson River

Delaware River

PENNSYLVANIA

NEW YORK •
PRINCETON •
TRENTON •

VALLEY FORGE •
PHILADELPHIA •

NEW JERSEY

Ohio River

Potomac River

MARYLAND

DELAWARE

Shenandoah River

WASHINGTON, D.C.

▲ Mount Vernon

▲ Ferry Farm

VIRGINIA

ATLANTIC OCEAN

• Yorktown

NORTH CAROLINA

Key:

– – – frontier (1763)

• town

▲ Washington's homes

▲ This map shows what the East Coast of
the U.S. looks like today. Look at where
the frontier was in 1763.

When he was just sixteen, George got the chance to help **survey** land on Virginia's western **frontier** . He had a fine time on the trip. Besides measuring land, he **swam horses** across flooded rivers. He roasted wild turkeys over open fires and slept under the stars.

Back home, **a new tragedy struck**. Lawrence **fell ill with tuberculosis** and died a year later. First George had lost his father. Now he had lost his beloved half brother. At age twenty, he was on his own.

▲ In the late 1740s, George helped to survey Virginia's western frontier. He had a good time there.

---

survey make a map of the

swam horses took horses

a new tragedy struck something terrible happened

fell ill with tuberculosis became very sick

Before You Move On

1. **Details** When was George born? Where did he grow up?

2. **Sequence** What did George do when he was sixteen?

227

America was still a colony at that time. That meant it was ruled by its parent country, Great Britain. The British army **defended** America's western frontier. Helping the army were groups of volunteer soldiers called militias. George joined the Virginia militia as **a major** in 1752.

George and his men marched with the British into the forests and mountains of the Ohio country. Both Great Britain and France **claimed this wilderness** was theirs.

George fought back bravely when the French attacked. Two horses **were shot out from under him**. Bullets ripped through his uniform. **His commanding officer** was killed, but George wasn't even **wounded**.

At last the French **gave up**. American settlers began to move into the Ohio country. His work done, George **put away his uniform**. He went back to Mount Vernon and became a farmer.

were shot out from under him were killed while George was riding them

His commanding officer The leader of the militia

wounded hurt

gave up stopped fighting

put away his uniform stopped being a soldier

Every **well-to-do** farmer in Virginia owned **slaves** then. With the help of his slaves, George raised crops of tobacco, wheat, and Indian corn.

Now that he had settled down, George decided to look for a wife. He found a pretty young **widow**, Martha Custis. Martha had two small children: John, who was called Jackie, and Martha, who was called Patsy.

George and Martha had no children of their own, but George **doted on** Jackie and Patsy. He ordered books and toys for them from faraway London.

The family lived happily for many years. Then Patsy got sick. Her mother and George took Patsy from doctor to doctor, but nothing helped. Patsy died when she was only seventeen.

George was still **grieving for** Patsy when he **got a new call to duty**.

Many Americans wanted to be free of Great Britain. They wanted to be **independent** and run their own country. Finally, fighting broke out between British troops and American volunteers. It happened at the little towns of Lexington and Concord in Massachusetts.

---

well-to-do rich

slaves people who were forced to work without pay

widow woman whose husband had died

doted on gave lots of love and attention to

grieving for feeling very, very sad about

got a new call to duty was asked to serve in the militia again

▲ After George and Martha married in 1759, she and her children came to live with him at Mount Vernon.

Before You Move On

1. **Details** How did George feel about his children?

2. **Traits** How would you describe George Washington so far?

America had never had a **Commander in Chief of its armed forces**. Now **Congress** decided it needed one. The members talked and talked and finally made their choice. They all agreed that the best man for the job would be George Washington.

George wasn't sure he could do it, and he hated to leave Mount Vernon. He also believed in American independence and wanted to help win it. So at last he said yes.

The fighting went well at first. George's men **drove the British out of** Boston. Then they moved south to build **defenses** around New York. Congress **declared** America's independence from Great Britain.

Then the British sent a large army to attack New York. They forced George and his men to give up the city and cross the Hudson River into New Jersey.

Commander in Chief of its armed forces leader of its army and navy

drove the British out of made all the British soldiers leave

defenses forts to protect them from the British

▼ On June 16, 1775, George became the Commander in Chief of the **Continental army**.

Continental army army of the American colonies

George **rallied** his army by planning a surprise attack on the British forces. Hidden by darkness, he led his men in boats across the icy Delaware River. At dawn on December 26th, they attacked the enemy camp at Trenton, New Jersey. Most of the soldiers in the camp were still asleep, and they **surrendered quickly**.

George won another battle at Princeton, but then he lost one near Philadelphia the following fall. With his men, he had to **retreat** to Valley Forge, Pennsylvania.

It was bitterly cold at Valley Forge. George lived in a stone house, but his soldiers had to sleep in tents until they could build **log huts**. The soldiers did not have enough food or clothing or shoes.

George and his men crossed the Delaware River on December 25, 1776. They defeated the British on December 26. ▶

rallied encouraged
surrendered quickly did not fight for very long
retreat move back
log huts small wooden houses

George wrote to Congress and begged for more supplies, but the supplies were slow to come. When they did come, George made sure every man got an equal share of clothing. He made sure the food was divided equally, too.

At last the long winter ended. The American army had **survived**, and new help was on the way. France **recognized** America as an independent nation. It sent troops to fight alongside the American soldiers.

George and his men were filled with fresh hope, but the war was far from over. The Americans and their French **allies** won some battles, but they lost many others.

George often wished he could go home to Mount Vernon, but he knew he could never leave his men. Nor could he give up the struggle for America's independence. So he stayed. Seeing his **determination**, most of his men stayed with him.

▲ George's men suffered terribly at Valley Forge. It was extremely cold during the winter of 1777–1778.

survived lived through the difficult times
recognized started to treat
allies friends
determination refusal to give up

Before You Move On

1. **Motive** Why did George agree to be Commander in Chief?

2. **Details** What did George do to help his men at Valley Forge?

At last came the chance George had been waiting for. A large British force was camped at Yorktown, Virginia. George and his men **surrounded** the British by land. A fleet of French ships blocked their escape by sea. With no hope of help, the British surrendered to George. He took more than 7,000 prisoners.

Yorktown was the greatest victory the American army had won. George's joy about it, however, soon turned to sadness. Martha's son, Jackie, was with the army at Yorktown. Just before the victory, he came down with a high fever, and soon afterward, he died.

A year and a half after Yorktown, the American Revolutionary War finally came to an end. Under General George Washington's leadership, the United States had won its freedom. No man in America was more loved than he. Many people even said that he should become King of the United States.

George would not hear of it. He hadn't fought for America's freedom against the King of England only to be **crowned king** himself. All he wanted, he said, was to **retire** to Mount Vernon. After saying **farewell** to his officers, that is what he did.

---

surrounded trapped, blocked
crowned king made a king
retire stop working and go home
farewell goodbye

▲ The British surrendered at Yorktown in 1781, but George was saddened by his son's death.

Before You Move On

1. **Motive** Why didn't George go home to Mount Vernon before the war was over?

2. **Paraphrase** Describe what happened at Valley Forge and at Yorktown.

237

▼ After the war, George returned to Mount Vernon.

George loved being a farmer again. He got up at dawn and ate a breakfast of **hoecakes** and tea. Then he rode from field to field to see what the workers were doing.

These happy days did not last long. Soon George got another call to duty. It was a call he **could not refuse**.

Delegates from twelve of the thirteen states met in Philadelphia to write a new plan, a constitution, for the **government** of the United States. The **Constitution** said the country should have a strong president, who would be elected for a **term** of four years.

Electors in each state cast ballots for America's first President. When the ballots were counted, all of the electors had voted for George Washington.

---

hoecakes corn pancakes

could not refuse had to say "yes" to

term time period

Electors in each state cast ballots People in each state voted

So once again George packed his bags and **set off** by himself. He traveled **by carriage** to New York City, which was then the capital of the United States.

When he took the oath of office, George did not wear his general's uniform or a fancy outfit made in England or France. Instead, he wore a plain brown suit made in America. That way, no one would think he wanted to be king.

Some people wanted to call George "His Highness." He said he **preferred** "Mr. President." So that is what America's presidents have been called ever since.

▲ In 1789, George became the first President of the United States. He wondered what it would it be like. No one had ever been President before.

---

set off left

by carriage in a wagon pulled by a horse

When he took the oath of office On the day he became president

preferred wanted to be called

Before You Move On

1. **Motive** Why did George Washington wear a plain brown suit when he became President?

2. **Details** What do Americans call their President?

Martha joined George in New York. A year later, the capital of the United States was moved to Philadelphia. George and Martha moved, too.

George discovered that it was as hard being President as it was being Commander in Chief of the Army, maybe harder. Some people believed the central government should **be strong**. Other people **feared** this would lead to a government like Great Britain's. They wanted the states to have more power.

George listened to both sides. He thought carefully. Then he made his decisions. Usually he decided in favor of a stronger central government.

▲ In 1789, George Washington took the oath of office. He became the first President of the United States.

---

be strong have more power than the state governments

feared were afraid or scared that

When his four-year term ended, George wanted to retire to Mount Vernon. The government leaders told him he could not. They said George was the only man who could keep the **country together** and lead it forward. So George ran again, and, in 1792, he was elected again.

▲ People disagreed about a lot of things. Only George's leadership could keep them from splitting the country apart.

country together states united

Before You Move On

1. **Point of View** Why did some people fear a strong central government?

2. **Motive** Why did George run for a second term as President?

George was over sixty years old now, and he **felt his age**. He feared that his memory was failing, and his false teeth bothered him. They were made from the teeth of a hippopotamus and did not fit well.

George was wearing his false teeth when he had his portrait painted by Gilbert Stuart. This is the picture of him that appears on every dollar bill. George looks very serious in the picture because his teeth were hurting him that day.

George's second term was coming to an end. He could look back with pride on his years as president. Great Britain had left the Ohio country, and more and more settlers were moving into it. American ships now sailed up and down the Mississippi River. Three new states, Vermont, Kentucky, and Tennessee, had joined the United States. The new capital city, Washington, named for George, was being **laid out** along the Potomac River.

Many people wanted George to run for a third term, but he refused. He said the time had come to retire **for good**. George went home to Mount Vernon.

Gilbert Stuart painted George's portrait in 1796. This is the picture that is on the dollar bill. ▶

---

felt his age was feeling tired and old
laid out planned
for good forever

George was happy to be home at Mount Vernon. Once more he got up at dawn and ate a breakfast of hoecakes and tea. Then he rode from field to field to see what the workers were doing, but something was troubling him.

During his years in the North, George had seen a world without slaves. Now he was back in the South, where slaves did most of the work on farms like Mount Vernon. Was it right? George wondered. Should slavery be allowed in a free country like the United States? He decided it should not.

George knew his neighbors would not agree with his ideas about slavery. But he could do something about it on his own. In **his will**, he said that after his death, and Martha's, all the slaves at Mount Vernon were to be freed.

▲ George was happy to be home at Mount Vernon, but he was **troubled** about slavery. He didn't think it was right.

---

his will the written directions George wanted people to follow after he died

troubled unhappy and worried

One day in December, George rode out in a freezing rain to inspect his fields as usual. The next day, he came down with a sore throat. The day after that, his throat was so swollen that he could not swallow. Breathing was difficult, and he could barely speak.

Doctors were called, but in those days there were no medicines that could cure George. "I am not afraid to **go**," he whispered to Martha. That night, near midnight, he died.

George Washington left behind no children of his own. Instead he left a nation. He had served as the nation's first commander in chief, and then as its first President. That is why he is known as "The Father of Our Country."

On December 14, 1799, George Washington died at Mount Vernon.

Before You Move On

1. **Paraphrase** How did America change while George was President?

2. **Problem** What did George worry about after he retired? Why?

go die

Meet the Author

James Cross Giblin

AWARD WINNER

James Cross Giblin wanted to find out what George was really like <u>as a person</u>. He discovered that he really admired George Washington's character. "The people tried to make George Washington a king," says Mr. Giblin, but "Washington refused to be crowned king. He would not wear his military uniform the day he became President. As President, he dressed as one of the people, wearing a plain brown suit."

Mr. Giblin has written more than 20 books for children. He has received awards for this book and many others.

Think and Respond

Strategy: Sequence

Make a time line of George Washington's life. Show the main events in his life and when they happened.

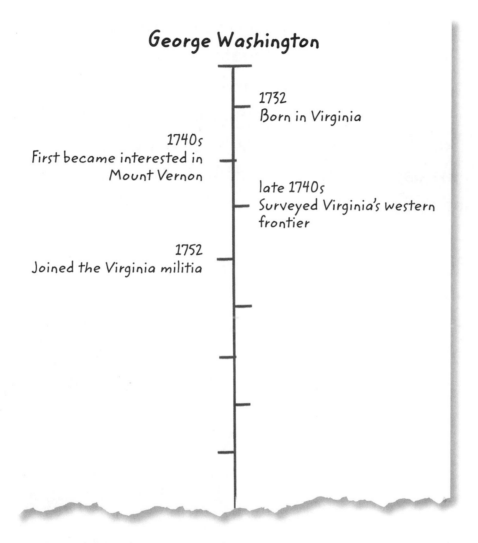

George Washington

1732
Born in Virginia

1740s
First became interested in
Mount Vernon

late 1740s
Surveyed Virginia's western
frontier

1752
Joined the Virginia militia

Interview a Hero

Imagine your partner is George Washington. Choose a five-year period from your time line. Ask George what he did during those years. Then switch roles.

Talk It Over

1 **Personal Response** What is the most important thing you learned about George Washington? What is the most interesting thing? Why?

2 **Cause/Effect** Why do you think most of the soldiers stayed with George Washington at Valley Forge?

3 **Motive** George loved being a farmer. Why did he leave his farm so many times?

4 **Speculate** If George Washington had written an autobiography, or a story about himself, how might it be different from this biography?

Compare Moods

Compare the mood, or feeling, of "George Washington" to the mood of "Joining the Boston Tea Party."

Content Connections

Make a Decision

small group

Imagine you are a soldier at Valley Forge. It is very cold. You need more food and clothing. Should you stay or leave? Make a group decision. Tell the class what you decided and why. Listen to other groups. What reasons do they give? Write them in a chart.

MATH

2×5

Graph Travel Time

partners

Calculate the time it takes to travel from Washington, D.C., to Philadelphia. Use this formula: distance ÷ rate = time. Complete the chart. Compare your answers with others. Show the information in a class bar graph.

Trip	Distance	Form of Travel	Rate	Time
Washington, D.C. to Philadelphia, Pennsylvania	130 miles	walking	4 miles per hour	
		horse	40 miles per hour	
		car	65 miles per hour	
		train	90 miles per hour	

Research Causes of the War

partners

Research the causes of the American Revolution. Take notes. Draw a picture of an action, or cause. Then draw one of the reactions, or effects. Discuss the pictures with your group. Ask and answer questions about the actions and reactions.

Action

Parliament Votes To Keep Tea Tax

Reaction

Boston Tea Party

WRITING

Write a Biography

Internet

on your own

Find out about a hero from the time of the American Revolution. Write a biography about the person. Add it to a class book of American Revolution heroes.

SAMUEL ADAMS

Samuel Adams was a leader of the American Revolution. He planned the Boston Tea Party and signed the Declaration of Independence.

Past Tense Verbs

Listen and sing.

Song

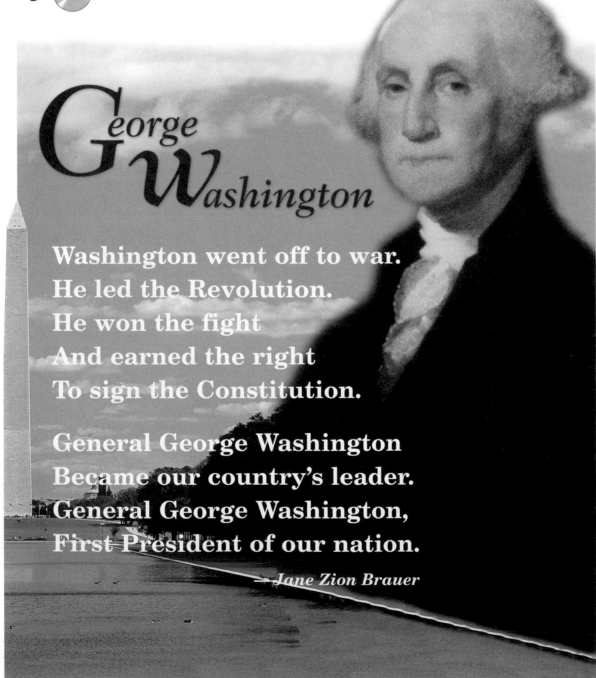

George Washington

Washington went off to war.
He led the Revolution.
He won the fight
And earned the right
To sign the Constitution.

General George Washington
Became our country's leader.
General George Washington,
First President of our nation.

— *Jane Zion Brauer*

Tune: "Yankee Doodle"

How Language Works

The **verb** in a sentence shows when the action happens.

Past Tense Verbs	Examples:
■ You can add **-ed** to many verbs to tell about the past.	Verb: **divide** In the Past: **divided**
■ Other verbs have a special form to tell about the past.	Verb: **become** In the Past: **became**

Practice with a Partner

Study the verbs in the box. Change each underlined verb to tell about the past.

1. The Revolutionary War <u>starts</u> in 1775.
2. Washington <u>is</u> Commander in Chief.
3. He and his men <u>fight</u> many battles.
4. They finally <u>win</u> the war.
5. Our country <u>becomes</u> an independent nation.

Now	In the Past
are	were
become	became
fight	fought
is	was
win	won

Put It in Writing

Write about George Washington when he was a boy. Describe where he lived and what he liked to do.

George had a pony. He lived on a farm. He rode around the farm.

Show What You Know

Talk About the American Revolution

In this unit, you read a story about an event that led to the American Revolution and a biography about America's first President. Look back at the unit. Which event do you think was the most interesting? Why? Talk about the event with your partner.

Make a Mind Map

Work with your group. Make a mind map to show what you learned about the American Revolution.

People	Thoughts and Feelings	Actions	Result
colonists	thought taxes were unfair	complained stopped buying English goods had the Boston Tea Party	They showed the king how much they hated the taxes.

Think and Write

What are other ways people can solve problems besides going to war? Write about it. Add the writing to your portfolio. Include work that shows what you learned about the American Revolution.

Read and Learn More

Leveled Books

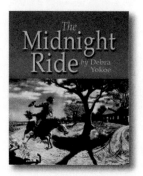

The Midnight Ride
by Debra Yokoe

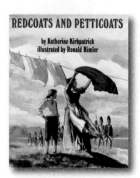

Redcoats and Petticoats
by Katherine Kirkpatrick

Theme Library

The Hatmaker's Sign
by Candace Fleming

Abigail Adams
by Alexander Wallner

Internet

Go to: www.hbavenues.com

Colonial Crafts

Liberty's Kids

American Revolution

From SEA to SHINING SEA

Make a Postcard

1. Make a postcard of a place in the U.S.
2. Put your postcard on a U.S. map.
3. What can you tell about the U.S. from your postcards?

U.S. National and State Parks

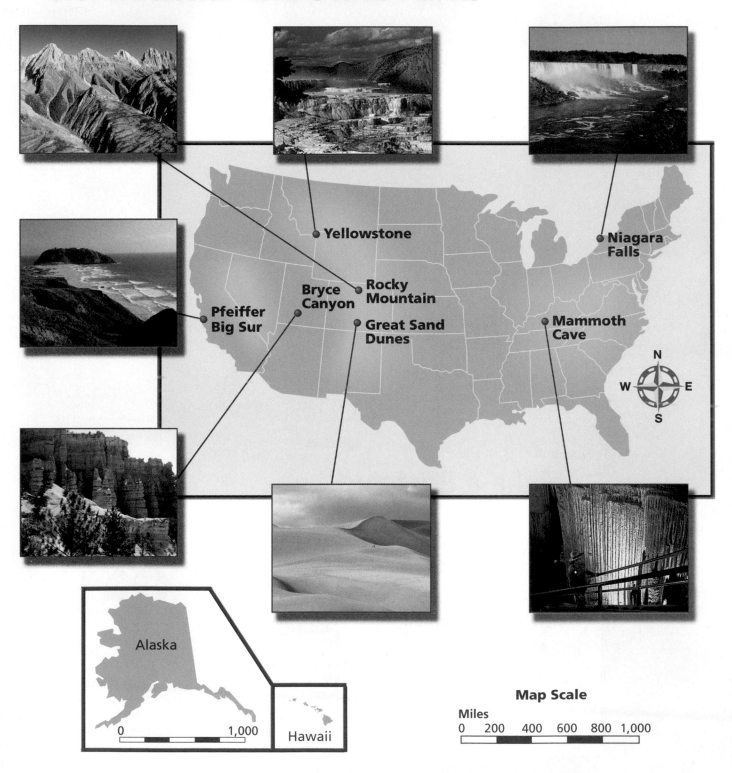

Yellowstone

Niagara Falls

Bryce Canyon

Rocky Mountain

Pfeiffer Big Sur

Great Sand Dunes

Mammoth Cave

N
W E
S

Alaska

0   1,000

Hawaii

Map Scale

Miles

0   200   400   600   800   1,000

How Landforms Are Made

▲ Ocean waves cut caves into sea cliffs.

▲ Glaciers wear down mountains to form valleys.

▲ Rivers carve canyons.

▲ Water moves rocks and soil to make islands.

▲ Wind blows sand into dunes.

▲ Wind and water break rocks down to create buttes and mesas.

257

EROSION CANYON

Act out this scene.

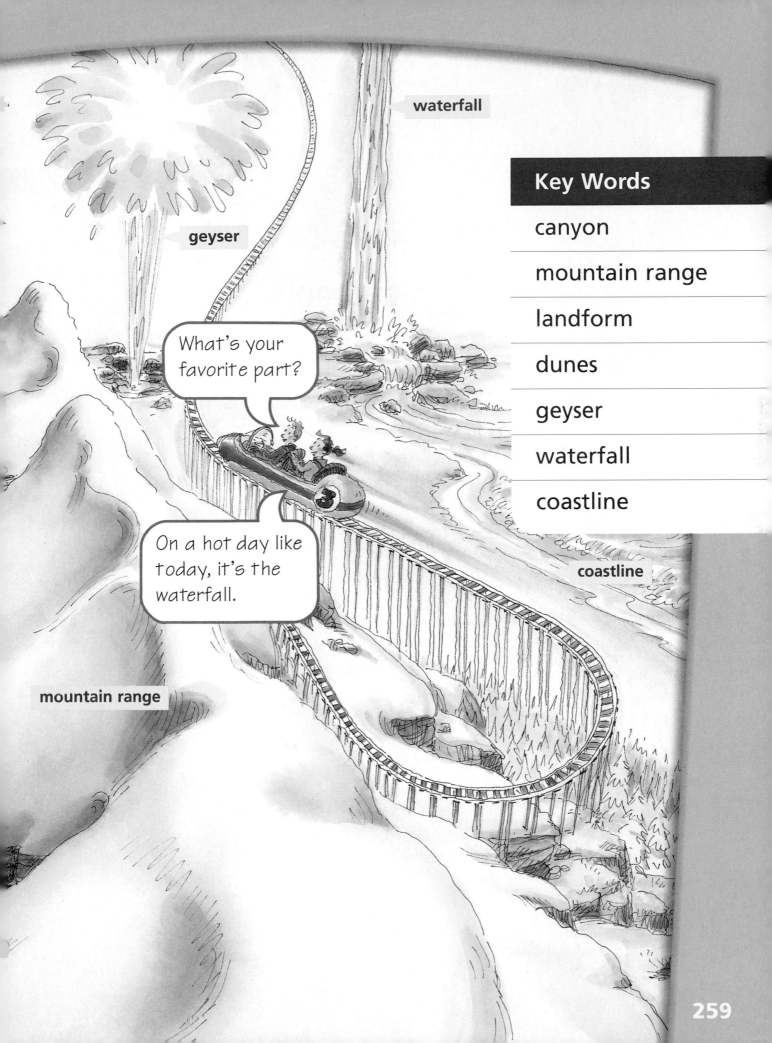

259

Read a Geography Article

A **geography article** is nonfiction. It can tell where places are and what they are like.

✔ Study the **maps** to find out where places are.

map
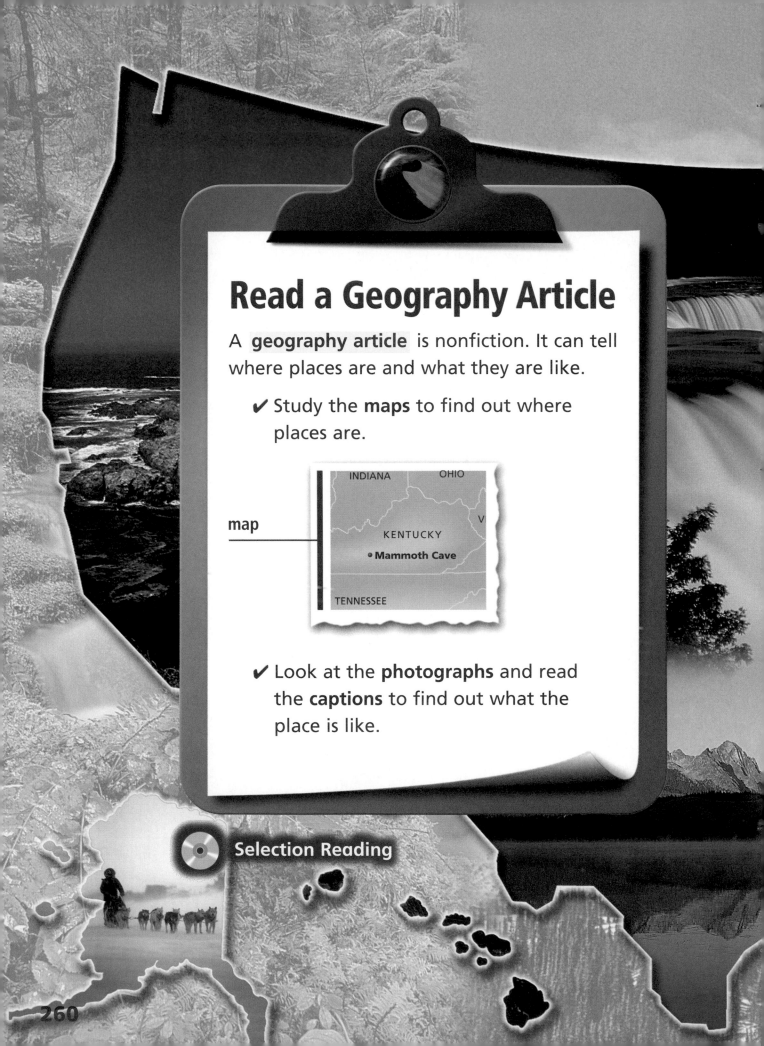

INDIANA OHIO

KENTUCKY
• Mammoth Cave

TENNESSEE

✔ Look at the **photographs** and read the **captions** to find out what the place is like.

Selection Reading

Greetings from AMERICA

by Elizabeth C. Sengel

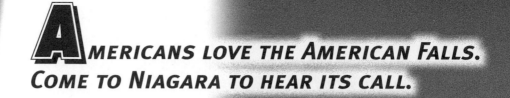

AMERICANS LOVE THE AMERICAN FALLS. COME TO NIAGARA TO HEAR ITS CALL.

You will often hear a **waterfall** before you see it. A cascade draws you toward it with a soothing, musical sound. A cataract roars as the water crashes into a pool below.

Nature makes waterfalls out of water and rock. Often, a waterfall forms where hard and soft rock meet. Water just bounces off hard rock as it rushes over, but the continual flow of water **wears down soft rock**. This process is called erosion. As the soft rock wears down, or erodes, a step or ledge forms in the river. Now the water has to tumble over the ledge. Over time, the falling water wears down more soft rock, creating a pool at the bottom of the falls.

Cascades are waterfalls with a small **volume** of water. They often drop from great heights and look like long silver ribbons. Cataracts are waterfalls with a large volume of water. Some spill over a ledge like water flowing over the side of a bathtub.

The American Falls is a cataract. A tour boat lets people see it from the bottom. ▶

---

wears down soft rock makes soft rock get smaller and smaller

volume amount

Greetings from NIAGARA FALLS

Horseshoe Falls

ONTARIO, CANADA

Toronto • Lake Ontario

Niagara River — • **Niagara Falls** NEW YORK

Lake Erie

FUN FACTS ABOUT THE FALLS

- Niagara Falls is actually two falls joined together: the American Falls in New York and the Horseshoe Falls in Canada. Both falls are about 17 **stories** high!

- American Falls is about as wide as three football fields. Horseshoe Falls is nearly half a mile wide!

- Since 1901, several people have gone over the falls in barrels. They meant to do it, too. The first person was Annie Edson Taylor. Was she brave or foolish? You decide.

- About 85 percent of Niagara's water goes over the Horseshoe Falls. The flow of water could fill 12,000 bathtubs every second!

◀ **Upper Yosemite Falls in California is a cascade. The water drops more than a quarter of a mile.**

stories floors of a house

Before You Move On

1. **Cause/Effect** What causes erosion?

2. **Comparison** How are cascades like cataracts? How are they different?

263

Mammoth Cave, deep and mysterious, Is full of wonders, strange and curious.

A cave is a natural hole in the Earth. Some caves are no larger than a fox's **den**. Others are big enough to hold an entire town!

Caves are made by wind or water. Ocean waves pound deep holes into rocky cliffs. Desert winds create holes as they **batter** hillsides with sand. Some caves form over a long time when water seeps, or drips, into the ground.

When a cave is very, very large, it is called a cavern. Caverns usually form within a soft rock called limestone. Water seeps into the limestone and creates small cracks in the rock. Over time, the cracks become tunnels. Water flows through the tunnels and **dissolves** more limestone. The tunnel gets wider and deeper until it becomes a cave. Thousands of years later, it may become a cavern.

Mammoth Cave has about 350 miles of tunnels and **chambers** that have been mapped. There are more to be explored. Who knows? Maybe you'll be the next person to discover one of its hidden wonders.

Stalactites and stalagmites are mineral cones that form when water with minerals in it drips from the roof of a cave. ▶

stalactite

Carlsbad Caverns, New Mexico

stalagmite

---

den hole, home
batter hit
dissolves softens and then washes away
chambers rooms

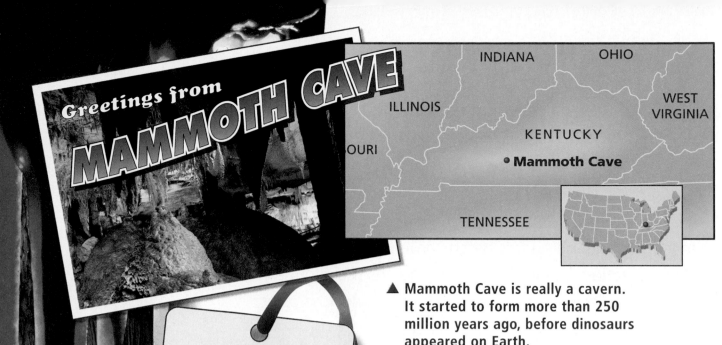

Greetings from
MAMMOTH CAVE

INDIANA   OHIO

ILLINOIS   WEST VIRGINIA

...OURI   KENTUCKY

● Mammoth Cave

TENNESSEE

▲ Mammoth Cave is really a cavern. It started to form more than 250 million years ago, before dinosaurs appeared on Earth.

EXPLORE MAMMOTH CAVE!

Bottomless Pit

Ruins of Karnak

Frozen Niagara

◀ **Stare** more than 100 feet down into a black hole. The light from a flashlight does not reach the bottom.

◀ Step down, down, down into a huge chamber. **Marvel at the shiny pillars.** It looks like an Egyptian temple!

◀ Be amazed by this huge rocky waterfall. It sparkles like a real waterfall!

Stare Look

Marvel at the shiny pillars You will be amazed by the bright posts

Before You Move On

1. **Graphic Aids** Where is Mammoth Cave?

2. **Cause/Effect** How is a cavern formed?

265

EVER-SHIFTING SEAS OF SAND
MARK THE SPOT WHERE HIGH DUNES STAND.

A desert is a large, open land where very little rain falls. The ground is very dry. People often think of sand when they think of a desert, but only a few deserts have sand. Most deserts are flat, stone-covered **plains**. Some deserts rise into the mountains. They may be covered with tall ponderosa pines, but the land is still dry. They are still deserts.

A sandy desert looks like a huge golden sea. The sand may **stretch** for miles and miles. Wind ripples the sand and blows it into hills, called **dunes**.

The Great Sand Dunes in Colorado began to form long ago when the Rio Grande River **changed its course**. A lot of sand was left behind. Winds blew the sand across the river valley until the sand hit the Sangre de Cristo Mountains in the Colorado Rockies.

The Great Sand Dunes are the tallest sand dunes in North America. Some of the dunes are more than 700 feet tall. Imagine playing in that sandbox!

---

plains lands without trees
stretch go on, continue
changed it course started flowing in a different direction

▼ The Sahara, in North Africa, is the largest desert in the world. Only a small part of the Sahara is sandy desert.

266

Greetings from the
GREAT SAND DUNES

COLORADO

UTAH

KANSA

Rio Grande River ● **Great Sand Dunes**

OKLAHOM.

NEW MEXICO

Desert Plants

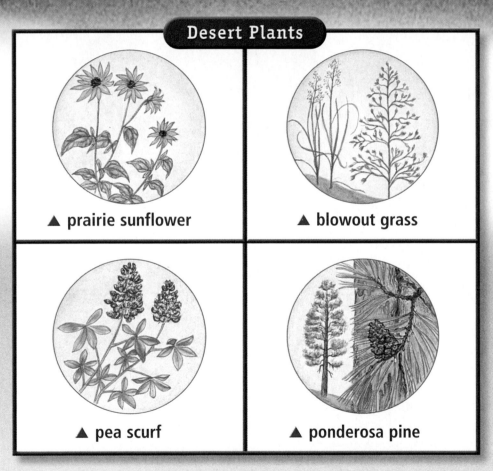

▲ prairie sunflower

▲ blowout grass

▲ pea scurf

▲ ponderosa pine

▲ Desert plants have **adapted to life** in a desert.
They can survive on small amounts of water.

_____

adapted to life learned to live and grow

Before You Move On

1. **Paraphrase** What is a desert?

2. **Cause/Effect** How did the Great Sand Dunes form?

ROCKY MOUNTAINS STAND WITH PRIDE.
THEY CALL THE PEAKS THE GREAT DIVIDE.

Mountains are the highest **landforms** on Earth. Many mountains were made by the movement of plates in the Earth's crust. Earth's plates move all the time, about as fast as your fingernails grow. Sometimes the plates crash into each other, forcing the land to wrinkle, fold, and push up.

Millions of years ago, plates crashed into each other with **tremendous** force. Great chunks of Earth's crust **heaved** upward. Wind and water then eroded the mountains into peaks and valleys.

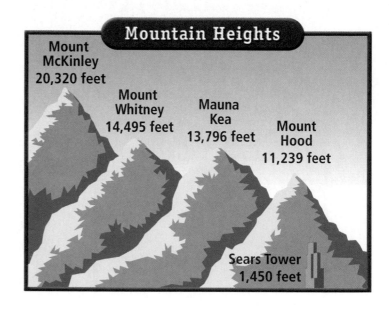

Mountain Heights

Mount McKinley 20,320 feet

Mount Whitney 14,495 feet

Mauna Kea 13,796 feet

Mount Hood 11,239 feet

Sears Tower 1,450 feet

The largest **mountain range** in North America is the Rocky Mountains. This range stretches more than 3,000 miles, from Alaska to New Mexico. Along the top of the Rockies is the Continental Divide. From these rugged, snow-capped peaks, rivers flow down one side to the east and down the other side to the west. That's why some people say this range divides the country in half.

---

tremendous huge
heaved pushed

Greetings from the ROCKY MOUNTAINS

Rocky Mountains

Americans love the Rockies. Many like to ski down the snowy mountains and swim in the sparkling lakes. There are many ways to **divide your time** in the Rockies!

◀ The tops of the Rocky Mountains form a long line, like a fence, that divides the continent of North America in two.

Before You Move On

1. **Cause/Effect** What happens when plates in the Earth's crust crash?

2. **Conclusion** Why is the top of the Rockies called the Continental Divide?

divide your time enjoy yourself

IN WYOMING, MONTANA, AND IDAHO, STEAMING GEYSERS FAITHFULLY BLOW.

A blast of steam **erupts** through a hole in the Earth! Steaming hot water soars hundreds of feet into the air like a giant fountain. Then, just as suddenly, the eruption stops. The steam **evaporates**, and all is quiet for a while, until the steam erupts again! This natural exploding fountain is called a **geyser**.

More than half of all the geysers in the world are in Yellowstone National Park. About 200 of these are active geysers that may erupt. Yellowstone sits on a huge "hot spot" where hot melted rock, called magma, lies just a few miles below ground. The magma heats up the underground water, and "whoosh!", a geyser blows its top.

The most famous geyser in Yellowstone is Old Faithful. It erupts **faithfully** about every hour. The jet of steam can rise as high as 180 feet into the air.

Jump back! There it goes again!

---

erupts blows out
evaporates mixes into the air around it
faithfully regularly

During an eruption, Old Faithful sends about 8,400 gallons of water into the air. That's enough for 330 showers! ▼

steam

OLD FAITHFUL GEYSER

▲ Yellowstone became a national park in 1872. It is the oldest national park in the world. It covers parts of Wyoming, Idaho, and Montana.

gas, ash, and melted rock

▲ Magma in the Earth's core creates both geysers and volcanoes. Old Faithful shoots out steam and hot water. Volcanoes, like Mount St. Helens, shoot out gas, ash, and melted rock.

Before You Move On

1. **Comparison** How are volcanoes and geysers alike? How are they different?

2. **Graphic Aids** Yellowstone covers parts of three states. Name them.

CASTLES OF ROCK GLOW IN THE SUN IN CANYONS WHERE COYOTES RUN.

A **canyon** is a deep valley. It may be narrow or wide, but it is always lower than the land around it. Some canyons are so narrow that you can reach out and touch both sides as you hike through them!

It takes nature millions of years to carve a canyon. Plates may lift up layers of rock. A river may cut deep into the Earth. Huge rivers of ice, called glaciers, may move down a mountain inch by inch, wearing down rock or **shoving** it out of the way. Sometimes, all these forces work together to create a canyon.

Bryce Canyon, in southern Utah, is one of the most amazing canyons in the United States. Over time, water has carved and eroded the soft limestone rocks.

Actually, Bryce is not one canyon. It is a group of valleys carved out by nature and then **sculpted** into fantastic shapes by rain, snow, and ice. It looks as if a child has been making sand castles.

---

shoving pushing
sculpted molded, shaped

This odd formation is called Thor's Hammer. ▶

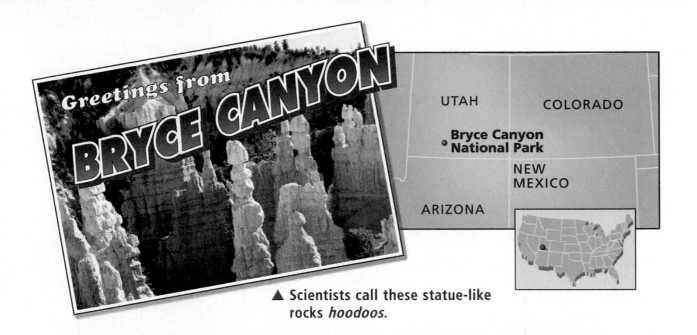

Greetings from **BRYCE CANYON**

UTAH

COLORADO

● Bryce Canyon
National Park

NEW
MEXICO

ARIZONA

▲ Scientists call these statue-like rocks *hoodoos*.

▲ Limestone comes from the skeletons of tiny sea animals and sandstone from grains of sand left long ago when water covered the area. This photo shows both limestone and sandstone layers.

▼ The Colorado River flows through the Grand Canyon. The river carved the canyon over millions of years.

Before You Move On

1. **Viewing** Describe Bryce Canyon to a partner.

2. **Main Idea/Details** What forces can work together to form a canyon?

273

At California's rocky shore, the mountains meet the ocean's roar.

Day after day, minute after minute, ocean waves crash against the land. The place where the ocean meets the shore is called a **coastline**. The coast of Maine is rocky. Beaches in Florida are flat and sandy. In other places, rugged cliffs **meet the sea**.

The shape of a coastline depends on many things. It depends on **ocean tides**, temperature and **climate**, winds, waves, and the kind of rock from which the land is made.

Coastlines are always changing. Ocean waves cause most of the changes, and waves are caused mainly by the wind. When the wind is light, the waves gently lap the shore. When the wind is strong, waves pound the shore like a giant fist or explode on the rocks like firecrackers!

Waves can carve out caves in cliff walls, or they can carve deeply into rock and break through to form an arch. The waves can also carry sand and pebbles from other places and build up a coastline.

---

meet the sea are right next to the ocean

ocean tides the pull of the Moon on the ocean waves

climate the pattern of weather

▲ An arch on Washington's rocky coast

▲ A sandy beach in Florida

Greetings from BIG SUR

NEVADA

Big Sur Coastline

Pacific Ocean

CALIFORNIA

Big Sur is a beautiful part of the California coastline where mountains run into the Pacific Ocean. Along the coastline, thundering waves have carved the rugged mountains into **spectacular** cliffs and sandy bays. Californians will tell you that Big Sur is the most beautiful coastline on Earth. If you go there, maybe you'll agree.

_____

spectacular incredible, amazing

▼ **At Big Sur, thundering waves have carved the rugged mountains.**

Before You Move On

1. **Details** Name four things that can change a coastline.

2. **Viewing** Compare the coastlines of Florida and California.

Americans love the American Falls.
   Come to Niagara to hear its call.

Mammoth Cave, deep and mysterious,
   is full of wonders, strange and curious.

Ever-shifting seas of sand
   mark the spots where high dunes stand.

Rocky Mountains stand with pride.
   They call the peaks the Great Divide.

In Wyoming, Montana, and Idaho,
   steaming geysers faithfully blow.

Castles of rock glow in the sun
   in canyons where coyotes run.

At California's rocky shore,
   the mountains meet the ocean's roar.

The falls, the caves, the dunes of sand,
The geysers, peaks, the canyon lands,
From mountains high to oceans deep,
This awesome land is ours to keep.

AMERICA

Before You Move On

1. **Author's Style** How does the author spell out America?

2. **Point of View** What does the author think about America?

Think and Respond

Strategy: Main Idea and Details

Make a main idea diagram. Write the details that support, or tell more about, the main idea.

Greetings from America

Main Idea

Water and wind change things in nature.

The **main idea** is what the article is mostly about

Details

Water erodes soft rock to form a waterfall in a river.

Water makes cracks in limestone, and they get wider to form a cave or a cavern.

The **details** give more information about the main idea.

Summarize

Use your diagram to summarize the article. Tell the main ideas. Leave out details that don't support the main idea.

Talk It Over

1 **Personal Response** Which place in this article would you most like to visit? Why?

2 **Prediction** Will the Great Sand Dunes look exactly the same 100 years from now as they do today? Explain.

3 **Conclusion** Many things in nature are changed by water and wind. Do these changes happen quickly? Explain your answer.

4 **Author's Point of View** What does the author think about America? What makes you think so?

Compare Purposes

Did the authors write "Planet Earth/Inside Out" and "Greetings from America" for the same reasons? Explain.

Both authors tell me how things on Earth formed, but one made me want to go and see them!

Content Connections

Describe Nature

partners

Look at a picture of a place in nature. Describe it to your partner. Now listen to a nature CD or tape. What do you hear? What do you think you could smell or touch there? Describe the place again. Which description does your partner like better? Why?

2×5

MATH

Estimate Distance

partners

Choose two places you would like to visit. How far would you have to travel if you drove from your home to both places and back again? Estimate the distance. Record your data in a chart. Tell how you got your answers.

Trip	Estimated Miles
Houston, Texas to to Niagara Falls	1,290
Niagara Falls to Mammoth Cave	553
Mammoth Cave to Houston, Texas	?

Give a Park Tour

Internet

Research a national park. Take notes about its main attractions or landforms. Print out or find pictures of the attractions. Add captions. Then give your class a tour of the park. Make them want to go there!

El Capitan is a sight you can't miss! It rises over 3,000 feet above Yosemite Valley.

Write a Visitor's Guide

Choose a place in your state, city, or town. Create a guide for visitors. Describe what the place is like, where it is, and why visitors shouldn't miss seeing it!

Lake Meredith, Texas

Visit the prettiest lake in Texas! Beautiful red-brown limestone cliffs rise around the lake. The water is clearer than most lakes, too.

Read Long Words

Some long words have a root word and a **prefix** . A **prefix** is a word part that is added to the beginning of a word. When you read a long word:

✔ Find word parts you know.
✔ Use the meaning of the word part to help you figure out what the whole word means.

Try the strategy.

Prefix	Example	Meaning
re	retell	tell again
dis	disagree	not agree; without agreement
pre	premade	made before
mis	misread	read incorrectly

The Mississippi River

Some people misunderstand how the Mississippi River was formed. The river took its present form about 10,000 years ago. At that time, glaciers covered the upper Mississippi Valley. As the glaciers moved, they picked up rocks and dirt and redeposited them. When the glaciers disappeared, the water cut channels into the soil. Today the Mississippi flows through these precut channels.

> I know what *cut* means. I also know that *pre-* means "before." When I put the two parts together, I can figure out that *precut* means "cut before."

Practice

Take this test and **read long words**.

Read the article. Then read each item. Choose the best answer

Everglades National Park is in southern Florida. People call the Everglades a "river of grass." You might stare at the miles of grass in <u>disbelief</u>, but there really is a river flowing slowly through it.

Since 1947, the park has been a safe place for many unusual plants, birds, and animals. Long ago, however, people <u>misunderstood</u> the Everglades. They thought it was a useless swamp and wanted to get rid of it. The birds and other animals who had lived there since <u>prehistoric</u> times were disappearing. Today, people are working to protect this unique place.

1 What does the word <u>disbelief</u> mean?

   A   without belief

   B   with incorrect belief

   C   with belief again

2 What does the word <u>misunderstood</u> mean?

   A   understood quickly

   B   understood completely

   C   understood incorrectly

3 What does the word <u>prehistoric</u> mean?

   A   not historic

   B   before history was written down

   C   incorrectly historic

 Test Strategy

Skip an item if you're not sure of the answer. Come back to it later. Make your best guess.

Vocabulary

Song

The Big Bunyans

There once was a family,
The four **mighty** Bunyans.
The teeth in their huge heads
Were bigger than onions.

They turned many **acres**
Of this mighty land
Into **scenic** attractions
That are grander than grand.

This tale of the Bunyans
Is entirely true,
All but the first part
And the rest of it too.

—Joyce McGreevy

Tune: "On Top of Old Smokey"

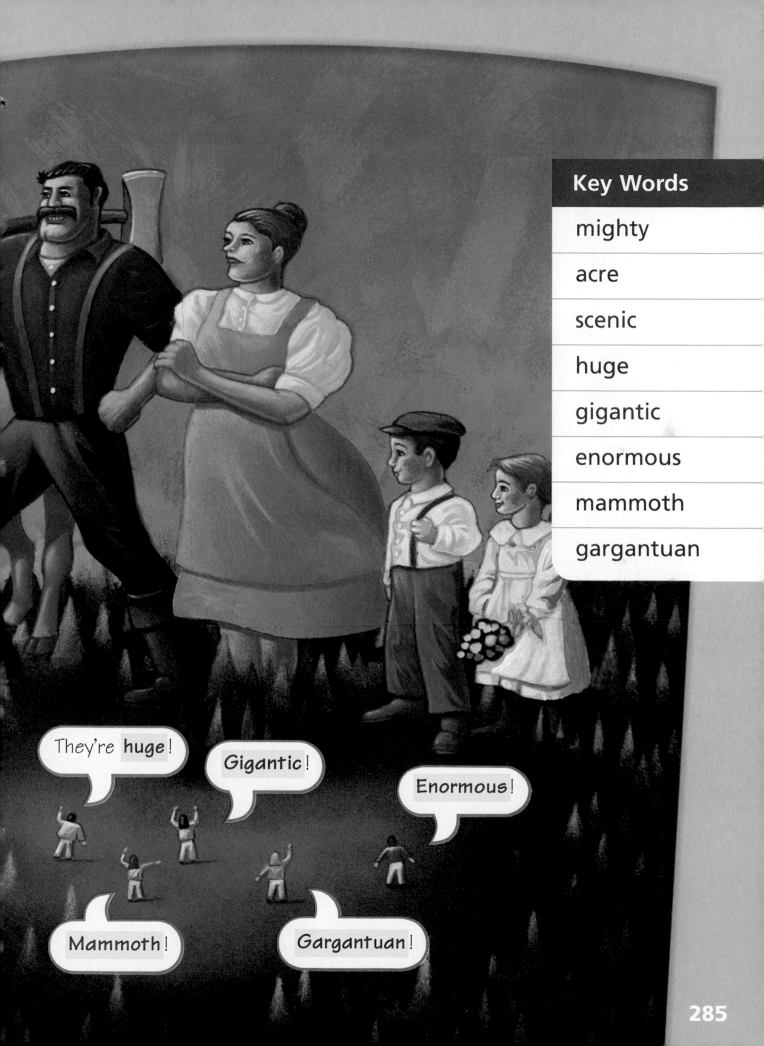

285

THE BUNYANS

by **Audrey Wood**
illustrated by **David Shannon**

Read a Tall Tale

Genre

A **tall tale** is a funny story. The characters and events are exaggerated, or larger and more important than they really are. This story tells how a family makes several U.S. landforms.

Characters

Paul Bunyan

Carrie Bunyan

Little Jean

Teeny

Setting

This story happens long ago in the United States.

UNITED STATES

 Selection Reading

1

Find out who Paul Bunyan is and how he meets his wife.

Storyteller's Note

Now I **suppose** you have heard about the **mighty logger**, Paul Bunyan, and his great blue ox named Babe. In the early days of our country, Paul and Babe **cleared the land** for the settlers, so farms and cities could **spring up**. You probably know that Paul was taller than a redwood tree, stronger than fifty grizzly bears, and smarter than a library full of books. Did you know, though, that Paul was married and had two fine children?

---

suppose think
mighty logger strong person who cut down trees
cleared the land cut down trees
spring up be built

One day Paul Bunyan was **clearing a road** through the forests of Kentucky when **a great pounding** began to shake the earth. Looking around, Paul discovered an **enormous** hole in the side of a hill. The **lumberjack** pulled up an **acre** of dry grass and made a torch to light his way.

Paul climbed inside the hole and followed the sound underground for miles, until he came to a large cavern. By the light of his torch, he saw a **gigantic** woman. She was banging a pickax against a wall.

---

clearing a road removing trees to make a road
a great pounding the force of something being hit hard
lumberjack person who cut down trees; logger

It was love at first sight.

"I'm Carrie McIntie," the gigantic woman said. "I was sitting on the hill when **my lucky wishbone** fell down a crack into the earth. I've been digging all day, trying to find it."

With a grin on his face as wide as the Missouri River, Paul reached into his shirt pocket. "I've got one, too," he said, pulling out his lucky wishbone. "Marry me, Carrie, and we'll share mine."

It was love at first sight He loved her as soon as he saw her

my lucky wishbone the small animal bone I carry for good luck

Carrie agreed, and their wedding invitations were mailed out right away.

The invitations were so large, only one needed to be sent to each state. Everyone could read them for miles!

The invitations said: "You are invited to the **mammoth** wedding of Paul Bunyan and Carrie McIntie." The couple was married in the enormous cavern that Carrie had carved. After the **ceremony**, folks began to call it "Mammoth Cave." The **giantess** had dug more than two hundred miles, making it the longest cave in the world. So, the name **fit perfectly**.

---

ceremony wedding, special event
giantess very large woman
fit perfectly was a good one

Paul and Carrie **settled down** on a farm in Maine, and soon there were two new Bunyans. While Pa Bunyan traveled with **his logging crew**, Ma Bunyan **worked** the farm and cared for their **jumbo** boy, named Little Jean, and their gigantic girl, named Teeny.

settled down decided to live

his logging crew the people who helped him cut down trees

worked took care of

jumbo very large

Before You Move On

1. **Cause/Effect** Why does Carrie dig Mammoth Cave?

2. **Inference** Why do you think Paul wanted to marry Carrie right away?

2

What are Paul
and Carrie's
children like?
What do
they do?

One morning when Pa Bunyan wasn't working, Ma
Bunyan cooked a **hearty** breakfast of pancakes and syrup, and
Teeny accidentally dumped a big bottle of syrup on her head.
Teeny's hair was so sweet, bears crawled into it and **burrowed
deep into** her curls. Try as they might, Pa and Ma Bunyan
couldn't wash them out.

"We'll need a **forceful** shower of water to get rid of those
varmints!" Ma Bunyan declared.

---

hearty big
burrowed deep into hid inside
forceful strong
varmints unwanted animals

Pa Bunyan had an idea. He placed his daughter on Babe, and he led them to the Niagara River in Canada. The **gargantuan** father scooped out a **huge** hole in the middle of the riverbed. As the great river roared down into the deep hole, Teeny cried out **in delight**, "Niagara falls!" Teeny showered in the waterfall, and the bears were **washed downstream**.

---

in delight happily
washed downstream taken away by the river

When Little Jean was five, he followed his pa to his logging camp in Montana. Thinking his son was too young to do much of anything, Paul set Little Jean down in **a barren** canyon in Utah to play for the day. When the lumberjack went to **fetch** him, he couldn't believe his eyes. Little Jean had carved the canyon into wonderful shapes.

Pa Bunyan **got tongue-tied** and said, "That's a mighty <u>brice</u> nanyon, coy. I mean, that's a mighty nice canyon, boy!" Somehow part of the **mix-up** stuck.

To this day, the canyon is known as Bryce Canyon.

---

a barren an empty

fetch get

got tongue-tied was so surprised that he could not talk clearly

mix-up mistake

After all that **sculpting**, Little Jean's shoes were full of sand. Pa knew Ma Bunyan wouldn't want her clean floors **dirtied up**, so he told Little Jean to sit down and empty out his shoes.

The sand from Little Jean's shoes blew away on the eastern wind and **settled down a state away**. It covered a valley ten miles long, making sand dunes eight hundred feet high. Everyone knows that's how the Great Sand Dunes of Colorado came to be.

---

sculpting cutting and carving
dirtied up to get dirty
settled down a state away fell on the ground in Colorado

Before You Move On

1. **Paraphrase** Tell a partner how Pa makes a waterfall.

2. **Cause/Effect** How does sand get into Little Jean's shoes? What happens when he takes the sand out?

297

3

Find out what happens as the Bunyan children get older.

One summer, Little Jean and Teeny wanted to go to the beach. Ma Bunyan told them to follow a river to the ocean. All the rivers **flowed** west back then, so they missed the Atlantic Ocean and ended up on the other side of the country instead.

Ma Bunyan **tracked them** out to the Pacific Ocean, where she found Teeny riding on the backs of two blue whales and Little Jean carving fifty **zigzag** miles of the California coast.

When Ma Bunyan saw what her son had done, she **exclaimed**, "What's the big idea, Sir?" From that time on, the **scenic** area was known as Big Sur.

---

flowed went
tracked them followed their footprints
zigzag crooked
exclaimed said with surprise

Ma Bunyan knew she had to put up a **barrier** to remind her children not to **wander off** too far. So, on the way home, everyone **pitched in and built** the Rocky Mountains. Teeny gathered and sorted out all the rivers, letting some flow east and others west. After that, the children had no trouble following the eastern rivers down to the Atlantic Ocean. And when they wanted to go exploring, Ma Bunyan would call out, "Now don't cross the Continental Divide, children!"

---

barrier wall
wander off go
pitched in and built helped to build

The best thing about **camping** is sleeping outdoors, and the worst thing is not having enough hot water. That's why the Bunyans always camped in Wyoming. By the time their camping years were over, Ma Bunyan had poked more than three hundred holes in the ground with her pickax and released tons of hot water from geysers. But Ma got tired of poking so many holes, so she made a geyser that blew every hour on the hour. After that, there was **a steady supply of** hot water to keep the giants' clothes and dishes sparkling clean.

Teeny named the geyser Old Faithful, and to this day, Old Faithful still blows its top every hour in Yellowstone National Park.

---

camping living outside for awhile
a steady supply of always enough

As our country grew up, so did the Bunyan children. When the kids left home, Ma and Pa Bunyan **retired to a wilderness area**, where they still live happily.

---

retired to a wilderness area stopped working and went to a part of the country where no one lived

Teeny **hitched a ride** on a whale over to England and became a famous **fashion designer**. Her colorful skirts made from hot air balloons were **a sensation** at the first World's Fair in London.

Little Jean traveled to Venice, Italy, where he studied art. Every day, the **gondoliers** would take their passengers down the Grand Canal to watch the giant artist **chiseling his marble sculptures**.

---

hitched a ride rode
fashion designer maker of new clothes
a sensation liked by almost everyone
gondoliers men who steered boats
chiseling his marble sculptures carving stone shapes

Before You Move On

1. **Problem/Solution** What barrier does the family build? Why?

2. **Cause/Effect** Why does Ma Bunyan poke holes in the ground?

Meet the Author

AUDREY WOOD

It's not surprising that **Audrey Wood** wrote about the Bunyans. She would feel right at home with a family like that. You see, Audrey once lived with the circus. The tallest man in the world bounced her on his knee. A family of little people took care of her and told her stories about Gargantua the Gorilla.

Young Audrey studied music, dance, painting, and drama. She read a lot. She loved books so much that she wanted to become an author.

Audrey grew up and married. When she read books to her son, she remembered her childhood dream. "That's when I began to write children's books seriously," she says.

Think and Respond

Strategy: Make Comparisons

Sometimes you can understand a story better if you make comparisons. Look for:

✔ how things are alike
✔ how things are different.

Make a comparison chart to show how landforms were made. Write the explanations from the tall tale. Then write the real explanations from the geography article.

How Were Landforms Made?

Landform	Tall Tale Explanation	Real Explanation
Mammoth Cave	Carrie lost her wishbone and dug for it.	Water dissolved the limestone rock.
Niagara Falls		
Bryce Canyon		
Great Sand Dunes		
Big Sur		
Continental Divide		
Old Faithful		

Retell the Story

Work with a partner to retell part of the story. Be the storyteller or the geographer. Exaggerate if you are the storyteller. If you are the geographer, tell only the facts. Then switch roles. Compare the stories.

Talk It Over

1 **Personal Response** Which part of the story do you think was the funniest? Why?

2 **Character Traits** Would you like to be friends with Little Jean and Teeny? Why or why not?

3 **Judgment** Do you think Ma and Pa Bunyan were good parents? Give examples.

4 **Mood** Talk about how this tall tale makes you feel. Find two examples that show how the author creates this mood.

Compare Ideas

How are the ideas in "The Bunyans" and "Piecing Earth and Sky Together" alike and different?

Content Connections

Give an Interview

partners

Pretend you are one of the Bunyans or a character you make up. Have a partner interview you to find out about your life. Answer the questions like the character would. Then interview your partner.

To start my day, I eat 275 flapjacks with five gallons of maple syrup.

Make a 3-D Model

small group

Choose a landform or waterway. Find facts about its height, length, and width. Use graph paper to plan your model. Then build it with clay or papier-mâché. Use the model to help you share the facts with the class.

Research a Cave
Internet

 small group

Find out about one cave in America. Where is it? How did it form? What minerals, plants, or animals can you find there? Make a fact card. Add your card to a class mural. How are all the caves alike?

Wind Cave
Hot Springs, SD
• Wind Cave is one of the longest caves in the world.

WRITING

Write to Entertain

on your own

Think of a new way to explain how a landform was made. Choose the best form:

- a new scene for "The Bunyans" tall tale
- a song or a poem
- step-by-step instructions

Be sure to add colorful and funny details.

Make a Lake
1. Find the biggest mountain you can.
2. Push it into a raging river.
3. Wait for one million years.
4. Give your new lake a name!

Adjectives and Adverbs

Listen and sing.

Song

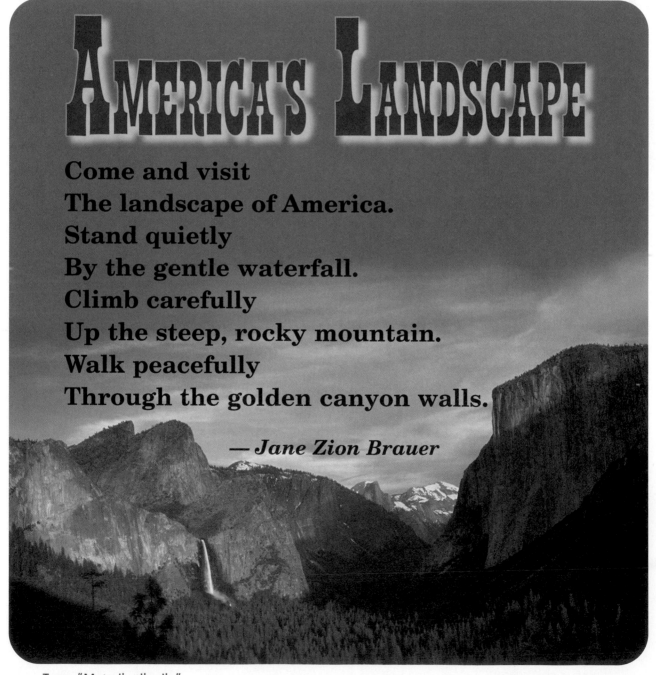

AMERICA'S LANDSCAPE

Come and visit
The landscape of America.
Stand quietly
By the gentle waterfall.
Climb carefully
Up the steep, rocky mountain.
Walk peacefully
Through the golden canyon walls.

— *Jane Zion Brauer*

Tune: "Matarile-rile-rile"

How Language Works

Adjectives and **adverbs** add details to sentences.

Adjectives	Example:
■ An **adjective** tells about a **noun** It often comes before the noun.	My family takes **long** <u>trips</u>.
Adverb	**Examples:**
■ An **adverb** tells how, where, or when. It usually tells more about a **verb**. It can come before or after the verb.	**How:** We **drive** <u>slowly</u> by car. **Where:** We **went** <u>down</u> into a canyon. **When:** <u>Yesterday</u> I **sent** you a postcard.

Practice with a Partner

Add an adjective in the blank. Say the sentence.

1. The _____ explorers go into the cavern.
2. They wear helmets with _____ lights.
3. They see _____ bugs on the walls.

Add an adverb in the blank. Say the sentence.

4. They crawl _____ through a narrow passage.
5. They look _____.
6. It is late. They will come back _____.

Put It in Writing

Pretend that you visit a place like Yellowstone or Big Sur. Describe what you see and do.

Gray steam goes high into the air. Then it quickly disapears again.

Show What You Know

Talk About Geography

In this unit, you read a geography article and a tall tale. Look back at the unit. What places do you want to visit? Why?

Make a Mind Map

Work with a partner. Make a mind map to show how forces of nature change Earth's surface.

Forces That Change Earth's Surface

Water	Winds	Magma	Glaciers	Earthquakes
erodes soft rock to form waterfalls				

Think and Write

Forces of nature can erode Earth's surface. How do some forces build up, or add to, the surface? Write a paragraph. Add it to your portfolio. Include work that shows what else you learned about the Earth.

Read and Learn More

Leveled Books

Giant Games
by Holly Melton

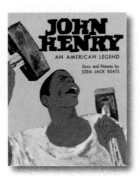

John Henry
by Ezra Jack Keats

Theme Library

America Is...
by Louise Borden

Clever Beatrice
by Margaret Willey

Internet

Go to: www.hbavenues.com

Landforms

National Parks

Map Scale

Unit 6 Launch

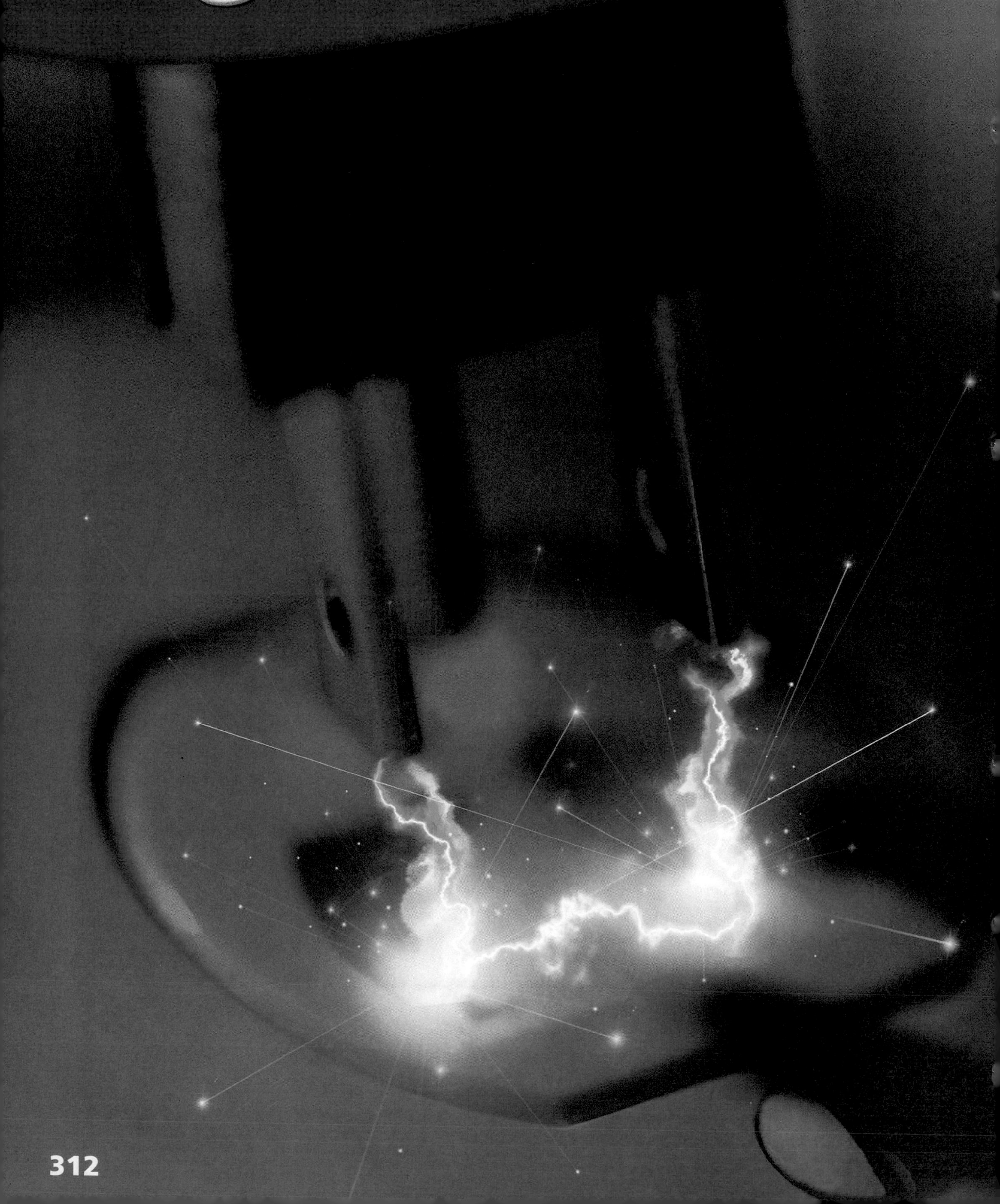

It's Electrifying!

Experiment with Electricity

1. Make small shapes out of paper.
   Put them on a desk.
2. Blow up a balloon.
   Rub it against your hair.
3. Use the balloon to make
   the shapes dance.
4. Talk with a partner
   about the results of
   your experiment.

Electricity Is All Around

Bedroom
air conditioner
lamp

Bathroom
heater
light bulb

Living Room
lamp

Kitchen
toaster
stove
oven
refrigerator

Magnetism

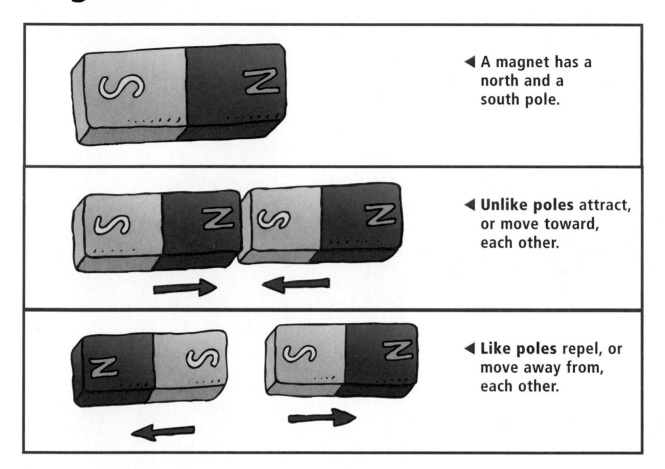

◀ A magnet has a north and a south pole.

◀ **Unlike poles** attract, or move toward, each other.

◀ **Like poles** repel, or move away from, each other.

Inside an Atom

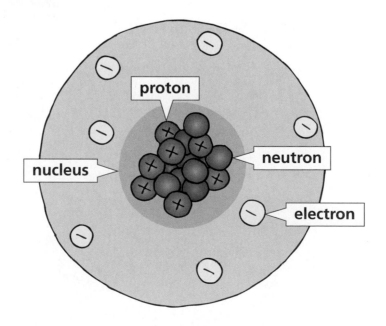

proton

nucleus

neutron

electron

Song 💿

LIGHTNING STRIKES!

In the stormy sky we see

Lightning strike suddenly,

This is electricity

On **exhibit**.

To **discover** something new,

And to **prove** what is true

To **accomplish** and **invent**,

We do **experiments**.

—Joyce McGreevy

Tune: "London Bridge"

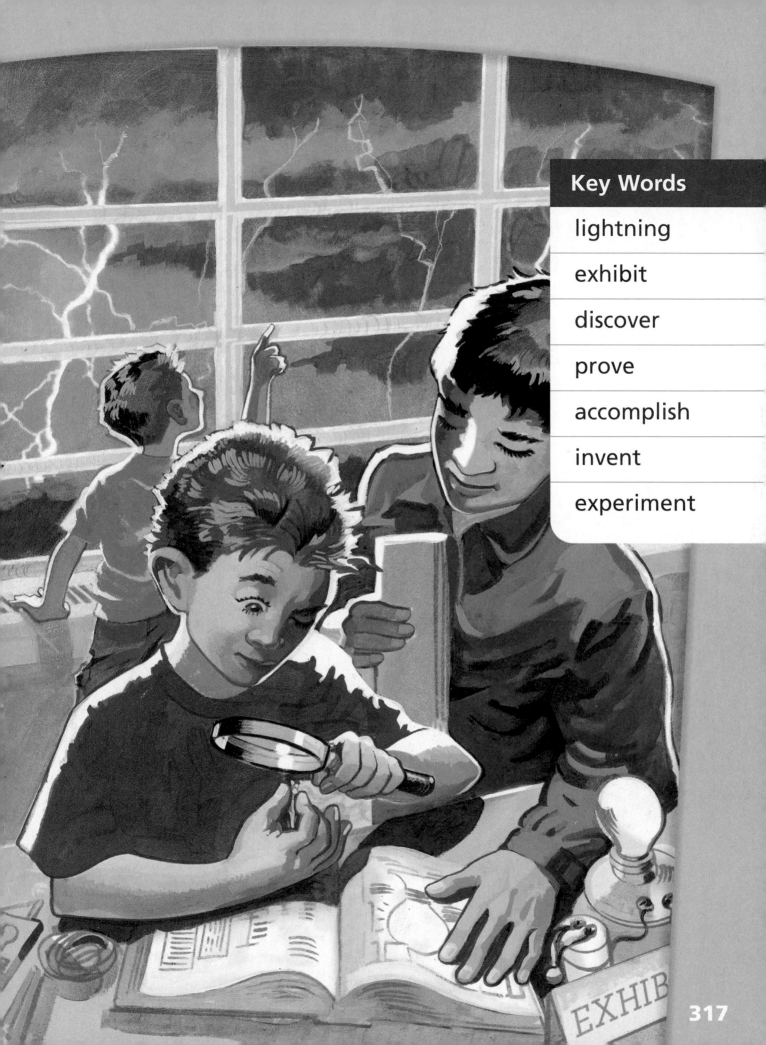

Key Words

lightning

exhibit

discover

prove

accomplish

invent

experiment

317

Ben Franklin's Experiment

by Adam Grant   illustrated by Scott Goto

Read a Play

Genre

A **play** is a story that is acted out. A **script** is the written form of a play. It tells what the characters say. In this play, a girl named Katrina meets a famous person from history.

Parts of a Play

A play has scenes, characters, and dialogue. Each scene may have a different setting.

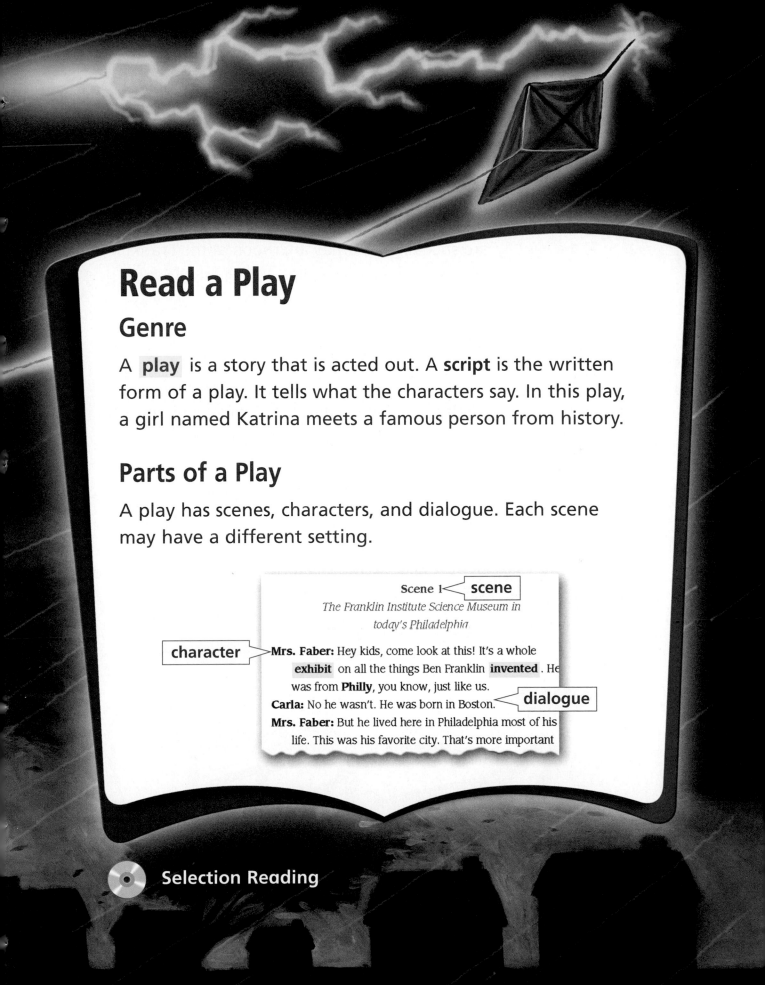

Scene 1 ← **scene**

The Franklin Institute Science Museum in today's Philadelphia

character → **Mrs. Faber:** Hey kids, come look at this! It's a whole **exhibit** on all the things Ben Franklin **invented**. He was from **Philly**, you know, just like us.

Carla: No he wasn't. He was born in Boston. ← **dialogue**

Mrs. Faber: But he lived here in Philadelphia most of his life. This was his favorite city. That's more important

Selection Reading

319

Katrina is at a science museum. Find out how she meets Ben Franklin.

Scene 1

The Franklin Institute Science Museum in today's Philadelphia.

Narrator: Katrina Faber, her sister Carla, and their parents are spending Saturday afternoon at the Franklin Institute Science Museum in Philadelphia.

Mrs. Faber: Hey kids, come look at this! It's a whole **exhibit** on all the things Ben Franklin **invented** . He was from **Philly**, you know, just like us.

Carla: No he wasn't. He was born in Boston.

Mrs. Faber: But he lived here in Philadelphia most of his life. This was his favorite city. That's more important than where someone is born, isn't it?

Mr. Faber: Wow! This is **pretty incredible**! Look at all the stuff he invented. Wood stoves . . . bifocals . . .

Katrina: What are bifocals?

Carla: Special glasses. The **lenses** are split across the middle. The top half is for seeing long distances, and the bottom half is for reading.

Philly Philadelphia, Pennsylvania
pretty incredible hard to believe
lenses glass parts of the eyeglasses

Katrina: You just read that off the display case. I could have done that.

Mr. Faber: Old Ben got so tired of having to **switch** from his regular glasses to his reading glasses that he just combined the two and invented bifocals. That was pretty smart, huh?

Katrina: I guess so.

---

switch change

Narrator: Katrina sits down on a bench. Her mom and dad and Carla wander off in different directions, looking at the different exhibits.

Mrs. Faber: Here's something about Franklin **discovering** electricity.

Narrator: Katrina sees a strange-looking man in the corner. He has very little hair and looks **pretty** old. He's wearing a shiny suit with **ruffles** at the wrists, and his pants only go down to his knees. His shoes have silver buckles on them. Still, Katrina is sure she's seen him somewhere before.

Stranger: It never happened.

Katrina: What?

Stranger: It never happened. I never discovered electricity.

Katrina: Hey! Who <u>are</u> <u>you</u>?

Stranger: What do you mean? You don't **recognize old Ben**? Ben Franklin?

Katrina: You can't be Ben Franklin. He was born about a million years ago.

Franklin: Young lady, how old is your grandfather?

Katrina: I don't know. Sixty-five, maybe.

---

pretty very

ruffles wide shirt cuffs

recognize Old Ben know Ben Franklin when you see him

Franklin: Would you offer him a seat if he were here?

Katrina: Sure!

Franklin: Well, I'm four times his age. So how about it? Hop up!

(*Katrina jumps up from the bench. Ben Franklin sits down and kicks off his shoes.*)

Katrina: Ben Franklin, right here in front of me. How did you . . . ?

Franklin: Never mind. **Curiosity killed the cat**, you know.

Katrina: What cat?

Franklin: Oh, brother! Forget it kid, it's just **an expression**.

So where were we? What were we talking about?

Katrina: Electricity.

Curiosity killed the cat You shouldn't ask so many questions

an expression something that people often say

Franklin: That's right. Your mother said I discovered it, but that's not quite true. The Greeks discovered electricity almost 3,000 years ago in 600 B.C.E. Of course, they didn't really know what to do with it. All they knew was that rubbing **amber** with a piece of wool would create static electricity. The same thing happens when you take your hat off in the winter and your hair stands straight up in the air.

Katrina: That's electricity?

Franklin: Sure. It's just like in your TV.

Katrina: How do you know about TV?

Franklin: I **keep up**.

Katrina: Oh. So, if you didn't discover electricity, what did you do?

Franklin: I figured out that **lightning** was made of electricity. Here, I'll show you. Close your eyes for a second.

---

amber a hard, brownish-yellow material from tree sap
keep up learn about all the new things

Before You Move On

1. **Conclusion** Why is there a museum named for Ben Franklin?

2. **Paraphrase** What does Katrina discover about Franklin and electricity?

2

The characters go back in time. What does Franklin show Katrina?

Scene 2

Ben Franklin's home in Philadelphia in 1752.

Narrator: When Katrina opens her eyes, she finds herself in the living room of a house. She sees Ben Franklin, with his shoes on, sitting in a chair and talking to a younger man.

Franklin: What are your plans today, son?

William: Nothing much. I've got some chores to do.

Franklin: How would you like to help me with an **experiment** ?

William: Sure.

Franklin: Good! It's going to be a rainy evening. It's perfect weather for our electrical experiment. Let's get started.

Narrator: Katrina watches as they make a kite out of two crossed strips of cedar wood and an old **handkerchief**. Then, she sees them attach a piece of wire to one of the wood strips. She wonders if they need her help, or if they can even see her.

---

handkerchief square cloth used to wipe the face

Franklin: Just think, William, electricity was discovered hundreds of years ago. Yet nobody really knows what it is, or how to use it, or if it <u>can</u> be used.

William: Is it magic?

Franklin: It's not magic. I **suspect** it comes from nature. My guess is that lightning is made of electricity. That's what I hope we can **prove** today.

William: How?

Franklin: Metal **attracts electricity**. I think it attracts lightning, too. We'll take this kite and tie a large metal key to it.

Narrator: Katrina follows the two men as they take the kite outside. Ben holds onto the string as William runs with the kite. The strong wind takes the kite high into the air. Ben goes into a **shed** to stay dry.

---

suspect think

attracts electricity makes electricity come near it

shed storage room

Franklin: William, look for a dark rain cloud and **direct me** to it.

Katrina: Hey wait! That's really dangerous! I heard about someone who got hit by lightning on a golf course and got badly hurt! Hey! Can you hear me?

Narrator: Ben and his son don't seem to hear Katrina's warning. The lightning flashes all around them, and finally it strikes the wire on the kite.

Franklin: Now! I'll simply touch the key with my knuckle. (*Touching the key*) Yeow!

William: Did you see that? Did you see that **spark** fly off that key? Did electricity travel down the string? Was that spark electricity?

Franklin: It certainly was! We've done it, William! We've proven that lightning is made of electricity!

direct me point
spark tiny flash of light

William: How does that help us?

Franklin: Do you remember last summer when those houses burned to the ground after they were hit by lightning? I think we can **prevent** fires like that.

William: How?

Franklin: We know that electricity is attracted to metal, and that lightning usually **strikes** the tallest thing around. If we put a tall metal pole on every house, the lightning will hit the pole instead of the house.

William: (*Turning to Katrina*) Hey, Katrina. It's time to go!

Katrina: What?

William: I said it's time to go!

---

prevent stop
strikes hits

Before You Move On

1. **Steps in a Process** Name the steps in Franklin's experiment.

2. **Character** How do you know Franklin cared about other people?

Katrina sees Franklin again. Find out what else she learns about him.

Scene 3

Franklin Institute Science Museum, today

Narrator: Katrina blinks and finds herself sitting on the bench at the Franklin Institute. Katrina's dad is shaking her on the shoulder.

Mr. Faber: Hey Katrina, it's time to go! I said, it's time to go! Have you been sleeping on this bench all afternoon?

Carla: I'll bet you've really learned a <u>lot</u>.

Katrina: I learned plenty today. For one thing, Ben Franklin didn't discover electricity. The Greeks did that in 600 B.C.E. Ben Franklin discovered that lightning is made of electricity, and he used that information to invent the lightning **rod**.

Mrs. Faber: Where did you learn that?

Katrina: Ben Franklin told me. I mean, I must have read it somewhere.

Carla: You read it somewhere? You?

---

rod pole

Mr. Faber: That's enough, you two. Let's **hit the road**.

Katrina: I need to get a drink of water first. I'll hurry.

Narrator: As Katrina goes to the water fountain, she sees someone carefully studying the electricity exhibit.

Katrina: Hey, Mr. Franklin, it's you again. What are you doing?

Franklin: I may be 200 years old, but I've still got things to learn.

Katrina: I told my parents about the lightning rod. That was great.

Franklin: That's nothing, kid. I did a lot of things. I **formed** the first fire department, **established** the first free library, invented the wood stove, signed the Declaration of Independence <u>and</u> the Constitution. I even went to France to raise money for the American Revolution.

Katrina: Wow! You did all those things? That's amazing! I can't even get all my homework done.

---

hit the road go
formed started
established began

Franklin: People can **accomplish** a lot if they believe in themselves and work hard. Nothing is so **complicated** that we can't understand it. All you have to do is slow down and think it through carefully. Pretty soon it'll make sense to you.

Katrina: I guess so.

Franklin: You guess so? Look, when I was young there were a million things we didn't understand about science and medicine. But I read everything I could, and I spent lots of time thinking about things. Try it. You'll be surprised what you discover.

Narrator: Ben Franklin pulls a penny from behind Katrina's ear and hands it to her. She looks at him in surprise.

Franklin: Here's a penny for your thoughts.

Katrina: How'd you do that?

Franklin: It's magic.

Katrina: Thanks, Mr. Franklin. Thanks for everything.

---

complicated hard to figure out

Here's a penny for your thoughts I'll give you a penny if you tell me what you're thinking (an expression)

Scene 4

Later that night in Katrina's bedroom.

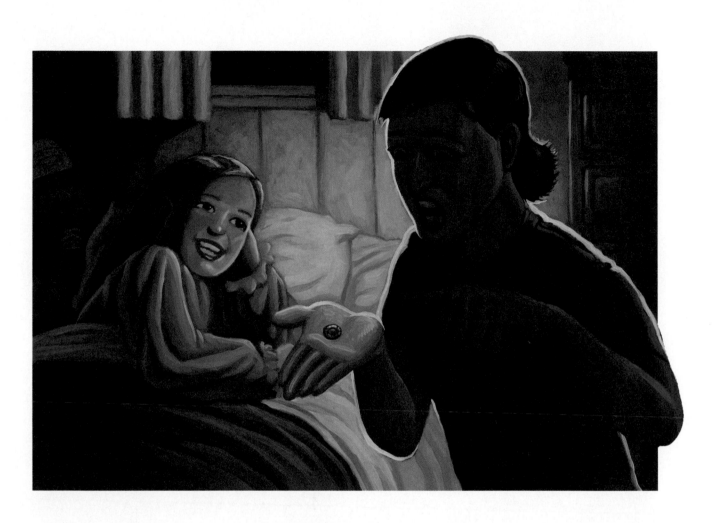

Mrs. Faber: I'm glad you had a good time at the museum today. You sure learned a lot.

Katrina: It was really fun.

(*Mrs. Faber sees the shiny penny on Katrina's desk and picks it up.*)

Mrs. Faber: This penny is from 1789. Where did you get this?

Katrina: (*Smiling*) An "old" friend gave it to me.

Before You Move On

1. **Character** What did Franklin believe that helped him do so much?

2. **Inference** Why doesn't Katrina tell her parents she met Franklin?

Light

Light,
light,
stretch
my sight,
bend back
corners
of the night.
Flicker, flash,
near and far,
turn on lamps,
& sprinkle stars.
One small flame,
a tiny spark . . .
or wide as day,
you scatter dark.

—Joan Bransfield Graham

Meet the Poet

Joan Bransfield Graham likes to write poems that look like the shape of the thing she writes about. She also likes to help other people be creative and has been a teacher, scout leader, and crafts instructor.

Before You Move On

Imagery What does the poem's shape remind you of? Why do you think the poet used this shape?

Think and Respond

Strategy: Make Comparisons

Compare what life was like when Ben Franklin was alive and what life is like today. Make a Venn diagram.

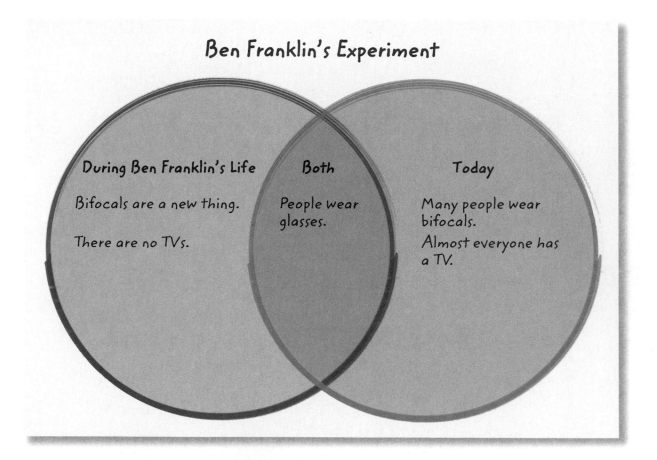

Ben Franklin's Experiment

During Ben Franklin's Life

Bifocals are a new thing.

There are no TVs.

Both

People wear glasses.

Today

Many people wear bifocals.

Almost everyone has a TV.

Interview Ben Franklin

Pretend you are Ben Franklin. Have your partner ask you questions about what life was like in the 1770s. Then switch roles.

Talk It Over

1 **Personal Response** What would you ask Ben Franklin if you met him?

2 **Fact/Fantasy** Which parts of the play could really happen? Which parts could not happen?

3 **Opinion** What is the most important thing Katrina learned from Ben Franklin?

4 **Formulate Questions** Brainstorm a list of questions you have about Ben Franklin, his life, electricity, or his inventions.

Compare Genres

Compare the biography "George Washington" with this play.

Content Connections

Sell an Invention

small group

Imagine you live in the past and have just discovered a new invention like the lightning rod. Try to sell the new product to your group. Use persuasive language. Tell why it will help them.

Gas lighting will make the streets brighter and safer!

SCIENCE

Make a Safety Checklist

partners

Electricity can be dangerous! Find out what people can do to be safe. Make a checklist. Include diagrams, signs, art, or photographs to support your information.

Don't pull a plug out of an outlet by pulling on the cord.

Words of Wisdom

large group

Ben Franklin said a lot of wise things! Discuss his sayings with your class. What other sayings or proverbs do you know? Choose your favorites to include in a class book.

The early bird catches the worm.

WRITING

Write a Report
Internet

on your own

Find out what one scientist discovered or invented. How did it change people's lives? Turn your notes into an outline. Then write a report to share with the class. Listen to all of the reports. Vote for the most important discovery.

The Amazing Light Bulb

They're cheap and easy to use. They're brighter and safer than candles. Imagine a world without them!

Summarize

A **summary** tells the most important information in what you read. To summarize:

✔ Tell the key events.
✔ Make sure you don't repeat any information.
✔ Keep your summary short.

Try the strategy. First make a list of the ideas in Part **1** of "Ben Franklin's Experiment." Then summarize them.

from Ben Franklin's Experiment

Narrator: Katrina sees a strange-looking man in the corner. He has very little hair and looks pretty old. He's wearing a shiny suit with ruffles at the wrists, and his pants only go down to his knees. His shoes have silver buckles on them.

Stranger: It never happened.

Katrina: What?

Stranger: I never discovered electricity.

Katrina: Hey! Who are you?

Stranger: What do you mean? You don't recognize Old Ben? Ben Franklin?

Katrina sees a man at the museum dressed in clothes from the past. She finds out that he's Ben Franklin!

Practice

Take this test and **summarize** "Ben Franklin's Experiment."

> **Read each item. Choose the best answer.**
>
> 1 **Read Part ❷ on pages 326–329 again. Which sentence belongs in a summary of Part ❷ ?**
>
>   **A**   Ben Franklin had a son named William.
>
>   **B**   Katrina sees Ben Franklin perform an experiment with a kite.
>
>   **C**   Katrina knows that lightning can be dangerous.
>
>   **D**   Many houses in Philadelphia burned down after they were hit by lightning.
>
> 2 **Which of the following is the best** · · · · · · · · summary of the whole play?
>
>   **A**   Ben Franklin appears at a museum. He teaches Katrina that the Greeks discovered electricity. He gives her a penny from 1789.
>
>   **B**   The Fabers visit a museum in Philadelphia. Katrina talks to Ben Franklin. She learns that Franklin didn't discover electricity, but he did invent bifocals and the wood stove.
>
>   **C**   The Fabers live in Philadelphia, where Ben Franklin once lived. They visit a museum with an exhibit about Franklin's inventions. Katrina talks to Ben Franklin.
>
>   **D**   The Fabers visit a museum. Katrina meets Ben Franklin. She learns about his experiment with lightning and his inventions. He encourages her to believe in herself.

 Test Strategy

Look for key words like *best* and *not*. They will help you find the correct answer.

It's ELECTRIC

A TV uses electricity. Have you ever wondered how it works?

1 A wire brings electricity to a TV. Electricity is a form of **energy** .

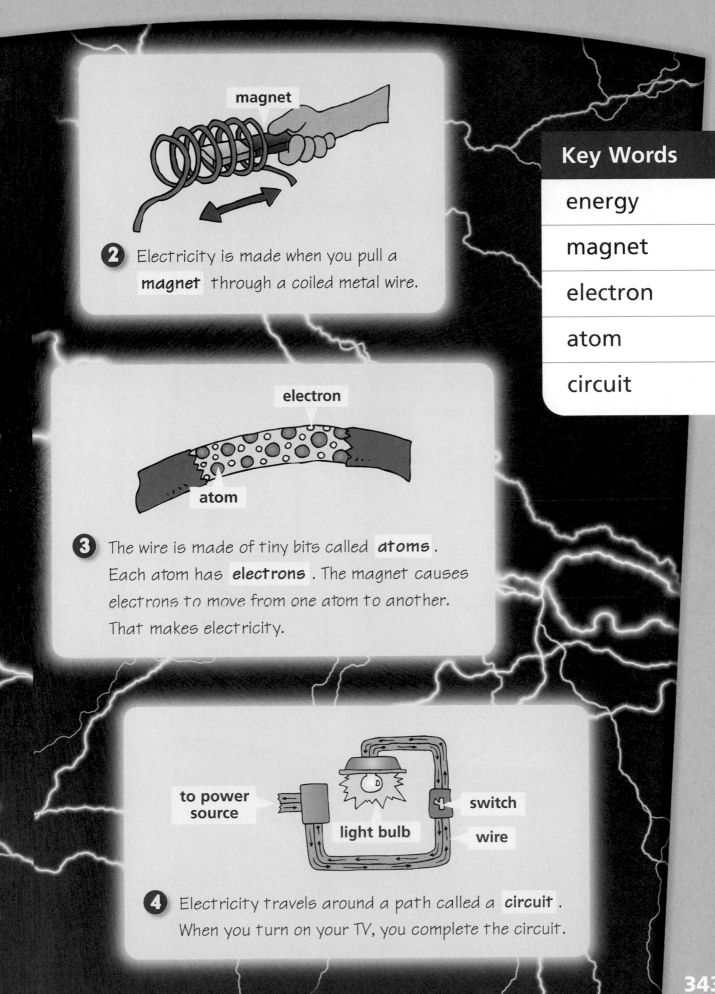

magnet

2 Electricity is made when you pull a **magnet** through a coiled metal wire.

Key Words

energy

magnet

electron

atom

circuit

electron

atom

3 The wire is made of tiny bits called **atoms**. Each atom has **electrons**. The magnet causes electrons to move from one atom to another. That makes electricity.

to power source

switch

light bulb

wire

4 Electricity travels around a path called a **circuit**. When you turn on your TV, you complete the circuit.

Read a Science Article

A **science article** is nonfiction. It can explain how things work and why.

✔ Look for **diagrams** with numbered steps. They show how something works.

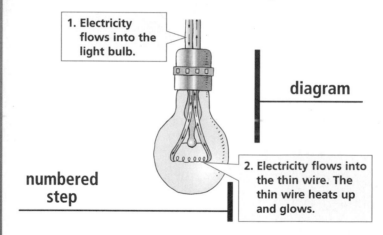

1. Electricity flows into the light bulb.

diagram

numbered step

2. Electricity flows into the thin wire. The thin wire heats up and glows.

✔ Look for **photographs** with **captions** to find out more information.

 Selection Reading

344

SWITCH ON, SWITCH OFF

by Melvin Berger

What Is Electricity?

It's time to go to sleep. You go to your bedroom. The room is dark. You flip up the switch on the wall. The light goes on.

You get into your pajamas. Just before you jump into bed, you flip down the switch. The light goes off. Flip up, and the light goes on. Flip down, and the light goes off. It seems like magic, but it's not magic at all. It's electricity!

Switch On   Switch Off

Electricity is a form of **energy**. Energy is the power to do work. You have a lot of energy. Your energy lets you walk, run, throw a ball, ride a bike, and sometimes even clean your room!

Electrical energy also does work. It lights your house. It brings you sound from your radio. If you have an electric stove, it cooks your food. If you have **an air conditioner**, it keeps you cool. Your energy comes from the food you eat, but electrical energy has to be made.

---

an air conditioner a machine that cools the air

Before You Move On

1. **Main Idea** What is electricity?

2. **Comparison** How is your body's energy like electrical energy? How is it different?

How Is Electricity Made?

Electricity moves by flowing through a metal wire. The wire is made up of billions of tiny bits, or particles. They are called **atoms** . Each atom is much too small to be seen. Yet each atom has even smaller particles. Some of these move in paths around the atom's center. They are the **electrons** .

A **magnet** can pull electrons away from an atom. When a magnet moves near a wire, it makes the electrons move out of their paths. They speed from atom to atom. The speeding electrons are what we call electricity.

▼ **When a wire is twisted into a coil, a magnet can move back and forth inside the coil. The magnet pulls electrons away from the atoms.**

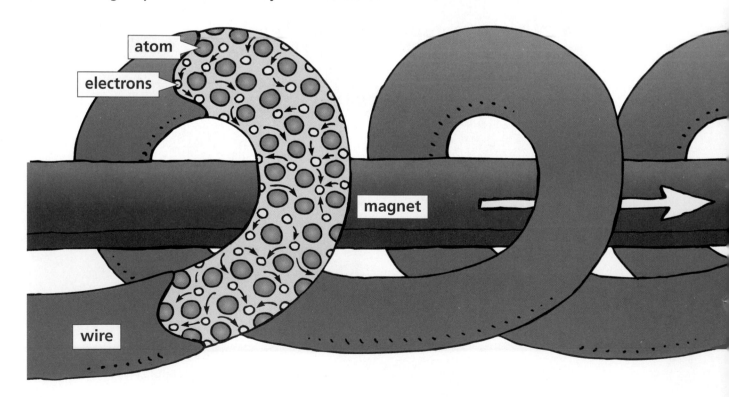

atom

electrons

magnet

wire

---

coil circle

Any machine that makes electricity is called a generator. It takes very big generators to supply electricity for a whole city. These generators have huge coils and giant magnets. Most generators spin a magnet inside the coils. Others spin coils between two magnets.

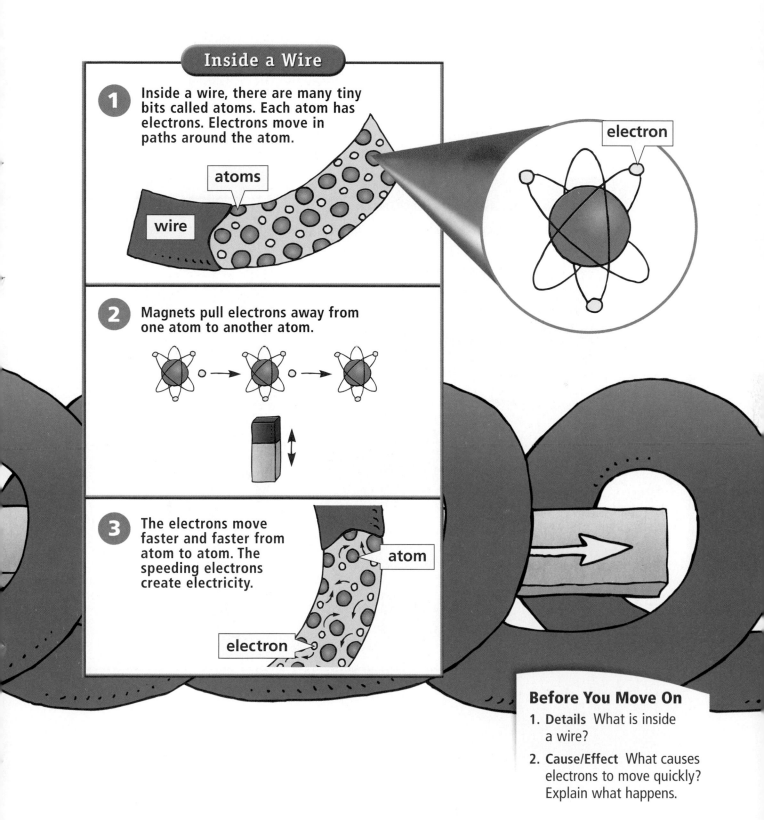

Inside a Wire

1 Inside a wire, there are many tiny bits called atoms. Each atom has electrons. Electrons move in paths around the atom.

atoms

wire

electron

2 Magnets pull electrons away from one atom to another atom.

3 The electrons move faster and faster from atom to atom. The speeding electrons create electricity.

atom

electron

Before You Move On

1. **Details** What is inside a wire?

2. **Cause/Effect** What causes electrons to move quickly? Explain what happens.

How Does Electricity Get to You?

Big generators need a lot of power to spin their coils or magnets. This power can come from wind, flowing water, or steam. As the coils or magnets spin, electricity flows in the coils.

The big wire coils are connected to other wires. These wires are strung along the tops of tall poles. The electricity travels through the wires for many miles.

From a Generator to Your Home

1. Wind, water, or steam power turns the propeller.

2. The propeller turns the magnet.

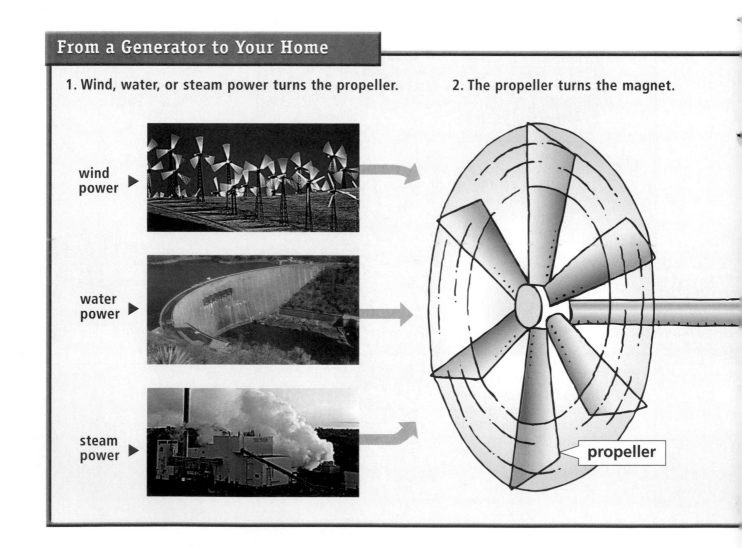

wind power ▶

water power ▶

steam power ▶

propeller

Shorter wires **branch off** from the long wires. They bring electricity to the homes, schools, stores, and other places that need it. One of these wires goes to your home. If you live in the country or in a small town, you can probably see the wire that brings the electricity into your home. If you live in a big city, you may not see the wire because it is under the ground.

Each wire is really made up of two **separate** wires. One brings the electricity from the generator into your house. The other takes the electricity back to the generator.

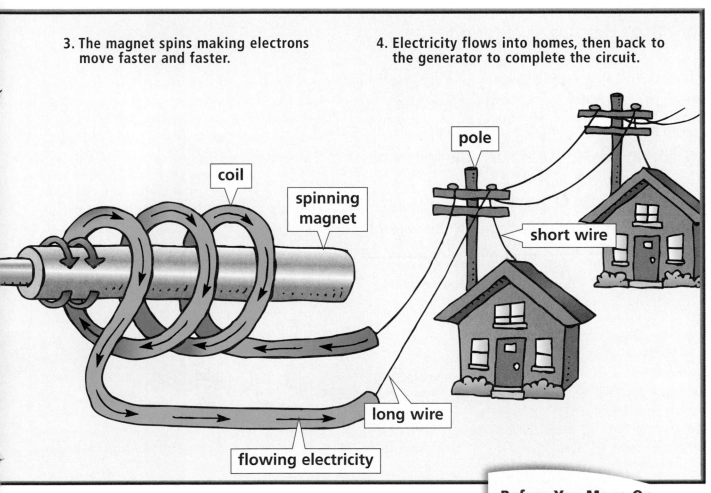

3. The magnet spins making electrons move faster and faster.

4. Electricity flows into homes, then back to the generator to complete the circuit.

coil

spinning magnet

pole

short wire

long wire

flowing electricity

Before You Move On

1. **Graphic Aids** What makes a generator's propeller spin?

2. **Steps in a Process** Where does electricity go after it leaves your home?

---

branch off go in other directions
separate different

What Is a Circuit?

Electricity always travels in a **circuit**. It only flows if it can get back to its starting point. If there is a **break in the circuit**, the electricity does not flow at all.

The circuit that comes into your house splits into many other circuits. It is like many small roads coming off a big highway. All the circuits in your house have breaks in them. The breaks let you turn the electricity on and off. That's what the switch is for!

The in and out wires of one circuit meet at the light switch in your room. When the switch is down, the break in the wire is open. No electricity can flow. The light is off.

Flip up the switch. The circuit is closed. Now the electricity can travel through the wire to the bulb on the ceiling. The light goes on.

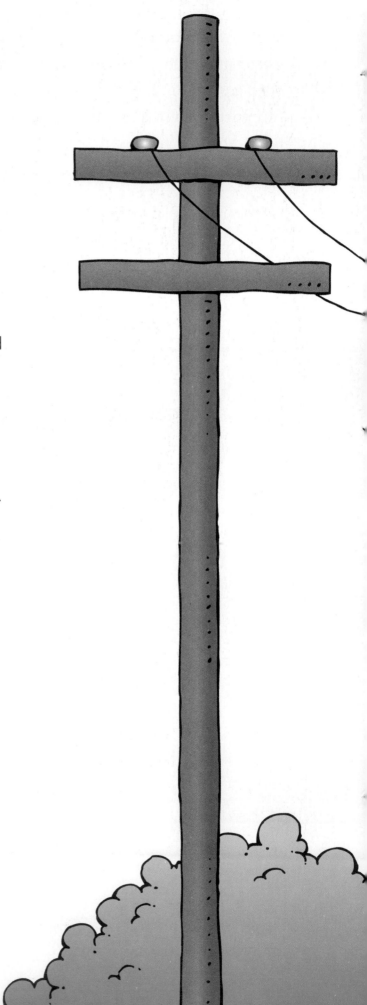

---

break in the circuit place where electricity cannot get through

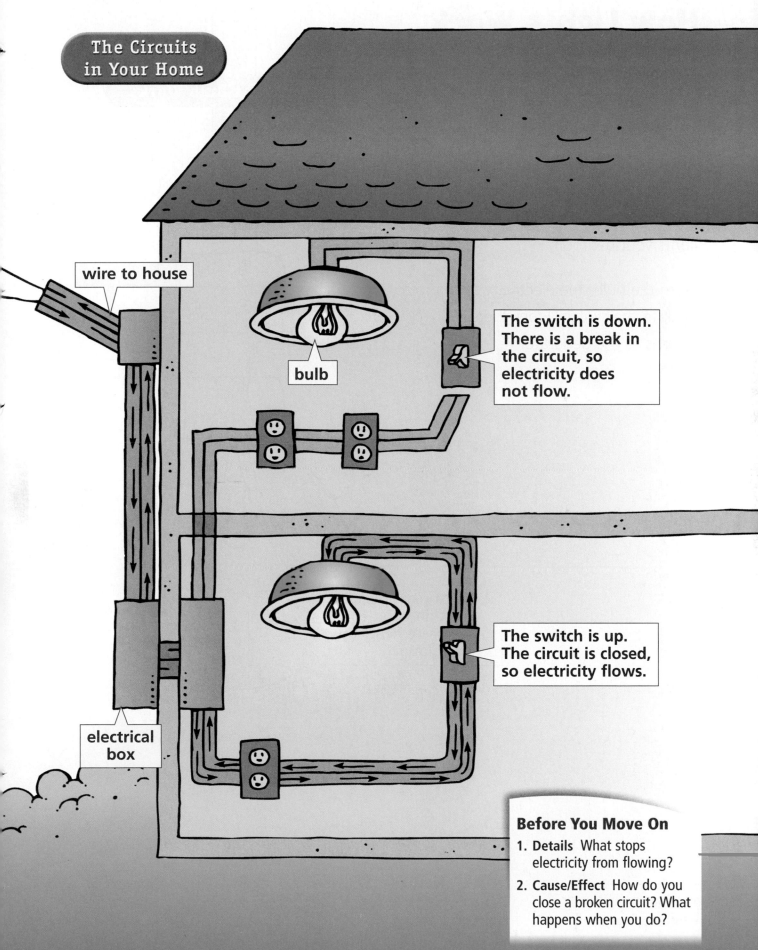

wire to house

bulb

The switch is down. There is a break in the circuit, so electricity does not flow.

The switch is up. The circuit is closed, so electricity flows.

electrical box

Before You Move On

1. **Details** What stops electricity from flowing?

2. **Cause/Effect** How do you close a broken circuit? What happens when you do?

How Lights Work

Inside the bulb, there is a very thin wire. The electricity must **squeeze** through this wire. When it does, the wire heats up. The wire quickly becomes **white-hot**. The glow of the white-hot wire in the bulb lights your bedroom.

From the bulb, the electricity zips back to the switch. From there it returns to the generator.

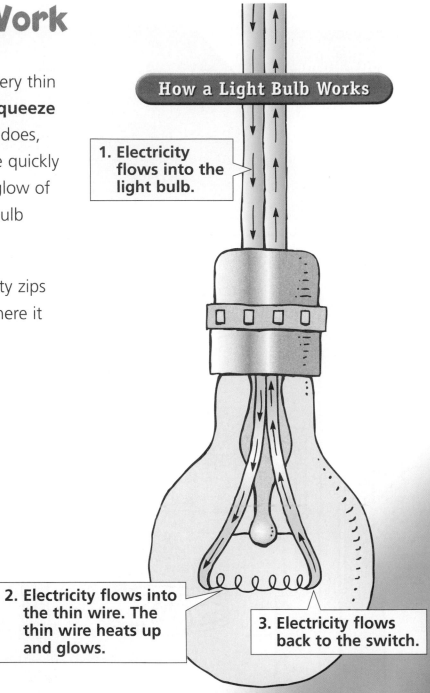

How a Light Bulb Works

1. **Electricity flows into the light bulb.**

2. **Electricity flows into the thin wire. The thin wire heats up and glows.**

3. **Electricity flows back to the switch.**

---

squeeze push its way
white-hot very, very hot

Maybe you have a lamp instead of a ceiling light. The lamp has a plug at the end of its cord. The plug has two metal prongs. Electricity can flow through the prongs just as it does through wires.

You fit the plug into an electrical outlet in the wall. The two wires of the house circuit are connected to the two holes of the outlet. When you put the plug in the outlet, the electricity can flow through the outlet, the plug, and the cord, and into the lamp.

The lamp has a switch. When you turn the lamp switch on, the electricity flows through the bulb and back out through the house circuit.

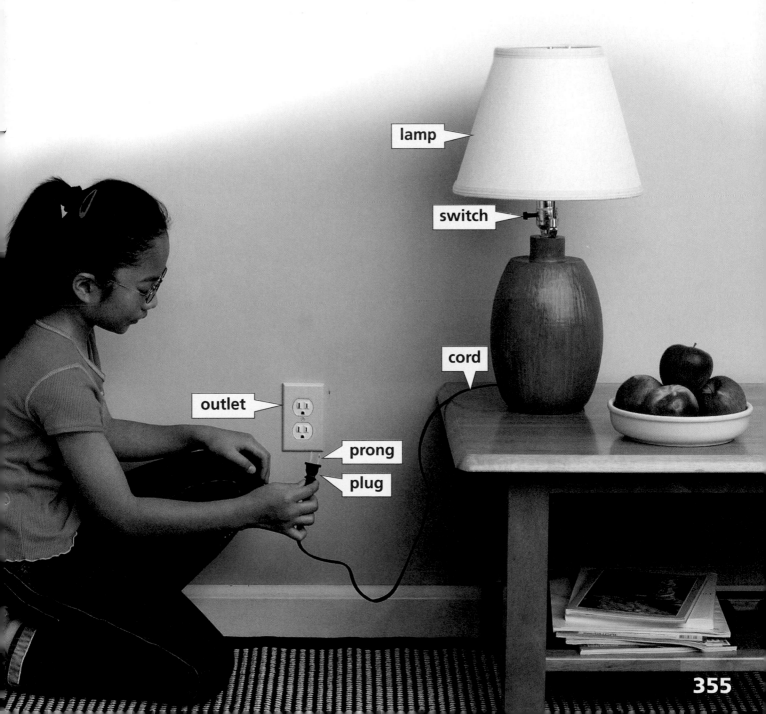

lamp

switch

cord

outlet

prong

plug

The next time you get ready for bed, stop and think. "Switch on" means you closed the circuit. The electricity flows.

"Switch off" means you broke the circuit. The electricity cannot flow. Then it is dark and time to sleep. Good night. **Pleasant dreams**.

Pleasant dreams Have happy dreams

Meet the Author

AWARD WINNER

   Melvin Berger knows there are a lot of complicated things in this world. He likes to make them easier to understand. "I like to answer the questions that I think kids want answered," says Mr. Berger.

   Melvin Berger mostly reads books, talks to the experts, and uses his own observations to explore new topics. He does some of his research on the Internet, too. In college, he studied electrical engineering, so he really knows what makes electricity ZAP!

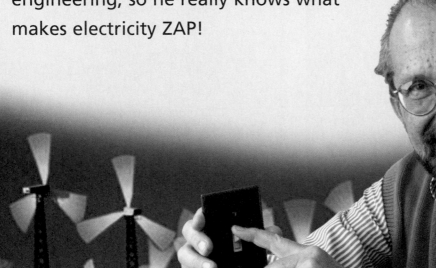

How to Make Your Own Electricity

bar magnet

Try this experiment to make electricity by yourself. You'll need a piece of electrical wire about two yards long. Ask an adult to help **strip the insulation off** the ends of the wire.

You'll also need a bar magnet and **a compass**. The compass will show whether or not you are making electricity.

electrical wire

compass

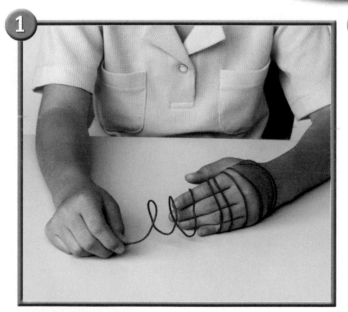

1

2

1. **Wrap one end of the wire around your hand about ten times, to make a coil. Slide the coil off your hand.**

2. **Now wrap the other end of the wire around the compass about five times. Leave the wire there.**

---

strip the insulation off take the plastic covering off

a compass an instrument that shows direction with a magnetic pointer

loop

3. Then **twist** the two metal ends of the wire together to make one big **loop**, or circuit.

4. Slide the magnet quickly back and forth inside the coil. Look at the compass as you do this. Do you see the **needle** move? This tells you that electricity is flowing.

Before You Move On

1. **Conclusion** What is the generator in the experiment? Explain.
2. **Cause/Effect** What happens if the ends of the wire are not connected?

twist join and attach

loop circle

needle pointer

Think and Respond

Strategy: Cause and Effect

Make a cause-and-effect chart. Show how electricity is made and how it flows.

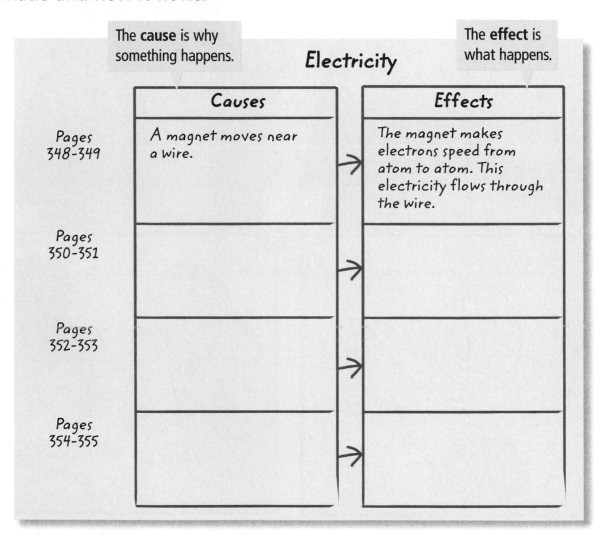

The **cause** is why something happens.

Electricity

The **effect** is what happens.

	Causes	Effects
Pages 348-349	A magnet moves near a wire.	The magnet makes electrons speed from atom to atom. This electricity flows through the wire.
Pages 350-351		
Pages 352-353		
Pages 354-355		

Give an Explanation

Choose one cause and effect from your chart and explain it to a partner. Draw pictures and add details to make your explanation clear.

Talk It Over

1 **Personal Response** Name all the things you switch on and off every day. Will you think about these things differently now? How?

2 **Speculate** What would your life be like without electricity? What would you miss most?

3 **Conclusion** Why is it important to know that generators use different kinds of power?

4 **Opinion** How well do you think the author explained the topic? Give examples to support your answer.

Compare Nonfiction

Compare "Switch On, Switch Off" and "Moving." Name ways that they are alike and different.

Both articles teach how things work.

Content Connections

partners

Check the Facts

Tell one fact about electricity, or tell something that is <u>not</u> true. Have your partner find information in "Switch On, Switch Off" that proves your statement is true or false. Then switch roles.

Most generators spin a magnet inside huge coils.

partners

Make a Magnet Boat

1. Glue sticks side by side. Glue more sticks crosswise.

2. Attach a magnet on top.

3. Move the boat around in water by moving a heavier magnet above it. What happens? Why?

4. Demonstrate for a younger child. Explain how magnetism works.

Plan to Conserve Energy
Internet

When you save energy, you save money. In a chart, calculate how much money you can save with energy-saving appliances. Use the Internet to find other ways to save energy. Share your information with the class.

Appliance	Energy Cost	Monthly Usage	Monthly Cost
fan	$.02 per hour	150 hours	$3.00
window air conditioner	$.16 per hour		$24.00

Write a News Report

What would it be like without electricity for 24 hours? Pretend it happened. Work with a partner to write a news report of an imaginary day. Deliver your report to your audience.

At 4:00 p.m., there were no batteries or candles left in local stores. By 5:00 p.m., the storm had arrived. Power lines were down all over town.

Helping Verbs

Listen and chant.

Chant

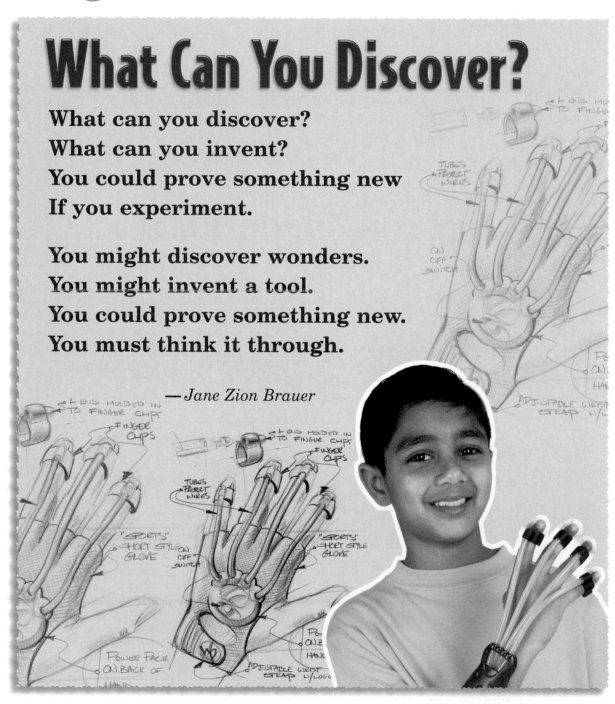

What Can You Discover?

What can you discover?
What can you invent?
You could prove something new
If you experiment.

You might discover wonders.
You might invent a tool.
You could prove something new.
You must think it through.

—*Jane Zion Brauer*

How Language Works

The verbs **can, could, may, might, must,** and **should** are **helping verbs.** They are always used with a **main verb.**

Helping Verbs	Examples:
1. Use **can** to tell what someone is able to do.	You **can be** an inventor.
2. Use **may, might,** or **could** to tell what is possible.	You **may invent** something. You **might have** a great idea. You **could think** of something new.
3. Use **must** or **should** to tell what has to happen.	You **should make** an invention. You **must share** your discoveries!

Practice with a Partner

Put a helping verb from the box in the blank. Say the sentence.

1. Some cars today _____ run on electricity.

2. There _____ be other fuel we can use, too.

3. One idea is that we _____ use power from the Sun.

4. Perhaps many cars _____ use natural gas in the future.

5. Someone _____ invent another type of fuel soon! It is important.

Helping Verbs
can
may
might
could
must
should

Put It in Writing

When all the electricity goes out during a storm, what can you do? Write about it.

I can read by the light of the Moon.

Show What You Know

Talk About Electricity

In this unit, you read a play and a science article about electricity. Look back at the unit. Find a photo or diagram that shows how electricity is made or how it flows. Use it to tell your group what you learned about electricity.

Make a Mind Map

Work with a partner. Make a mind map to summarize what you learned about electricity.

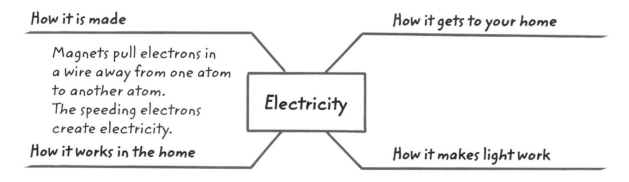

Think and Write

What questions do you still have about electricity? Write a list. Add it to your portfolio. Include work that shows what you learned about electricity.

Read and Learn More

Leveled Books

Power Out
by Sherilin Chanek

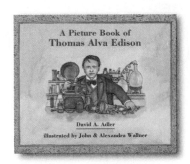

**A Picture Book of
Thomas Alva Edison**
by David A. Adler

Theme Library

**Science
Experiments with
Electricity**
by Sally Nankivell-Aston

Flicker Flash
by Joan Bransfield Graham

Internet
Go to: www.hbavenues.com
Electrical Safety
Wise Words
Save Energy

Going Places

with Patricia McKissack

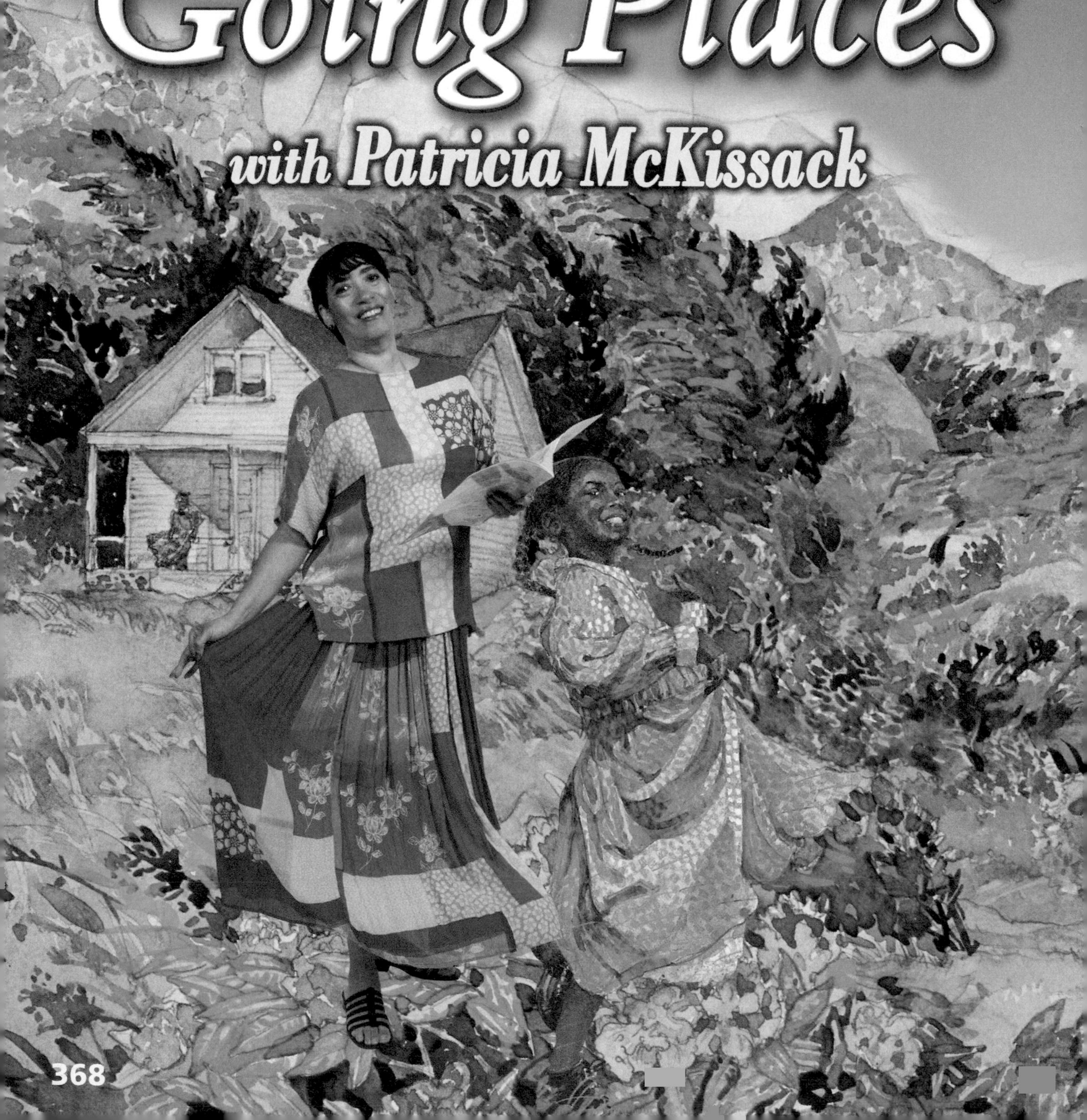

Put Yourself in a Story

1. Draw a picture of a place that is special to you.
2. Now add a picture of yourself.
3. Use the picture to tell a story to a partner.

America in the 1950s

In many states, African Americans were treated unfairly.

▲ African American children couldn't go to the same schools as white children.

▲ In some states, African Americans had to ride in the back of the bus.

America in the 1960s

People worked to change the laws. People wanted to be treated fairly. They wanted their civil rights.

▲ Students held "sit-ins" at restaurants. They refused to leave until the restaurants served them.

▲ More than 200,000 people marched to ask government leaders to change the laws.

Civil Rights Leaders

▲ The Civil Rights movement grew strong in 1955 when Rosa Parks refused to give up her bus seat to a white man.

▲ Martin Luther King, Jr., was one of the most important leaders. He led many marches and gave powerful speeches.

▲ President Johnson signed the Civil Rights Act of 1964 to make it law.

The Civil Rights Act

Congress passed The Civil Rights Act of 1964. This law gives every American the same rights.

Eighty-eighth Congress of the United States of America

AT THE SECOND SESSION

Begun and held at the City of Washington on Tuesday, the seventh day of January, one thousand nine hundred and sixty-four

An Act

To enforce the constitutional right to vote, to confer jurisdiction upon the district courts of the United States to provide injunctive relief against discrimination in public accommodations, to authorize the Attorney General to institute suits to protect constitutional rights in public facilities and public education, to extend the Commission on Civil Rights, to prevent discrimination in ... assisted programs, to establish a Commission on Equal Employ-...

A Visit To Remember

FRED WILLINGHAM

November 9

Dear Uncle José,

　Last week our class had a long **conversation** about Dr. Martin Luther King, Jr., and civil rights. Do you know that we have civil rights **protection** because of his work?

Then we went on a **special** trip to the King Center. My **favorite** part was listening to his speeches. Now I'm **determined** to read every book in our **public** library about him!

The King Center is such a **welcoming** place, too. Maybe we can go there when you visit.

Love,
Alma

Key Words

conversation

protection

special

favorite

determined

public

welcoming

The King Center, Atlanta, Georgia

Goin' Someplace Special

by Patricia C. McKissack

illustrated by Jerry Pinkney

Read a Story

Genre

A **historical fiction** story takes place in the past. Some of the people and events are real, but the story is fiction because the writer made up some of the details.

Dialogue

In this story, 'Tricia Ann and the other characters speak in **dialect**. The author wrote the words to sound the way people in that part of the U.S. often speak.

'Tricia Ann

Setting

This story takes place in Nashville, Tennessee, in the 1950s.

Nashville, Tennessee

Selection Reading

'Tricia Ann wants to go someplace alone. Will Mama Frances let her go?

'Tricia Ann was **about to burst with excitement**. Crossing her fingers and closing her eyes, she **blurted out** her question. "Mama Frances, may I go to Someplace **Special** by myself, today? Pretty please? I know where to get off the bus and what streets to take and all."

Although it had another name, 'Tricia Ann always called it Someplace Special because it was her **favorite** spot in the world.

"Please may I go? Pretty please with marshmallows on top?"

_____

about to burst with excitement very excited
blurted out quickly asked
favorite spot favorite place

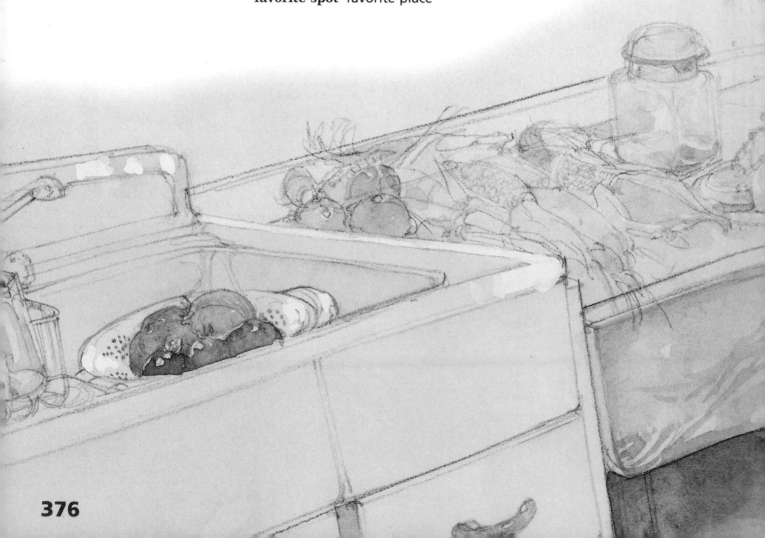

"I don't know if I'm ready to **turn you loose in the world**," Mama Frances answered, tying the sash of 'Tricia Ann's dress. "**Goin' off** alone is a mighty big step."

"I'm ready," the girl said, taking a giant leap across the floor. "See what a big step I can make?"

_____

turn you loose in the world let you go to town by yourself

Goin' off Going to town

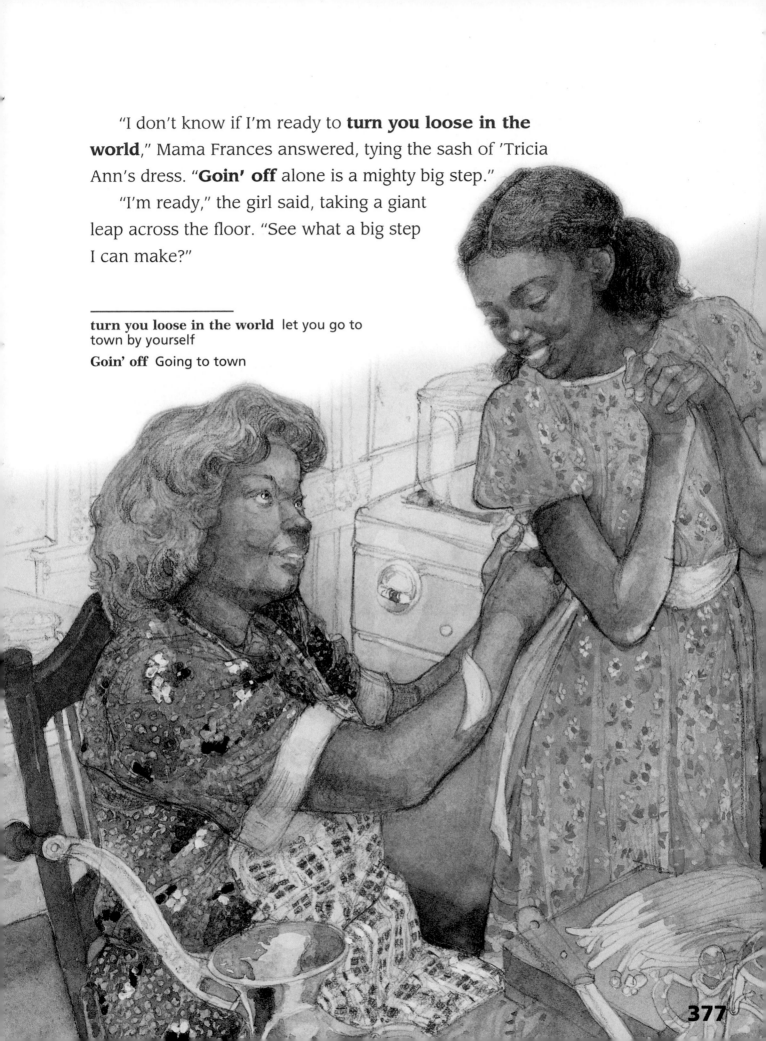

377

Mama Frances **chuckled**, all the time studying her granddaughter's face. "I **trust you'll be particular** and remember everything I've told you."

"I will. I will," 'Tricia Ann said, **real confident-like**. Suddenly, her smile grew into a full grin. "So you're saying I can go?"

"I **reckon** . . . but you **best hurry on 'fore** I change my mind."

---

chuckled laughed
trust you'll be particular hope you will be careful
real confident-like very sure about herself
reckon think so
best hurry on 'fore better go before

Pulling her pocketbook up on her shoulder, 'Tricia Ann **blew her grandmother a thank-you kiss**. Then she rushed out the door and down the sidewalk.

"And no matter what," Mama Frances called after her, "**hold yo' head up and act like you b'long to somebody**."

---

blew her grandmother a thank-you kiss kissed her hand and blew the kiss to her grandmother

hold yo' head up and act like you b'long to somebody hold your head up and show people that you are proud of yourself

Before You Move On

1. **Goal** What does 'Tricia Ann want to do?

2. **Inference** Why isn't Mama Frances sure if 'Tricia Ann should go?

At the corner, a green and white bus came to a jerky stop and hissed. When the doors folded back, 'Tricia Ann **bounded** up the steps and dropped in the **fare**, same as when Mama Frances was with her.

The girl **squared her shoulders**, walked to the back, and took a seat behind the **Jim Crow sign that said: COLORED SECTION**.

---

bounded ran

fare money for the bus ride

squared her shoulders stood straight

Jim Crow sign that said: COLORED SECTION sign that showed where African American people had to sit

'Tricia Ann had seen signs like that all her life. She **recalled** the first time she and Mama Frances had taken this bus ride. Her grandmother had told her, "Those signs can tell us where to sit, but they can't tell us what to think."

"I'm **gon'** think about Someplace Special," 'Tricia Ann said to herself and turned to look out the window.

---

recalled remembered
gon' going to

Stop by stop, the bus began to fill. At the Farmer's Market, people crowded on, carrying bags of fruits and vegetables. Mrs. Grannell, Mama Frances's friend from the sewing club, climbed on board. As she **inched her way** toward the back, 'Tricia Ann noticed that there were no seats left behind the Jim Crow sign. So she stood up and gave Mrs. Grannell hers.

"It's not fair," she said, **glaring** at the empty seats up front.

"No, but that's the way it is, Honey," said Mrs. Grannell.

"I **don'** understand why," she began. But by now the bus had reached 'Tricia Ann's stop in front of Capitol Square in the **heart** of downtown.

---

inched her way moved slowly
glaring looking angrily
don' don't
heart center, middle

The doors swung open, and she hurried off.
"**Carry yo'self proud**," Mrs. Grannell called out
the window as the bus pulled away.

Holding her hat, 'Tricia Ann leaned back as far as
she could to see Peace Fountain's **magnificent** water
show. It made her **dizzy** to watch the sprays that shot
high into the air, but she liked the feeling and turned
'round and 'round with her arms outstretched.

Carry yo'self proud Show pride
in yourself

magnificent beautiful

dizzy feel like she was spinning

Then, giggling, she **staggered on wobbly legs** to a nearby bench.

Instantly, 'Tricia Ann leaped to her feet. On the bench was a sign that said: **FOR WHITES ONLY**.

Her face fell, and she wished for Mama Frances's strong hand to hold. "Silly signs," she muttered as she **strutted away on sober legs**.

---

staggered on wobbly legs walked in a shaky way

FOR WHITES ONLY This bench is for white people only

Her face fell She stopped smiling

strutted away on sober legs walked away in a sad and angry way

At the edge of the square, she greeted Jimmy Lee, a street vendor. "**What's got yo' face all clouded up like a stormy day**?" he asked, handing 'Tricia Ann a free pretzel.

"Jim Crow makes me so mad!" she said. "My grandfather was **a stonemason on** Peace Fountain. Why can't I sit down and enjoy it?"

Jimmy Lee pointed to a sign in Monroe's Restaurant window. He said, "My brother cooks all the food they serve, but do you think we can sit at one of their tables and have a **BLT** and a cup of coffee together?"

What's got yo' face all clouded up like a stormy day Why do you look so angry

a stonemason on one of the men who built

BLT bacon, lettuce, and tomato sandwich

Then with a chuckle he whispered, "Not that I'd want to eat anything Jesse cooks. That man **can't even now scald water**." The light changed, and 'Tricia Ann carefully started across the street. "Don't let those signs **steal yo' happiness**," Jimmy Lee called after her.

---

can't even now scald water can't cook well (an expression)

steal yo' happiness make you unhappy

Before You Move On

1. **Obstacle** What happens to hurt 'Tricia Ann's feelings?

2. **Mood** Has the mood, or feeling, of the story changed? Explain.

3

What almost makes 'Tricia Ann turn around and go home?

'Tricia Ann pulled her shoulders back and **fixed her thoughts on** being inside that warm and welcoming place where there were no signs. Hurrying up Tenth Avenue, she passed the gas station, and stopped to buy a **pop** to wash down Jimmy Lee's pretzel.

At the second light, the Southland Hotel rose up in front of her, **as spectacular as a palace**. Mr. John Willis, the hotel's doorman, saw her. "**I b'lieve an angel done slipped 'way from heaven**," he said, smiling.

---

fixed her thoughts on thought about

pop soda, soft drink, cola

as spectacular as a palace big and beautiful like a king's home

I b'lieve an angel done slipped 'way from heaven You look very pretty today (an expression)

'Tricia Ann smiled back. Mr. John Willis always said the nicest things. "No, sir. It's just me."

"Your mouth is smiling, but your eyes aren't," he said.

Just then, a long white car with two police **escorts** pulled up in front of the hotel. A man with black shiny hair and shy eyes stepped out. Suddenly people were everywhere, screaming and **begging for his autograph**. 'Tricia Ann got caught in the crowd and swept inside.

So often she'd wondered what it would feel like to walk on the royal red carpet that covered the double-winding staircase, or to stand in the light of the chandelier that looked like a million diamonds strung together. Now, there she was, right in the middle of the Southland Hotel's grand lobby.

escorts cars to protect it

begging for his autograph asking him to write his name on his picture

Somebody pointed at her. "What is she doing in here?"

It seemed as if the whole world had stopped talking, stopped moving, and was staring at her. The manager pushed his way to the front of the crowd. "What makes you think you can come inside? No colored people are allowed!" He **shooed the girl away with his arms**.

'Tricia Ann backed out, shaking her head. "I didn't mean . . . ," she said, trying hard not to cry.

shooed the girl away with his arms waved his arms to make 'Tricia Ann go away

Hurrying past Mr. John Willis, 'Tricia Ann ran straight into the **Mission Church ruins** where Mama Frances often stopped to rest. There in the **protection** of the walled garden, the girl **let the tears come**. "Getting to Someplace Special isn't worth it," she sobbed. "I'm going home."

Mission Church ruins garden of an old church
let the tears come cried

"My flowers have been watered already," said a voice above her. It was Blooming Mary, an **elderly** woman who took care of the garden **with neither permission nor pay**. Everybody said she **was addled**, but Mama Frances didn't agree. "Blooming Mary is a kind and gentle **soul**," she'd told 'Tricia Ann.

"Are you lost, child?" the woman asked.

Trying to **steady her voice**, 'Tricia Ann answered. "No, ma'am, I just wish my grandmother was here to help me get to Someplace Special."

elderly old

with neither permission nor pay even though she was not asked or paid to do it

was addled did not think clearly

soul person

steady her voice speak clearly

"You can't get there by yourself?"

"It's too hard. I need my grandmother."

Blooming Mary nodded and thought **on the matter**.

Then she said, "I believe your granny <u>is</u> here, just as my granny is here with me even as I speak. Listen close. Tell me what you hear."

All 'Tricia Ann heard was the **distant** buzz of a bumblebee. What was Blooming Mary talking about?

Yet as she listened closer, she began to hear her grandmother's steady voice. "You are somebody, a human being. You are no better, no worse than anybody else in this world."

---

on the matter about 'Tricia Ann's problem
distant faraway

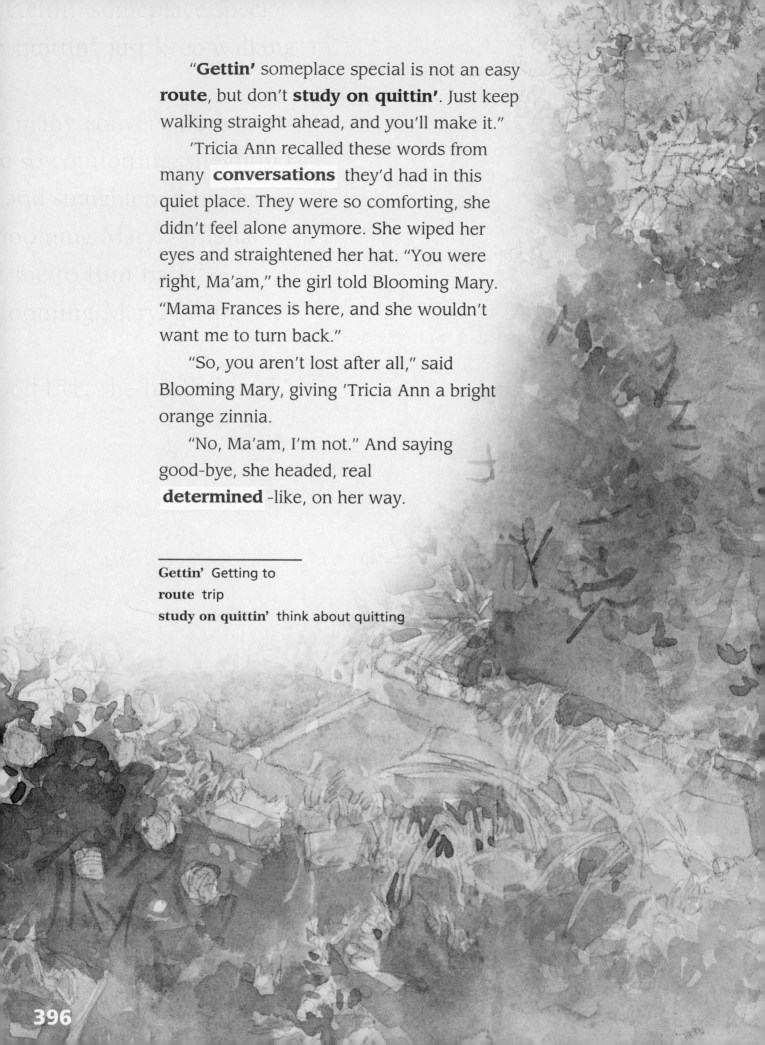

"**Gettin'** someplace special is not an easy **route**, but don't **study on quittin'**. Just keep walking straight ahead, and you'll make it."

'Tricia Ann recalled these words from many **conversations** they'd had in this quiet place. They were so comforting, she didn't feel alone anymore. She wiped her eyes and straightened her hat. "You were right, Ma'am," the girl told Blooming Mary. "Mama Frances is here, and she wouldn't want me to turn back."

"So, you aren't lost after all," said Blooming Mary, giving 'Tricia Ann a bright orange zinnia.

"No, Ma'am, I'm not." And saying good-bye, she headed, real **determined** -like, on her way.

Gettin' Getting to
route trip
study on quittin' think about quitting

Before You Move On

1. **Obstacle** What event makes 'Tricia Ann want to go home?

2. **Turning Point** How does 'Tricia Ann feel after she leaves the garden?

 wo blocks later 'Tricia Ann came to the Grand Music Palace, where a group had gathered for the **matinee performance**. As the girl approached, a little boy spoke to her. "Howdy, I'm Hickey, and I'm six years old today. You comin' in?"

Before 'Tricia Ann could answer, an older girl grabbed his hand. "Hush, boy," she said **through clenched teeth**. "Colored people can't come in the front door. They have to go 'round back and sit **up in the Buzzard's Roost**. Don't you know anything?" his sister whispered.

Hickey looked at 'Tricia Ann with wide, wondering eyes. "Are you going to sit up there?"

"In the last three rows of the balcony? Why, I wouldn't sit up there **even if watermelons bloomed in January**. Besides, I'm going to someplace very, very special," she answered, and then 'Tricia Ann skipped away.

"I want to go where she's goin'," she heard Hickey say as his sister pulled him through the door.

---

matinee performance afternoon show

through clenched teeth in an angry voice

up in the Buzzard's Roost in the back of the theater on the upper floor

even if watermelons bloomed in January and I will never change my mind (an expression)

At the corner, 'Tricia Ann saw a building **rising above all that surrounded it**, looking proud in the summer sun. It was much more than bricks and stone. It was an idea. Mama Frances called it a doorway to freedom. When 'Tricia Ann looked at it, she didn't feel angry or hurt or **embarrassed**. "At last," she whispered, "I've made it to Someplace Special."

Before bounding up the steps and through the front door, 'Tricia Ann stopped to look up at the message **chiseled** in stone across the front: **PUBLIC** LIBRARY: ALL ARE WELCOME.

---

rising above all that surrounded it that was taller than the buildings near it

embarrassed afraid that people might laugh at her

chiseled cut, carved

Before You Move On

1. **Conclusion** What makes the library special?

2. **Outcome** How do you think 'Tricia Ann feels about herself now?

Meet the Illustrator

Jerry Pinkney

AWARD WINNER

Jerry Pinkney would rather draw than anything else. "When I'm working on a book, I wish the phone would never ring. I love doing it," he says. Mr. Pinkney has illustrated more than 75 books.

Mr. Pinkney grew up in a place different from the South in *Goin' Someplace Special*. However, with Patricia McKissack's help, he was able to understand the deep hurt 'Tricia Ann felt. As he worked, he first pictured each event in his mind. Then he used pencils and watercolors to capture 'Tricia Ann's feelings and her brave journey to the library.

Think and Respond

Strategy: Goal and Outcome

Some stories tell how a character reaches a goal.
In these stories, look for:

- ✔ the goal
- ✔ the obstacles
- ✔ the turning point
- ✔ the outcome.

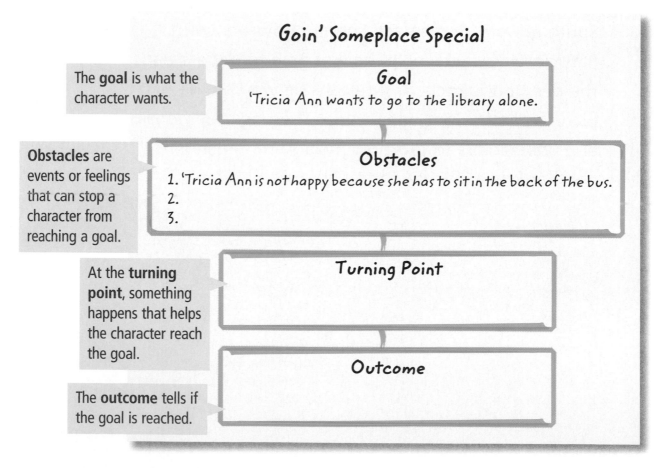

Goin' Someplace Special

The **goal** is what the character wants.

Goal
'Tricia Ann wants to go to the library alone.

Obstacles are events or feelings that can stop a character from reaching a goal.

Obstacles
1. 'Tricia Ann is not happy because she has to sit in the back of the bus.
2.
3.

At the **turning point**, something happens that helps the character reach the goal.

Turning Point

The **outcome** tells if the goal is reached.

Outcome

Make a story map for "Goin' Someplace Special."

Draw Conclusions

What can you say about 'Tricia Ann? Talk about the things
'Tricia Ann did and what they tell you about her.

Talk It Over

1 **Personal Response** What is your favorite place? Why is it special to you?

2 **Generalization** How did 'Tricia Ann's friends help her? What can you say about friendship?

3 **Inference** Mama Frances called the library "a doorway to freedom." What did she mean?

4 **Opinion** This story tells about a real time in history. Is it important to learn about history? Why?

Compare Issues

How is fairness an issue in both "Goin' Someplace Special" and "Joining the Boston Tea Party"?

Both 'Tricia Ann and the colonists had to face things that were not fair.

Content Connections

Role-Play a Conversation

small group

Mama Frances wasn't sure if 'Tricia Ann was ready to go off alone. Role-play the conversation between Mama Frances and 'Tricia Ann. Was Mama Frances right to be worried? Talk about it.

Mama Frances shouldn't worry. 'Tricia Ann has gone to the library many times.

Research Expressions

small group

Do people talk the same way all over the United States? Send an e-mail to students in another region of the country. Tell how people say something where you live. Ask how people say it in their region.

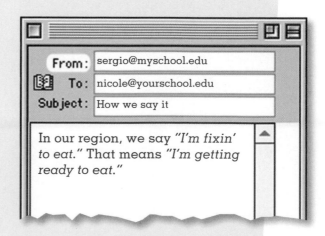

From: sergio@myschool.edu
To: nicole@yourschool.edu
Subject: How we say it

In our region, we say "I'm fixin' to eat." That means "I'm getting ready to eat."

Study American Music

Internet

small group

The library isn't the only thing that's special about Nashville, Tennessee. The city is also famous for its country music. Use the Internet and other sources to make a multimedia report about this kind of music.

Country music is one of the most popular kinds of music in America.

WRITING

Write a Story

on your own

Think about all the realistic fiction stories you've read. Now write your own story. Make up the characters, setting, and plot. Use dialogue to make your characters seem real.

The Longest Friday

Kelli couldn't wait for the school day to end. "I'm fixin' to go with my family to San Antonio this weekend!" she told her friend Mia. "We're going to visit Aunt Ana."

Make Predictions

When you guess what will happen next in a story, you **make a prediction**. To make predictions:

- ✔ Read carefully and look for story clues.
- ✔ Think about what you already know.
- ✔ Make a guess about what will happen next.
- ✔ Continue reading to find out if your prediction is right.
- ✔ Change your prediction if you discover new information.

Try the strategy.

from *Goin' Someplace Special*

"I don't know if I'm ready to turn you loose in the world," Mama Frances answered, tying the sash of 'Tricia Ann's dress. "Goin' off alone is a mighty big step."

"I'm ready," the girl said, taking a giant leap across the floor. "See what a big step I can make?"

Mama Frances chuckled, all the time studying her granddaughter's face. "I trust you'll be particular, and remember everything I've told you."

Most kids can't go off alone, so I predicted that Mama Frances wouldn't let 'Tricia Ann go. Then I changed my prediction because Mama said she trusted 'Tricia Ann.

Practice

Take this test and **make predictions** about "Goin' Someplace Special."

Read each item. Choose the best answer.

1 **What do you think 'Tricia Ann will do after she's finished at the library?**

   A   She will go back to the hotel.

   B   She will go to the Grand Music Palace.

   C   She will go home to her grandmother.

   D   She will sit on a bench and watch the fountain.

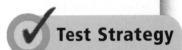

Test Strategy

Check your answers if you have time. Reread the questions and the answers you marked.

2 **Think about Mama Frances. Read these details about her.**

> Mama Frances says that going someplace special isn't easy, but you shouldn't stop trying to get there. Mama Frances calls the library "a doorway to freedom."

What will Mama Frances do the next time 'Tricia Ann wants to go to the library?

   A   Mama Frances will let 'Tricia Ann go to the library alone again.

   B   Mama Frances will not let 'Tricia Ann go to the library alone again.

   C   Mama Frances will tell 'Tricia Ann to stay away from Blooming Mary.

   D   Mama Frances will tell 'Tricia Ann not to call the library "Someplace Special."

Getting to Someplace Special
by PATRICIA C. McKISSACK

Vocabulary

Song

Partnership!

When you **inspire** someone,
When you **respect** them, too,
You **make a difference**. Yes!
You know, you really do!
When you **encourage** someone
To be their very best,
That is a **partnership**!

Tune: "The Hokey Pokey"

When you **compromise**,
And give up just a bit,
Of what you really want
So that both of you can win
And share a little, too,
Of what each of you needs,
That is a partnership!

—*Joyce McGreevy*

Key Words

inspire

respect

make a difference

encourage

partnership

compromise

LIBRARY HOURS
MONDAY thru FRIDAY
8:30 a.m. to 9:00 p.m.
SATURDAY
8:30 a.m. to 5:00 p.m.
SUND
1:00 p.m. t

Read an Autobiography

An **autobiography** is the story of a person's life written by that person.

✔ Study the **photographs**. They help you see what people and places in the author's life were like.

photograph

caption

▲ Fred and Patricia McKissack share a story with students.

✔ Read the **captions** to learn more about what the photographs show.

 Selection Reading

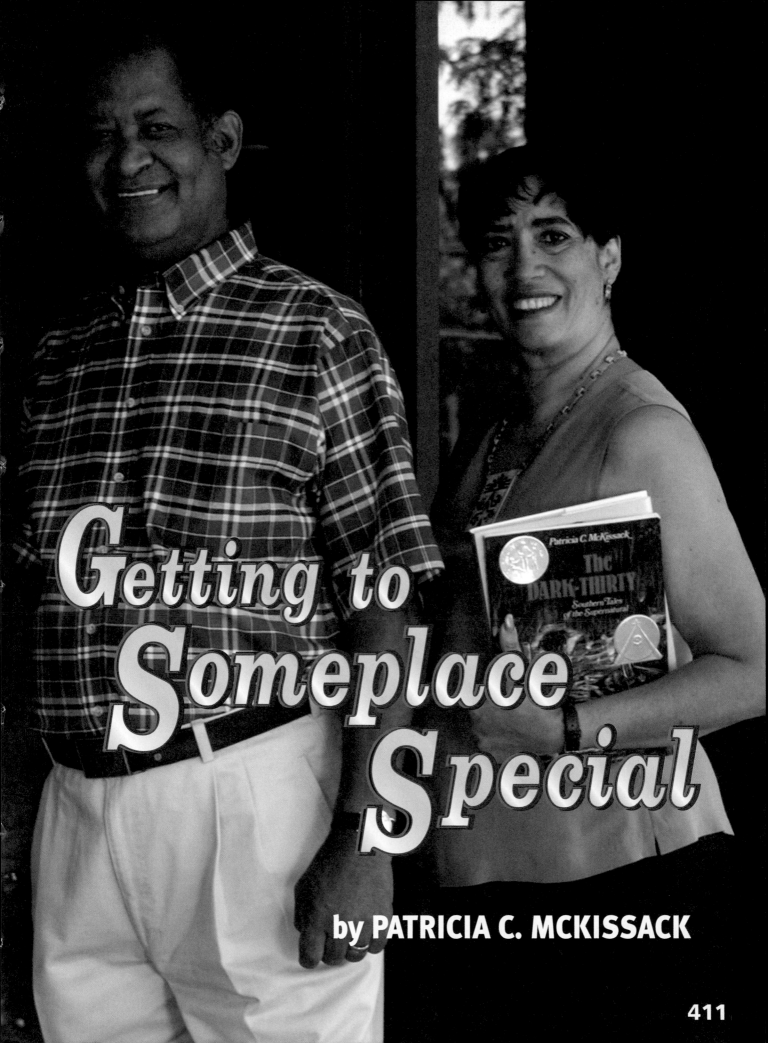

Getting to Someplace Special

by PATRICIA C. MCKISSACK

▲ Fred and Patricia McKissack share a story with students.

A Love of Books

My husband, Fredrick McKissack, and I have written more than 75 children's books since 1980. People often ask what **inspired** us to become writers. We always answer, "Reading."

We both love to read. Our parents and teachers **encouraged** our love of books. So, we each spent a lot of time in the Nashville Public Library, although we didn't know each other then because we lived on opposite sides of town. The Nashville Public Library was a beautiful building, but it wasn't always easy to get there. Getting to someplace special usually isn't.

Like most southern cities in the 1950s, Nashville, Tennessee was segregated. That meant blacks and whites couldn't eat at the same restaurants, play together in parks, live in the same neighborhoods, or go to the same schools. Segregation signs were posted everywhere: on public restrooms, on drinking fountains, and on buses. The signs **were humiliating**.

---

were humiliating made us feel bad

Some libraries were segregated in the 1950s, but the Nashville Public Library welcomed everyone. ▶

At least the Nashville Public Library was not segregated. In the late 1950s, **the board of directors decided to integrate** all of their neighborhood libraries. Fred and I both saw and felt all kinds of **racial bigotry and discrimination** on the way to the library.

Once we got there, however, it was **well worth the effort**. We felt welcome, so we went regularly to get more books. The more we read, the more we learned about ourselves and the world we lived in. The library was a very special place then, and it still is.

---

board of directors decided to integrate leaders agreed to allow both blacks and whites in

racial bigotry and discrimination hurtful words and actions because we were black

well worth the effort enjoyable to go even though people treated us badly on the way there

Before You Move On

1. **Conclusion** What did both Patricia and Fred like to do as children? Why?

2. **Comparison** How was the library different from other places?

Map of the
**SOUTHERN
UNITED STATES**

Early Years

I was born in Smyrna, Tennessee, on August 9, 1944. Shortly afterward, my family moved to St. Louis, Missouri. During the summer I turned ten, my parents **divorced**. Mother moved my brother Robert Nolan, my sister Sarah Frances, and me back to Tennessee. She found a job and rented an apartment in the Preston-Taylor Housing Projects in Nashville. Daddy stayed in St. Louis. We visited him every summer and on some holidays.

Fred was born in Nashville on August 12, 1939. His father, his grandfather, his great uncle, and five other uncles were all **architects and engineers**. Among the many **construction projects of** McKissack and McKissack, Inc., were libraries at Fisk University, Tennessee State University, Meharry Medical College, and other **historic black colleges**.

---

divorced ended their marriage

architects and engineers people who plan and build buildings

construction projects of buildings planned and built by

historic black colleges schools that were started for African Americans

Fred graduated from Pearl High School in Nashville, Tennessee, in 1957. ▶

◀ Patricia graduated in 1961.

College Years and New Careers

Fred and I lived in the same city and attended the same high school, but we didn't know each other in those days. Fred **became a marine** after high school and then entered Tennessee State University after that. We both entered the university at the same time, and that's where we finally met.

Fred **majored in civil engineering** and worked for his family's company. I studied English. We married after we graduated from college in 1964.

Within a few months, we moved to St. Louis, **my old hometown**, because of Fred's job. Our sons, Fred, Jr., Robert, and John were born there. A few years later, Fred opened his own construction company, and I started to teach eighth-grade English in Kirkwood, Missouri.

---

became a marine joined the United States Armed Services; was a soldier

majored in civil engineering studied how to plan and build buildings

my old hometown where I lived as a child

Before You Move On

1. **Sequence** Why did Fred and Patricia start college at the same time?

2. **Graphic Aids** Look at the map. Use it to tell about Patricia's life so far.

My Writing Begins

While I was teaching, I took my first steps toward becoming a writer. Once again, the library played **a significant** role in my life. Let me explain. Before I was a parent or a teacher, I was a listener. Mother recited the poetry of Paul Laurence Dunbar to me when I was a little girl. "Little Brown Baby" was my favorite poem. I never got tired of hearing it. Later, I taught it to my sons.

As a teacher, I wanted to share Dunbar's life and poetry with my students. When I went to the library to check out a biography of him, I couldn't find one for young readers. In fact, in 1971, there weren't a lot of books about African Americans in any of the libraries I visited. Since I needed a biography of Paul Laurence Dunbar, I decided to write it myself. That was **easier said than done**. I'd never written a book before.

◄ Patricia, age 8, with her mother and father.

Paul Laurence Dunbar ▲ was born in 1872.

a significant an important
easier said than done not easy to do

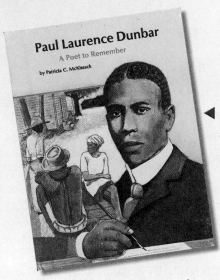

◀ Patricia McKissack wrote
*Paul Laurence Dunbar:
A Poet to Remember* in 1971.
It was published in 1984.

After I gathered facts about Dunbar from old newspapers, magazines, and books written for adults, I wrote the biography. It took a long time. Yet when my students read the **manuscript**, they asked, "Who wrote this? It's terrible. It's so boring!" I was embarrassed.

In nonfiction, all the information must be true. Well, I had listed the facts, but I had not told a good story.

It was time to revise my biography. I shortened it. I added words. I moved sentences around. I went to the library to make sure that everything was **accurate**. Each time I worked on my manuscript, it got better and better. The next time I shared Dunbar's biography with my students, they enjoyed it.

I learned a very **valuable** lesson from this experience. Rewriting is the most important part of the writing process. I'm happy to say that today there are a number of good books about Dunbar in the library, and one of them is mine.

---

manuscript writing
accurate correct, right
valuable useful

Before You Move On

1. **Paraphrase** Why did Patricia decide to become a writer?

2. **Main Idea** What lesson did Patricia learn about writing?

417

We Work Together

Time passed quickly. By 1980, I had sold a few poems and short stories. Then, in 1981, Fred encouraged me to follow one of my dreams and write **full time**. He even offered to help me do research and think of ideas. That was the beginning of a new **partnership** for us.

Fred and I work together well because we enjoy what we do. Fred likes to do research. He **digs up** forgotten facts, looks up information in old **record books**, and reads old diaries. He spends hours in libraries, museums, **historical societies** and historic homes and buildings. He's very careful that his facts are correct.

---

full time every day as my job

digs up finds

record books books that list dates, names, and other facts

historical societies groups that study history

▼ While they were researching their book, *A Picture of Freedom,* Patricia and Fred visited plantations like this one.

I like to write. I use the facts that Fred finds to tell a good story. Sometimes we spend as much time researching fiction as we do nonfiction. *A Picture of Freedom: The Diary of Clotee a Slave Girl* is historical fiction, but Fred and I spent two years researching it. We drove to Virginia to study **plantation life** at several historic houses. We visited museums and libraries. We wanted to **reconstruct** Clotee's world just as it was in 1859. The story was so realistic that a few readers thought Clotee was a real person!

▲ Patricia and Fred share ideas as they work together.

Fred and I are often asked, "How do you work together?" **Respect** and **compromise** . Fred and I agree about most things, but sometimes we don't. We might disagree about how a book should begin or end, what a character should say and do, or if a fact is important or not. When this happens, we **put all of our ideas and feelings on the table**. Then, we discuss them one by one. Sometimes my idea is chosen. Sometimes Fred's is. Occasionally, we come up with a new idea just by talking it through.

---

plantation life farm life in the 1800s in the Southern states

reconstruct show

put all of our ideas and feelings on the table say everything we are thinking

Before You Move On

1. **Main Idea** Why does the story about Clotee seem real to some people?

2. **Conclusion** Why do the McKissacks work well together?

▲ Sometimes illustrators of Patricia McKissack's books make her characters look like her. Flossie looks a lot like Patricia when she was a girl.

Stories from Childhood

Some of my picture books are about animals that talk, such as *Flossie and the Fox, A Million Fish…More or Less*, and *Nettie Jo's Friends*. These stories come from my childhood. All of my grandparents were wonderful storytellers. My mother's father, Daddy James, told delightful stories about little girls who could **outsmart** foxes and catch the wind. Since the girl in his stories had my name, I thought I was just as clever and brave as she was. In a way, I feel like the story characters Flossie, Mirandy, and Nettie Jo are the daughters I never had. I created them from my childhood memories.

---

outsmart   be smarter than

My mother's mother, Mama Frances, told **hair-raising** stories at the hour of the dark-thirty. That's the last half-hour beforc it gets all the way dark. She'd tell a scary story, then send me into the dark, dark house to get her a drink of water. I loved being deliciously frightened as I **set out** on the journey through the living room and dining room, then back to the **pitch-black** kitchen. Even now I can feel the fear as it starts in my toes and moves up my back like a zipper. I write about some of those scary times in my books.

---

hair-raising scary
set out went
pitch-black very dark

Before You Move On

1. **Comparison** How were Patricia's grandparents alike?

2. **Inference** Do you think Patricia likes scary stories?

421

My St. Louis grandparents, Mama Sarah and Papa Lucious, taught me to love music and flowers. They took me fishing, and they sent me to camp where I made friends that are still **dear**. Ezel, a character in *Mirandy and Brother Wind*, is based on a youngster who was at camp with me years ago. He, truly, could not walk and chew gum at the same time. Many of the characters in our books are based on family members, friends, or combinations of people we know.

▲ Patricia McKissack's characters are often based on people she knows. Ezel is a boy she met at camp.

---

dear close to me

▼ Fred and Patricia McKissack share their love of books with children all over the country.

Making a Difference

The people who have illustrated my picture books have been some of the best: Rachel Isadora, Jerry Pinkney, Scott Cook, Floyd Cooper, James Ransome, Brian Pinkney, and others. It **thrills me** to see how an illustrator understands my words and the way they "see" my characters. It's amazing how closely their art matches the way I see my characters, especially since we don't often get to talk to each other.

Fred and I have tried to **make a difference** through our writing. Nashville Public Library was open to us when many places **rejected us** because of the color of our skin. Still, as African American children, we **longed for** a book that was about our culture. We wanted a book with pictures of characters who looked like us and the people in our neighborhood. Now there are many more books like that available in libraries all over the world. Fred and I are pleased that we have helped to present those images that show our culture.

Getting someplace special might not be easy, but it's well worth the effort.

---

thrills me makes me very happy
rejected us wouldn't let us come in
longed for wanted, wished for

Before You Move On

1. **Generalization** Where do writers get ideas for books?

2. **Cause/Effect** What difference have the McKissacks made?

My People

The night is beautiful,
So the faces of my people.

The stars are beautiful,
So the eyes of my people.

Beautiful also is the sun.
Beautiful, also, are the souls of my people.

—*Langston Hughes*

Meet the Poet

Langston Hughes celebrated African American life and culture through his poetry, novels, plays, essays, and children's books. He lived and worked in Harlem, a neighborhood in New York City, in the 1920s.

Before You Move On

Conclusion What is the poem mostly about?

Content Connections

Tell a Story

small group

Make up a story character. Make a filmstrip or cartoon to show events in the character's life in order. Be the character and tell your group about your life. Answer questions from your listeners.

> I was born on planet Volax. My home was underground.

ART

Illustrate Poetry

Partners

Choose a favorite poem. Talk about it. What is the poet's message? How does the poem make you feel? Illustrate the poem to show your ideas.

Little bird, soaring so high,
I fly away with you in my dreams...

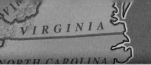

Make a Time Line

Internet

partners

Find out more about the events and people involved in the Civil Rights movement. Download images or create your own to show what happened in the 1950s and 1960s. Create a class time line.

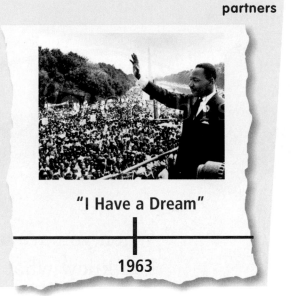

"I Have a Dream"

1963

WRITING

Write to Persuade

on your own

Choose a book or story by Patricia McKissack. Choose the best way to persuade others to read it:

- a book review
- an ad
- a letter

Try to use correct spelling, capitalization, punctuation, and grammar.

A Picture of Freedom: The Diary of Clotee, a Slave Girl
by Patricia C. McKissack

You will like the brave character in this book, and you will learn a lot about history. You must read it!

Join Sentences

Listen and sing.

Song

When You Are a Writer

When you are a writer,
You know what to write.
If you are a writer,
You write what is right.

Because you're a writer,
You write with delight.
You write what you know,
And you write what is right.

—Jane Zion Brauer

Tune: "Five Hungry Mice"

Drama
Fantasy
Adventure
Mystery

How Language Works

Use a **conjunction** to put two sentences together.

Conjunctions	Examples:
1. Use **when** to tell how ideas are related in time.	I went to the library. I got three books. **When** I went to the library, I got three books.
2. Use **because** to relate a cause and its effect.	I can get books. I have a library card. I can get books **because** I have a library card.
3. Use **if** to tell how one thing depends on another.	A book is overdue. I have to pay a fine. **If** a book is overdue, I have to pay a fine.

Practice with a Partner

Choose a conjunction to join the sentences. Say the new sentence.

Conjunctions
when
because
if

1. I write stories. I want to tell about my life.
2. I write about hiking. I love to hike.
3. I bring a notepad and a pencil. I go hiking.
4. I see something interesting. I jot down notes.
5. You want to tell about your life. Write stories!

Put It in Writing

Write about a special place or something special you want to do. Put some of your sentences together. Use *when*, *because*, or *if*.

When I sit under my favorite tree, I feel peaceful.

Show What You Know

Talk About the Unit

In this unit, you read a story by Patricia McKissack and an autobiography about her life. Look back at the unit. Choose your favorite illustration or photograph. Describe it to your group. Why did you choose that picture?

Make a Mind Map

Work with a group. Make a mind map to show what you learned about Patricia McKissack and her writing.

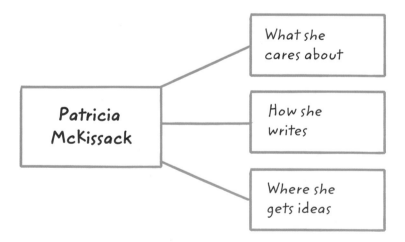

Think and Write

What do you think about the work the McKissacks do? Write a paragraph. Add it to your portfolio. Include work that shows what else you learned about the McKissacks.

Read and Learn More

Leveled Books

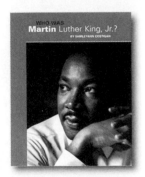

Who Was Martin Luther King, Jr.?
by Shirleyann Costigan

Tomás and the Library Lady
by Pat Mora

Theme Library

The Honest-to-Goodness Truth
by Patricia C. McKissack

Martin's Big Words
by Doreen Rappaport

Internet

Go to: www.hbavenues.com

Country Music

Civil Rights Movement

Great African Americans

We the People

Make a Flag

1. Design a stamp. Draw something on your stamp that tells about you.
2. Use your stamp to make a class flag. Tell the class about your stamp.
3. Talk about what your class flag shows about the U.S.

Social Studies Words

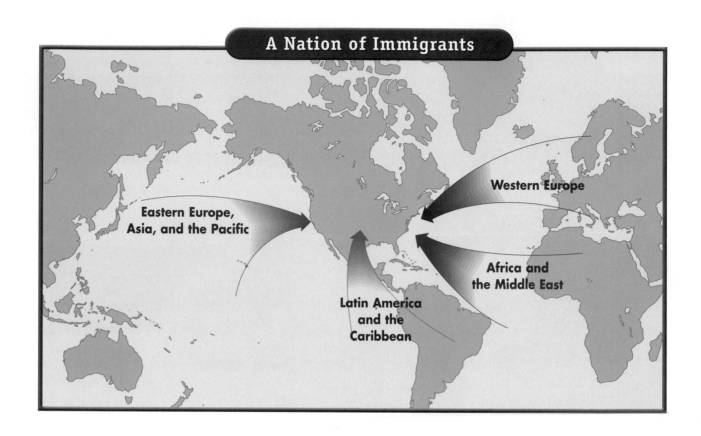

A Nation of Immigrants

Western Europe

Eastern Europe, Asia, and the Pacific

Latin America and the Caribbean

Africa and the Middle East

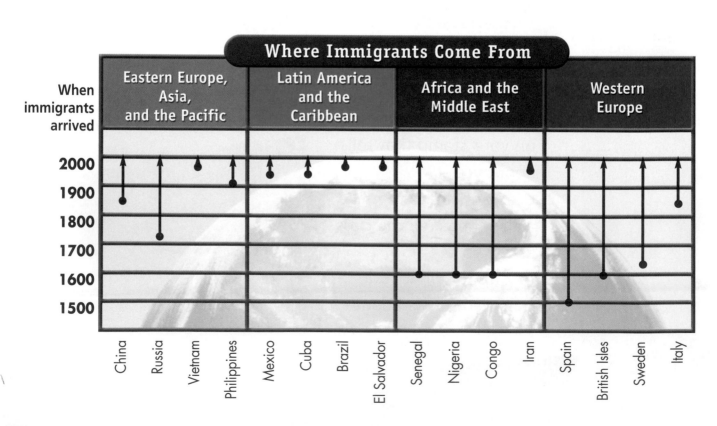

Where Immigrants Come From

When immigrants arrived	Eastern Europe, Asia, and the Pacific				Latin America and the Caribbean				Africa and the Middle East				Western Europe			
2000																
1900																
1800																
1700																
1600																
1500																

China · Russia · Vietnam · Philippines · Mexico · Cuba · Brazil · El Salvador · Senegal · Nigeria · Congo · Iran · Spain · British Isles · Sweden · Italy

U.S. Culture Is Diverse

Music

▲ mariachi band

▲ salsa band

▲ Caribbean steel band

Crafts

▲ Nigerian embroidery

▲ Japanese fabric

▲ Guatemalan weaving

Buildings

▲ Russian church

▲ Native American pueblo

▲ Islamic mosque

Dance

▲ lion dance

▲ hula

▲ tango

Vocabulary

CAMP BENEATH THE STARS

I remember how we **harvested**

In the fields of California

And the **migrant** workers' voices

In our **camp** beneath the stars.

Sometimes we **settled down** for

A season in the sunshine,

Where *mi familia* labored

'Til it came time to **move on**.

—Shirleyann Costigan

---

mi familia my family (in Spanish)

Tune: "Adiós, mi chaparrita"
(Good-bye, My Little One)

438

Key Words

harvest

migrant

camp

settle down

move on

439

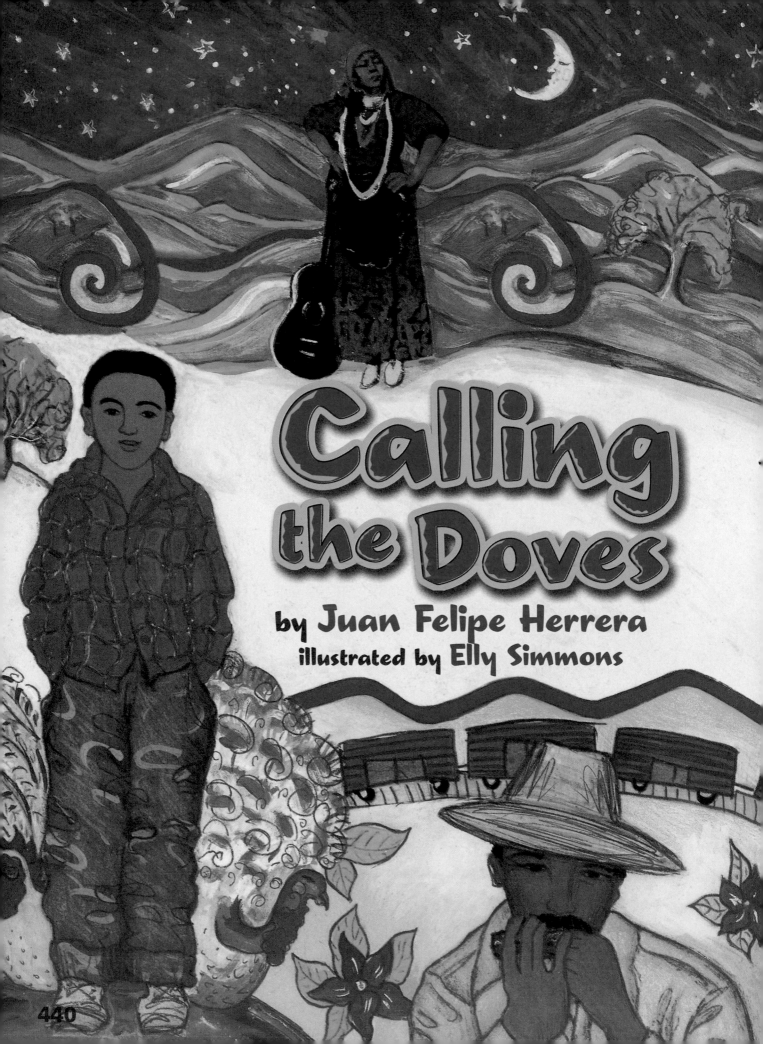

Calling the Doves

by Juan Felipe Herrera

illustrated by Elly Simmons

Read a Story

Genre

In a **personal narrative**, an author tells a story about events in his or her own life. In this story, Juan Felipe Herrera tells about his family's life as migrant farmworkers.

Characters

Juanito

Juanito's mother and father

Setting

The story happens in California during the early years of the author's childhood.

California

 Selection Reading

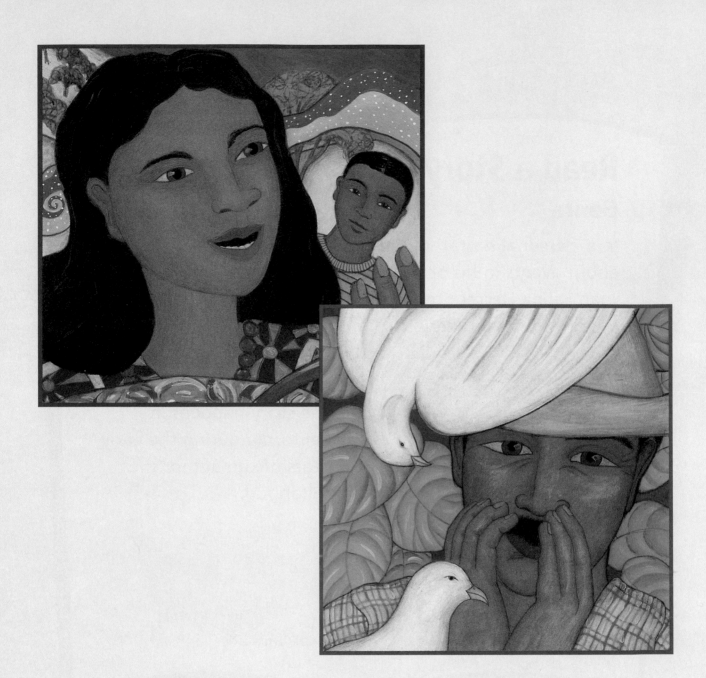

I was born in the tiny town of Fowler, "the raisin capital of the world." My mother and father were **migrant** farmworkers, and I grew up traveling with them through the mountains and valleys of California.

This story is dedicated to my mother Lucha and my father Felipe, who loved the open sky and the earth when it is tender. They taught me that inside every word there can be kindness.

This story is dedicated to I wrote this story for

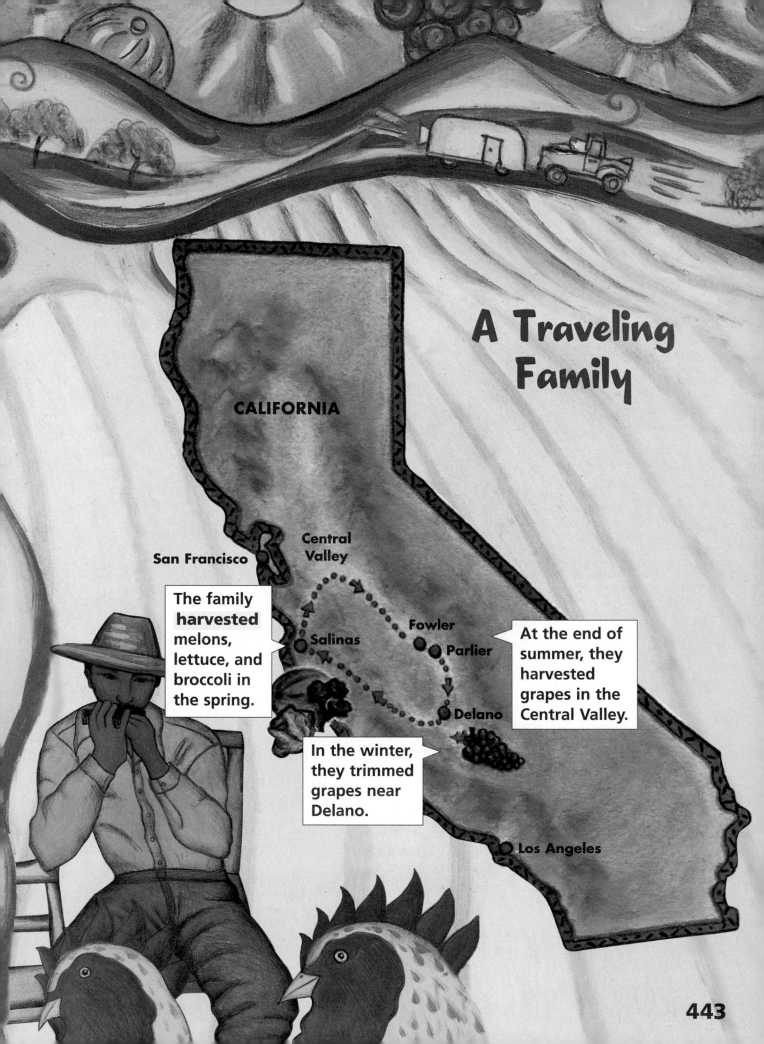

A Traveling Family

CALIFORNIA

San Francisco

Central Valley

The family **harvested** melons, lettuce, and broccoli in the spring.

Salinas

Fowler

Parlier

At the end of summer, they harvested grapes in the Central Valley.

Delano

In the winter, they trimmed grapes near Delano.

Los Angeles

Juanito's family travels a lot. Find out what their life is like.

"You were born on the road, like your father."

My mother would tell me this when we had to **move on** to another **labor camp**.

My mother Lucha, my father Felipe, and me.

I would **gaze** across the fields at the *campesinos*, the farmworkers, as my father drove our old army truck through the back roads of California.

In their bright colors, *campesinos* dotted the land like tropical birds.

---

labor camp place where a lot of farmworkers live
gaze look

Whenever we stopped, we set up a *carpa,* or a tent. My father would pull out a thick green **canvas**, like a giant tortilla dipped in green tomato sauce. Mama would unroll it while we looked for branches to **pin the ends into** the ground.

We slept huddled together under blankets and quilts. I would look up and see the stars sparkle through the tiny holes of the canvas.

---

canvas heavy piece of cloth
pin the ends into keep the cloth on

My mother would cook breakfast outside, in the open. It was often *huevos con papas*, which are scrambled eggs or fried eggs with potatoes.

A frying pan, a **griddle** to cook the tortillas, and a jar of forks and knives were **the necessary ingredients**. And, of course, wood for the fire.

The sky was my blue spoon. The wavy clay of the land was my plate.

------

griddle flat pan

the necessary ingredients all she needed to make the food

One day my father decided to build us a one-room house on top of **an abandoned car**. He hammered **two-by-fours and plywood onto the old chassis** and dipped his brush into buckets of white paint.

From the distance, my house looked like a short loaf of bread on wheels. Inside it was a warm **cave of conversations**. Mexican songs and auctions **blared** from a box radio on the wall.

---

an abandoned car a car that no one wanted

two-by-fours and plywood onto the old chassis
wooden boards onto the frame of the old car

cave of conversations place to talk

blared sounded loudly

At noon time, on a lunch break from driving the tractor, my father made **bird calls**.

He would put his hands up to his mouth and whistle deeply as if he had a tiny **clarinet** inside the palms of his hands.

"This is how a dove sings," my father would say.

Sooner or later a real dove would fly in and **perch itself** on a nearby tree.

---

bird calls sounds like a bird makes
clarinet musical instrument
perch itself sit

Sometimes my mother would surprise us at dinner and **recite** poetry.

Over a plate of *guisado* (a spicy tomato stew) and a hard flour tortilla, she would rise to her feet with her hands up as if asking for rain.

Rhyming words would **pour out** of her mouth and for a moment **the world would stop spinning**.

After dinner, my father would play the harmonica and tell stories about coming to the **States** from Chihuahua, Mexico.

---

recite say

Over a plate of *guisado* While we were eating stew

pour out come quickly out

the world would stop spinning everything seemed to stop

States United States

Before You Move On

1. **Cause/Effect** Why does the family travel so much?

2. **Paraphrase** What happy memories does Juanito have about his family's life?

449

The road changed with the seasons. In the winter, in Delano, my parents **trimmed grapevines**. By springtime we headed to Salinas to pick melon, lettuce, and broccoli.

When summer began, we drove back to Delano and Parlier to **prune** the grapes so that a few would grow the sweetest.

By the end of summer, as the leaves turned colors, we traveled through the Valley picking the grapes. We laid them out on the ground to dry on long sheets of paper between the vines.

In time, with the sun, the **tiny fiery planets would stop glowing** and shrink into dark raisins.

---

trimmed grapevines cut the grapevines smaller

prune cut off

tiny fiery planets would stop glowing small, round red and purple grapes would dry up

In the mountain valleys around Lake Wolfer, my father would get paid in sacks of sweet potatoes and buckets of freshwater fish instead of money.

He worked for **old retired people** like Mr. Kelly the Irishman, who paid him with rabbits, and Mrs. Jameson, who paid him in trays of corn biscuits. Instead of toys, he would bring home bags of avocados and flying turkeys.

The turkeys shook their red noses and flapped their **peppery** feathers and ran after me.

---

old retired people older people who had stopped working

peppery black and white

Before You Move On

1. **Details** What different jobs did Juanito's parents do?

2. **Inference** Why do you think Juanito's father accepted food as pay?

3

What other happy memories does Juanito have about his family's life?

I loved the night.

"Can you hear the wolves in the mountains?" my mother would ask me.

The wolves were the mountain singers. I imagined them sniffing at the moon. In long howls and high notes, they cried in the dark like lost children.

I would **cup my hands to** my mouth and join them.

---

cup my hands to put my hands around

A *fiesta* in the mountains was a **rare treat**. The other *campesinos* would invite us. They worked as gardeners like my father or housekeepers like my mother.

We would gather under a large *carpa* as big as a circus tent **huddled up against** a mountain slope. I remember stove fires, guitars and my father's harmonica, and sweet tortillas the size of my hand that tasted like licorice candy.

The men would lift me up in their arms and offer me *churros con canela y azucar*, which are Mexican donuts with cinnamon and sugar.

It was a home-made city of brown faces with smiles and music.

---

fiesta party (in Spanish)
rare treat special thing that didn't happen often
huddled up against close to

"It's time to **settle down**. It's time Juanito goes to school," my mother finally said to my father.

I was eight years old and I **had gathered the landscapes of the Valley close to my heart**: my father curling a tractor around the earth, my mother holding her head up high with song.

Our little square loaf house **swerved down the spiral of the mountains** into the cities of Southern California.

As the cities came into view, I knew one day I would follow my own road. I would let my voice fly the way my mother recited poems, the way my father called the doves.

---

had gathered the landscapes of the Valley close to my heart remembered the things I saw as we moved around

swerved down the spiral of the mountains traveled down the mountain roads

Before You Move On

1. **Character** Why did Juanito like *fiestas*?

2. **Figurative Language** Juanito thought, "…one day I would follow my own road." What did he mean?

Meet the Author

Juan Felipe Herrera

AWARD WINNER

Juan Felipe Herrera grew up in the mountains and valleys of California. He misses his parents who inspired him with poetry and song. He misses living in the open fields and sleeping under the stars. In 1993, he wrote *Calling the Doves* to tell about his memories.

Today, Mr. Herrera is a college professor, writer, actor, and musician who lives by these words: "Always believe in yourself. Don't forget where you come from, and don't be afraid of life."

Think and Respond

Strategy: Make Inferences

Sometimes you need to make a guess, or an inference, about why characters in stories do things. Make a chart.

1. Show how the characters are related.

2. Show what the characters did.

3. Think about what each character is like.

4. Think about what they do at the end of the story and why.

Calling the Doves

Character and Relationship to Juanita	Actions	Traits	Outcome and Reason
Lucha, mother	cooks good food creates a warm home wherever they are recites poetry	good cook and housekeeper kind loves her family loves poetry	She decides they must settle down so Juanito can go to school. She loves Juanito and wants to do what is best for him.
Felipe			

Interview a Character

Pretend you are Juanito. Have your partner ask you about your life before you started school. Give answers from the story.

Talk It Over

1 **Personal Response** Do you like the illustrations in this story? Choose one and tell why you like it or don't like it.

2 **Personal Experience** Juanito went to school for the first time when he was eight. Do you think that was hard or easy for him? Give reasons.

3 **Conclusion** What did Juanito's parents teach him? How did these things help him?

4 **Opinion** Is happiness more important than money? Explain.

Compare Characters

Compare Juanito with the boy in "Grandma's Records." How were their lives the same?

Content Connections

LISTENING/ SPEAKING

Describe Your Day

partners

With a partner, take turns being Juanito. Role-play a conversation with a relative. Describe what your day of travel was like.

How was your day?

It was hot, Uncle Raul! We drove with the windows open. I saw fields of big, purple grapes. They smelled sweet.

ART

Create a Pattern

on your own

1. Choose an object from a picture in the story.

2. Draw it over and over again to make a pattern.

3. Write sentences to describe it. Use a simile or metaphor.

The dove's feathers are as white as new snow. Its song is soft and sleepy.

Research a Crop
Internet

Use the Internet and other sources to find out about one crop. Show your information on fact cards, and on visuals such as diagrams. Display your work on a poster or in a book. Share it with the class.

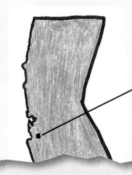

Where are the best strawberries grown?

Some of the finest strawberries are grown in the Pajaro Valley in California.

Write a Personal Narrative

"Calling the Doves" is a personal narrative. Write a personal narrative about an experience you had as a younger child. It might be about moving to a new city or country. Mail or e-mail your story to a friend.

My First Day at Lincoln School
I was scared. It was my first day in an American school, and I only knew a few English words.

Form Generalizations

A **generalization** is a statement that tells about many situations or people. To form generalizations:

✔ Think about the facts the writer gives.
✔ Use the writer's examples to make a general statement. The words *many*, *some*, or *usually* can help you make a generalization.
✔ Make sure your statement applies to more than one situation.

Try the strategy.

My Friends

Several of my friends are from other countries. Juanita came from Mexico to the United States to go to high school. Ivana came from Russia to get a college education. Bashar is from Jordan. He is going to a community college here.

I can make the general statement that some people come to the United States to get an education.

Practice

Take this test and **form generalizations** .

Read the article. Then read each item. Choose the best answer.

Sometimes, many people from a country immigrate to the U.S. all at once. In the 1840s a disease killed potato crops in Ireland and parts of Europe. Families began to run out of food. They wanted to work in the U.S. and have enough food for their families. At the same time, nearly one million Germans came to the United States. Their crops were dying, too, and there were not enough jobs.

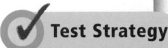

Test Strategy

Look for key words like *which* and *best*. They will help you find the correct answer.

In the 1960s and 70s, there was a war in Vietnam. In 1975, about 600,000 Vietnamese came to the U.S. In the 1980s, there was a war in El Salvador. Half a million Salvadorans immigrated to the U.S.

1 What is the best generalization for the first paragraph?

   A   People usually immigrate to the United States.

   B   Some immigrants come to the U.S. for a better life.

   C   Potatoes were a very important food for many European people.

2 What is the best generalization for the second paragraph?

   A   Most people do not like war.

   B   People usually leave their home countries.

   C   People often immigrate to keep their families safe from war.

LETTERS BETWEEN FRIENDS

September 9

Dear Shanté,

I can't believe we're moving to Nebraska. I feel like an **explorer** going off into a new land.

My mom and dad are excited about their new jobs here, and I'm happy that we live near my favorite aunt. She tells me stories about our **distant relatives** from Japan.

What's new with you?

Your friend,
Tamiko

September 17

Dear Tamiko,

Thanks for your letter! We have a new girl in our class. Her name is Farha. She's an **immigrant** from Pakistan. I think we're going to be friends. How do you like your new school?

Your friend,
Shanté

P.S. Don't worry. I still miss you.

Key Words

explorer

distant relative

immigrant

culture

pioneer

descendant

settler

September 30
Dear Shanté,

I'm learning about the **culture** of the **pioneers** . (Pioneers were the first European people to move here.)

I met a girl named Sarah. She's a **descendant** of a family of **settlers** (people who moved here after the pioneers).

Your friend,
Tamiko

P.S. Don't worry. I still miss you, too.

Read a History Article

A **history article** is nonfiction. It can tell about people, places, and events in the past.

✔ Look for **graphs**. Graphs use words, numbers, and shapes to show data.

graph

Africa and All Other 1%
Scandinavia 6%
Great Britain 11%
Ireland 12%
Other Europe 3%
Canada and Latin America 10%
Asia 2.5%
Germany 16%
Italy and Southern Europe 15.5%
Russia and Eastern Europe 10%
Poland and Central Europe 13%

Immigration to America
1820 to 1925
(Total: 36,307,892)

✔ Study the **maps**, **photographs**, and **illustrations** to get more information.

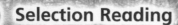 **Selection Reading**

464

Coming to America

by Betsy Maestro

Set Your Purpose

Find out when and why different groups of people came to America.

The First People Arrive

★ ★

America is a nation of **immigrants**. Immigrants are people who come to a new land to make their home. Many scientists believe that Native Americans are **distant relatives** of hunters who arrived in North America thousands and thousands of years ago. If they are right, then Native Americans were the first immigrants to arrive in what was truly a new world.

As many more thousands of years passed, the **descendants** of the first hunters moved around North and South America. They settled in small villages and later built big cities. By the time the first European **explorers** came to America, millions of people lived in the great **civilizations** of the Americas.

Many people lived in great cities throughout the Americas before Europeans arrived. ▶

---

civilizations nations; places where people share the same culture, art, and language

466

Monterey Museum of Art, courtesy of Betty Hoag McGlynn

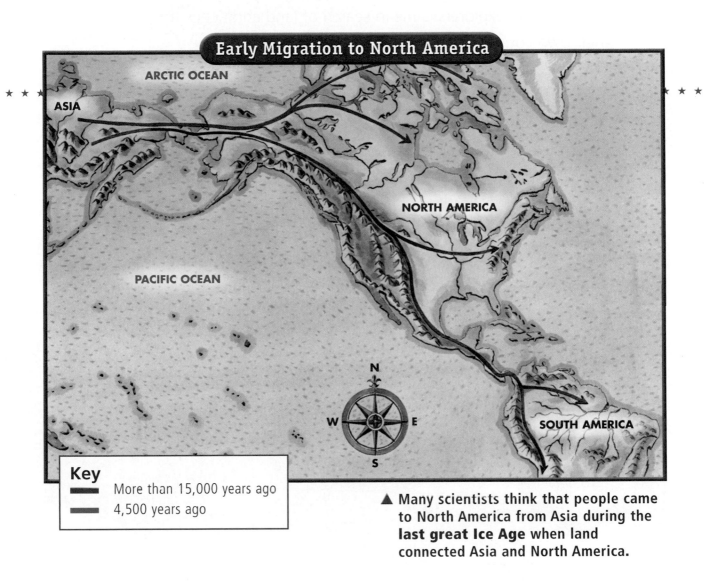

Early Migration to North America

ARCTIC OCEAN

ASIA

NORTH AMERICA

PACIFIC OCEAN

N
W   E
S

SOUTH AMERICA

Key
More than 15,000 years ago
4,500 years ago

▲ Many scientists think that people came to North America from Asia during the **last great Ice Age** when land connected Asia and North America.

last great Ice Age time thousands of years ago when much of Earth was covered with ice

Why Did People Come?

★ ★

European explorers came in search of land and riches for their own countries. Soon, stories about the fascinating "New World" spread throughout Europe. In time, **settlers** followed the explorers' **routes** across the great ocean.

These European immigrants came to make new homes in the Americas. They came in search of a better life. They wanted a life free of the trouble and **hardship** they had left behind. In their native countries, they often had little money and could not worship their God in the way they wished. The immigrants hoped for freedom and **good fortune** in their new lives.

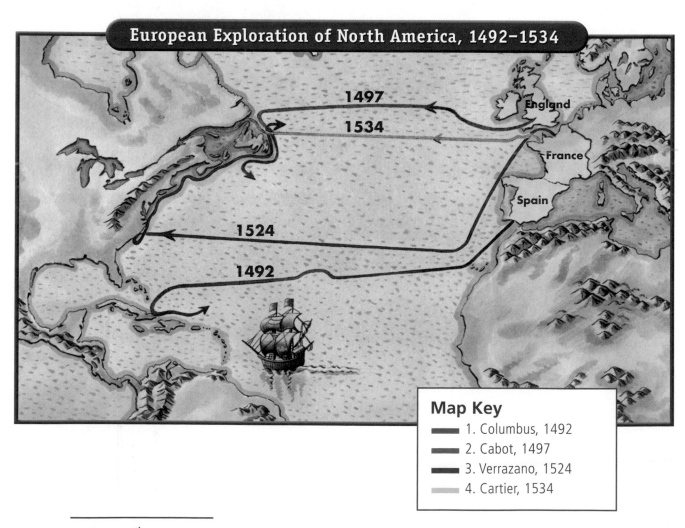

European Exploration of North America, 1492–1534

1497
1534
1524
1492

England
France
Spain

Map Key
— 1. Columbus, 1492
— 2. Cabot, 1497
— 3. Verrazano, 1524
— 4. Cartier, 1534

---

routes paths
hardship difficult times
good fortune happiness, success

©Scala/Art Resource, NY

▲ **Beginning in 1619, many Africans were brought to the Americas and forced to work as slaves.**

Not all immigrants came to America because they wanted to. Beginning in 1619, millions of Africans were brought to the Americas **against their will** and were forced into slavery. Instead of finding freedom, these Africans lost theirs, and most never returned to their homelands, so very far away.

---

against their will by force; not by choice

Before You Move On

1. **Cause/Effect** Why did European immigrants come to America?

2. **Comparison** How were slaves different from other immigrants?

469

Where Did Immigrants Settle?

During the 1700s, settlers continued to come to America. Their hopes for the future gave the immigrants courage to face the long and difficult sea voyage.

New **arrivals** sometimes settled near the ports where they first landed. New York, Boston, Philadelphia, Charleston, Baltimore, and New Orleans were all growing cities. As early as 1700, about eighteen languages could be heard in the streets of New York City.

▲ In the late 1800s, New York was a busy, growing city.

◀ Immigrants arrive at a port in New York in the early 1900s.

---

arrivals immigrants

Toward the middle of the 1800s, other adventurous immigrants became part of the westward movement. After arriving in the United States, they traveled on, by boat, train, and wagon. They headed for new **frontiers** in the Midwest and the Great Lakes **region**. Between 1836 and 1869, thousands of immigrants moved further west on the Oregon Trail.

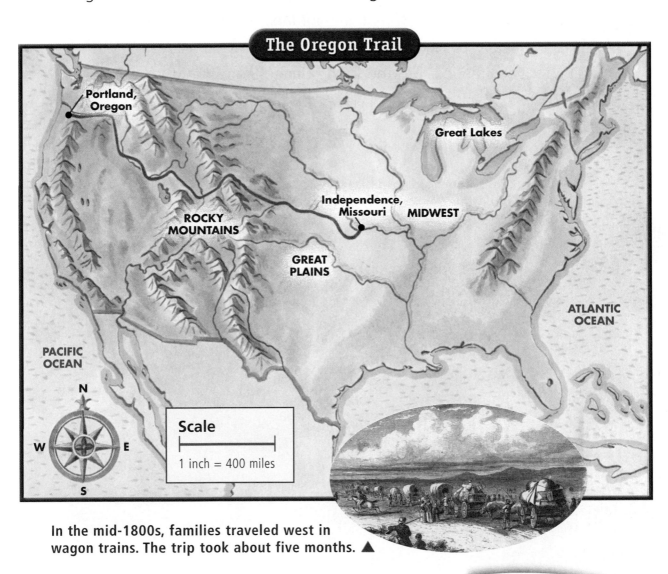

The Oregon Trail

Portland, Oregon

Great Lakes

ROCKY MOUNTAINS

Independence, Missouri

MIDWEST

GREAT PLAINS

ATLANTIC OCEAN

PACIFIC OCEAN

N
W   E
S

Scale
1 inch = 400 miles

In the mid-1800s, families traveled west in wagon trains. The trip took about five months. ▲

Before You Move On

1. **Details** Many immigrants arrived by boat during the 1700s. Where did they settle?

2. **Paraphrase** What was the westward movement?

---

frontiers places where few people lived
region part of the country

People Continue to Arrive

Soon other **pioneers** moved even further west. Pioneers moved all the way to California, where Chinese and Mexican immigrants had already settled. Early Chinese settlers helped to build the first **transcontinental** railroad. When it was completed in 1869, westward travel increased. The United States had become a **vast** nation, spreading from the Atlantic to the Pacific Ocean.

Although life was hard for new immigrants, it still was better than the **perils** and poverty they faced in their native countries. So immigrants continued to come to the United States. Thousands poured into the many ports, from New York City to San Francisco, every year.

▼ **In the 1860s, thousands of Chinese settlers helped build the transcontinental railroad.**

---

transcontinental cross-country
vast very, very big
perils dangers

▲ From the late 1700s to the middle 1800s, Spanish farmers and ranchers helped to create the **culture** of the west.

▲ About 1880, children began to work long hours in the **textile mills of** the Northeast.

▲ Chinese workers won praise for their work on the railroad. In the late 1800s, they were offered work on many other projects.

▲ Families worked together in the orchards of the West. In this photograph, a family packs apricots in the 1920s.

---

textile mills of factories that made cloth in

Before You Move On

1. **Sequence** Who had settled in California before the railroad was built?

2. **Graphic Aids** What kinds of work did immigrants do?

Immigration Centers Open

★ ★

On January 1, 1892, the United States government opened an immigration center on Ellis Island near New York City. **Officials** counted and questioned the new arrivals. They saw that those admitted were healthy and ready to become **useful citizens**.

◄ **Between 1892 and 1954 more than 12 million immigrants arrived at Ellis Island. Ellis Island closed its doors in 1954.**

From 1910 to 1940, immigrants also arrived at Angel Island near San Francisco, California. ▶

Officials People who worked for the United States government

useful citizens people who would be good, working members of a community

▶ The Statue of Liberty has been an inspiration to artists as well as immigrants. Francis Hopkinson Smith painted this.

As big passenger ships entered New York harbor, the immigrants saw the Statue of Liberty, **a welcome and inspiring sight**. On the busiest days, so many ships arrived in New York harbor that there were long waits just to get to Ellis Island.

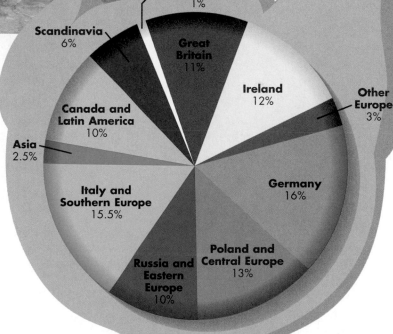

Africa and All Other 1%

Scandinavia 6%

Great Britain 11%

Ireland 12%

Other Europe 3%

Canada and Latin America 10%

Asia 2.5%

Germany 16%

Italy and Southern Europe 15.5%

Poland and Central Europe 13%

Russia and Eastern Europe 10%

Immigration to America
1820 to 1925
(Total: 36,307,892)

a welcome and inspiring sight a symbol that made them feel good about coming to the United States

Scandinavia the countries of Denmark, Sweden, Norway, and Finland

475

◀ Immigrants wait at Ellis Island in the early 1900s.

Everyone had to be examined. ▶

Once on the island, there was more waiting! With thousands arriving each day, long lines formed everywhere.

First the immigrants were given a quick examination by doctors. Those with health problems were marked with colored chalk. The doctors would examine these persons more closely.

Immigrants with **permanent health problems** were often sent back to their native country. But most of the new arrivals **passed inspection** and moved on to the next step.

---

permanent health problems sicknesses that would never go away

passed inspection were told they were healthy enough

Many immigrants struggled to answer questions in English. ▶

◀ Immigrants were happy when they were allowed to enter the United States.

Now the immigrants were asked a long list of questions. Since most of the immigrants did not speak English, they needed help in understanding and answering the questions. **Translators** did what they could to help the inspectors and newcomers understand one another. Mothers often spoke for children who might be too little or too scared to speak.

Usually the **ordeal** was over within a day. At last, the immigrants could enter their new country.

Translators People who spoke more than one language

ordeal trouble, painful experience

Before You Move On

1. **Graphic Aids** How does the graph help you understand immigration?

2. **Details** What happened to immigrants after they arrived at Ellis Island?

477

Immigration Today

★ ★

▲ Today, most immigrants arrive in the United States by plane.

▼ Joining others who share a common heritage helps people become more comfortable in a new country.

Today, few immigrants arrive by ship. Instead, they fly into an international airport in the United States.

All newcomers have a hard time at first. This is true whether they came in the 1600s or have just arrived. It isn't easy to start a new life in **an unfamiliar country**. Most immigrants have to learn a new language and a new way of life.

New Americans make their lives a little better by finding friends from their native country. It helps them to feel more **at home** in a strange, new country.

Today's new immigrants come to the United States from Russia, Asia, Mexico, South and Central America, the Middle East, the West Indies, and Africa. They are still coming for the same reason people have always come. They come to make a better life for themselves and for their children.

---

an unfamiliar country a place you've never been to before

at home like they belong; comfortable

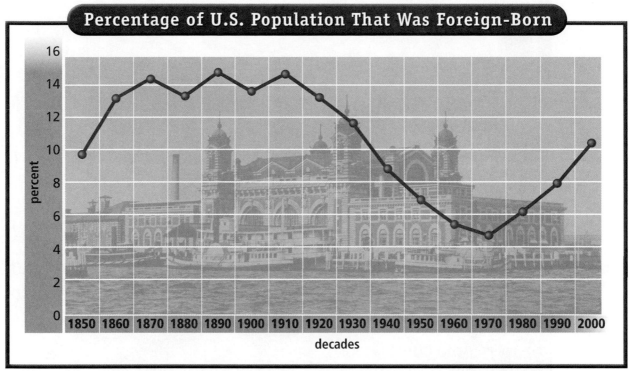

Percentage of U.S. Population That Was Foreign-Born

percent / decades

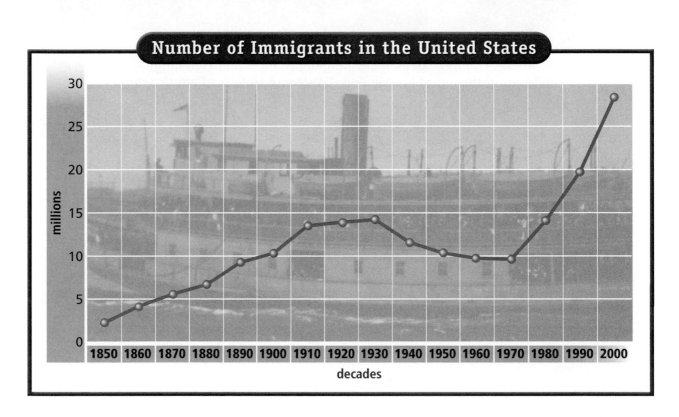

Number of Immigrants in the United States

millions / decades

---

decade period of ten years

▲ America's children speak many languages, including sign language. The children in the mural are signing, "Welcome to César Chavez School."

America has been called a great "melting pot," in which many cultures, or ways of life, have blended together. However, today's Americans have also learned to celebrate their differences. There is a growing appreciation and understanding of the special character and **unique** contributions of each **cultural or ethnic group**. Everyone, from the first Americans thousands of years ago to those who came only yesterday, has **left a lasting mark on** this great land.

---

unique one-of-a-kind

cultural or ethnic group group that has the same traditions, culture, or country of birth

left a lasting mark on changed something about

▼ Albert Einstein

▲ Madeleine Albright

▲ Gloria Estefan

▲ I.M. Pei

▲ Sammy Sosa

Immigrants settled and farmed this land before it was a country. Others created a new nation and founded its government. Immigrants built the cities, roads, and railways of America. They have **toiled** in its fields, its factories, and its mills. Immigrants, too, have made the music of this land, written its books, and recorded its beauty in paintings. The spirit of American strength and **independence** is the spirit of its people, and the spirit of its immigrants and their children.

---

toiled worked hard
independence freedom from control by others

Before You Move On

1. **Details** What countries do today's new immigrants come from?

2. **Viewing** What do the pictures on pages 480–481 tell you about America?

481

Meet the Author

Betsy Maestro

Betsy Maestro's inspiration for writing *Coming to America* came from her own family history. Her mother's parents came from Russia to the United States in 1915. Today, Ms. Maestro and her family live in New England, but they have visited most regions in the United States.

"The United States is a very special country," Ms. Maestro says. "The people who live here came from all around the globe and more are still coming. We don't look alike, we don't think alike, we don't have the same beliefs, and yet we all live together in peace."

TRAVELER'S SONG

My loving mother, thread in hand,
Mended the coat I have on now,
Stitch by stitch, just before I left home,
Thinking that I might be gone a long time.
How can a blade of young grass
Ever repay the warmth of the spring sun?

—Meng Jia

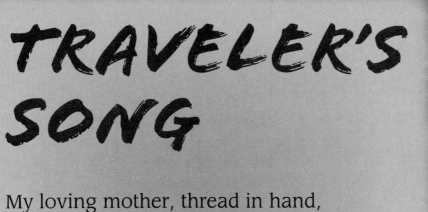

Before You Move On
Personal Response How does the poem make you feel?

Think and Respond

Strategy: Classify

Make a chart. Show who came to America, when, and why.

Immigration to America

Time Period	Who Came	Why They Came
thousands of years ago	Native Americans	to hunt and settle in the new land
1000–1600s	European explorers, European settlers	
1600s	African slaves	
1700s	more Europeans	
mid-1800s		
1820–1925		
1925–today		

Form Generalizations

Why do most people come to America? Support your answer with evidence or examples from the article. Compare your answer with a partner's answer.

Talk It Over

1 **Personal Response** Why did your family or ancestors come to the United States?

2 **Conclusion** Americans "celebrate their differences." What does this mean? Give examples.

3 **Author's Purpose** Why do you think Betsy Maestro wrote this article?

4 **Personal Experience** What would you tell a newcomer about the United States?

Compare Issues

How is freedom an issue in both "George Washington" and "Coming to America"?

In both selections, people want freedom.

Content Connections

Create Culture Squares

small group

Use art to tell about yourself.

1. Fold a paper twice to get four squares.

2. Draw a picture or a design, or write words in each square. Tell about yourself and your heritage.

3. Explain each square to your group.

ART

Immigration Events

on your own

Draw a storyboard to show the sequence of events on one family's trip to the U.S. in the early 1900s. Include what happened after they arrived. Compare your storyboard with others.

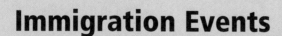

SOCIAL STUDIES

small group

Make a Q & A Book
Internet

Research one group of immigrants. When did they come to the U.S.? Why? What did they bring with them? Use your notes to make pages for a class book about immigration. Add pictures and graphics to support your ideas.

Q. Why did so many Irish immigrate to the U.S. in the 1840s and 1850s?

A. They came here because there wasn't enough food in Ireland.

WRITING

on your own

Write a Letter

Immigrants traveled by ship to America in the early 1900s. What was the journey like? Imagine being on the trip. Write a letter to one of your relatives.

Dear Olga,
   I do not feel well. I hope we arrive in America soon.
   This ship is terrible. We stay in a big, dark room that is very crowded. It smells so bad!

Verb Tense

Listen and sing.

Song

Immigrants from Many Lands

Immigrants have come
from many lands.
He has come. She has come.
Oh-h-h! Immigrants have come
from many lands.
They have come. We have come.
They have settled in a new place.
They have made
the new place their place.
Oh-h-h! Immigrants have come
from many lands.

—*Jane Zion Brauer*

Tune: "She'll Be Coming 'Round the Mountain"

How Language Works

A **verb** in a sentence shows when the action happens.

Present Perfect Tense	Examples:
1. Use **has** or **have** with the **past participle** of a verb to form the present perfect tense.	<table><tr><th>Present</th><th>Past</th><th>Past Participle</th></tr><tr><td>live</td><td>lived</td><td>lived</td></tr><tr><td>learn</td><td>learned</td><td>learned</td></tr><tr><td>go</td><td>went</td><td>gone</td></tr></table>
2. Use the **present perfect tense** to: • tell about something that happened in the past and is still going on. • tell about something that happened in the past, but you are not sure when.	My family **has lived** in Texas since 1990. We **have learned** English. We **have gone** back to Mexico many times.

Practice with a Partner

Use **has** or **have** and the red verb to finish each sentence.

built 1. We _____ a new life in America.

found 2. My parents _____ good jobs.

done 3. I _____ well in school.

gotten 4. My sister _____ good grades, too.

Put It in Writing

Write about someone you know who has come to the U.S. Tell what he or she has learned to do.

My neighbor has learned how to drive a car.

489

Show What You Know

Talk About Immigration

In this unit, you read a story about an immigrant family and a history article about immigration. Look back at the unit. Find a picture or a photo. Use it to tell a group as much as you can about immigration.

Make a Mind Map

Work with a partner. Make a mind map to show what you learned about immigration to America.

Immigrants to the U.S.

How are they alike?	How are they different?
Want a better life many have hardship in their native countries	native countries cultures

Think and Write

What do you like best about living in America? Why? Write a paragraph. Add it to your portfolio. Include work that shows what you learned about immigration.

Read and Learn More

Leveled Books

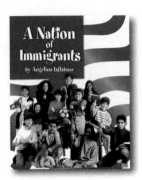

A Nation of Immigrants
by Angelina Ixtlahuac

All Across America
by Daphne Liu

Theme Library

The Upside Down Boy
by Juan Felipe Herrera

Journey to Ellis Island
by Carol Bierman

Internet

Go to: www.hbavenues.com

Immigrant Stories

Immigration Time Line

The Immigrant Journey

Picture Dictionary

The definitions are for the words as they are introduced in the selections in this book.

Pronunciation Key

Say the sample word out loud to hear how to say, or pronounce, the symbol.

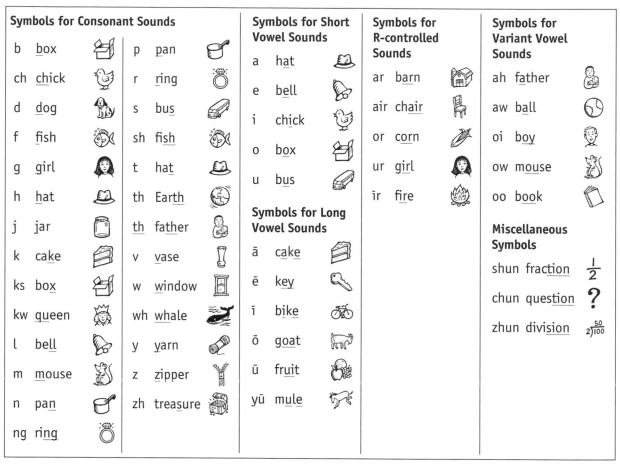

Symbols for Consonant Sounds

b	box		p	pan
ch	chick		r	ring
d	dog		s	bus
f	fish		sh	fish
g	girl		t	hat
h	hat		th	Earth
j	jar		th	father
k	cake		v	vase
ks	box		w	window
kw	queen		wh	whale
l	bell		y	yarn
m	mouse		z	zipper
n	pan		zh	treasure
ng	ring			

Symbols for Short Vowel Sounds

a	hat
e	bell
i	chick
o	box
u	bus

Symbols for Long Vowel Sounds

ā	cake
ē	key
ī	bike
ō	goat
ū	fruit
yū	mule

Symbols for R-controlled Sounds

ar	barn
air	chair
or	corn
ur	girl
ir	fire

Symbols for Variant Vowel Sounds

ah	father
aw	ball
oi	boy
ow	mouse
oo	book

Miscellaneous Symbols

shun	fraction	$\frac{1}{2}$
chun	question	?
zhun	division	$2\overline{)100}^{50}$

Parts of an Entry

The **entry** shows how the word is spelled.

The **pronunciation** shows you how to say the word and how to break it into syllables.

The **picture** helps you understand more about the meaning of the word.

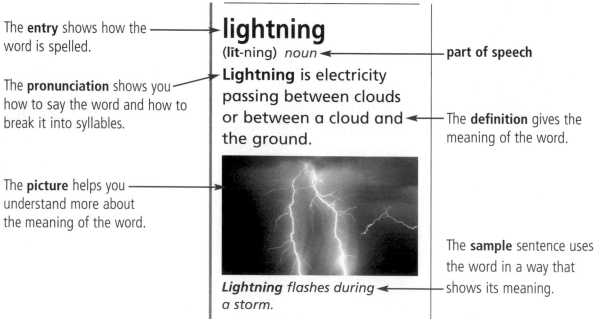

lightning
(līt-ning) *noun*

Lightning is electricity passing between clouds or between a cloud and the ground.

Lightning flashes during a storm.

part of speech

The **definition** gives the meaning of the word.

The **sample** sentence uses the word in a way that shows its meaning.

A

accomplish

(u-**kom**-plish) *verb*

When you **accomplish** something, you finish doing it.

> **Things to Do Today**
>
>   Do homework.
> ✔ Feed cat.
>   Volunteer at library.
> ✔ Clean bedroom.

*I check off the things I **accomplish** each day.*

acre

(ā-kur) *noun*

An **acre** is a piece of land that measures 43,560 square feet.

soccer field

*The size of a soccer field is about one and one-half **acres**.*

adventure

(ad-**ven**-chur) *noun*

When you have an **adventure**, you do something different and exciting.

*Our first camping trip is an **adventure**!*

album

(**al**-bum) *noun*

An **album** is a collection of songs on a record, tape, or CD.

record
album cover

*There are ten songs on this record **album**.*

ancestor

(**an**-ses-tur) *noun*

Your **ancestors** are people in your family. Ancestors usually lived long ago.

*This family has an old picture of their **ancestors**.*

atom

(**at**-um) *noun*

An **atom** is the smallest part of something. Everything is made up of atoms.

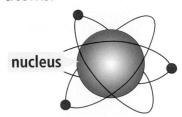
nucleus

*The nucleus is the center of an **atom**.*

audience

(**aw**-dē-uns) *noun*

An **audience** is a group of people who watch a movie or a show.

audience
musicians

*The **audience** cheers during the music concert.*

B

band

(band) *noun*

A **band** is a group of musicians who play together.

guitar
piano
drums
flute

*Miguel plays the guitar in our jazz **band**.*

beauty
(**byū**-tē) *noun*

A thing of **beauty** is something that is very nice to look at.

*This garden is a thing of **beauty**.*

bone
(bōn) *noun*

A **bone** is one of the hard parts of the skeleton. Bones help give the body its shape.

bone

*The hand has many **bones**.*

Ⓒ

camp
(kamp) *noun*

A **camp** is a group of tents, trailers, or small houses where people live for a short time.

*Migrant workers live at this **camp** in the summer while they pick grapes.*

canyon
(**kan**-yun) *noun*

A **canyon** is a deep, narrow piece of land with steep walls.

canyon wall

river

*Sometimes a river flows at the bottom of a **canyon**.*

capture
(**kap**-chur) *verb*

When you **capture** a memory or special feeling, you find a way to keep it.

*This photo **captures** the joy of a birthday party.*

circuit
(**sur**-kit) *noun*

A **circuit** is the complete path of an electric current.

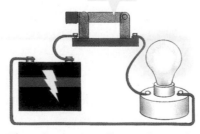

switch

*Electric current flows through this **circuit**.*

clever
(**klev**-ur) *adjective*

❶ A **clever** person is smart and thinks quickly.

*The **clever** boy figures out how to get the ball.*

❷ Some people are **clever**, or skillful, with their hands.

*She can fix the bicycle. She is **clever** with her hands.*

coastline
(**kōst**-līn) *noun*

The **coastline** is the place where the ocean meets the land.

ocean wave

*Strong ocean waves pound the California **coastline**.*

colony
(**kol**-u-nē) *noun*

A **colony** is land in one place that belongs to a country in another place.

The Thirteen Colonies

These 13 colonies in America belonged to Great Britain in the 1700s.

comfort
(**kum**-furt) *verb*

When you **comfort** someone, you make that person feel better.

This boy cut his leg. His mother tries to comfort him.

compromise
(**kom**-pru-**mīz**) *noun*

When people reach a **compromise**, each gives up something to satisfy the other.

Juan and Marta reach a compromise. They agree to get a small dog.

Congress
(**kong**-gris) *noun*

The members of **Congress** make laws for the U.S.

Members of Congress vote on different laws.

constitution
(**kon**-sti-**tū**-shun) *noun*

A **constitution** is a set of rules for a country to follow.

The U.S. Constitution was written in 1787.

contest
(**kon**-test) *noun*

A **contest** is a race or game that you try to win.

Which frog will win the contest?

conversation
(**kon**-vur-**sā**-shun) *noun*

When two or more people talk together, they have a **conversation**.

The teachers are having a conversation.

core
(kor) *noun*

The **core** is the center part of the planet Earth.

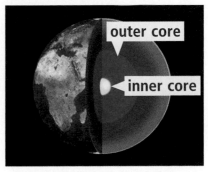

The inner core of the Earth is very hot.

D

courage

(**kur**-ij) *noun*

When you have **courage**, you do something even if you are afraid.

It takes **courage** to climb a mountain.

crust

(krust) *noun*

The **crust** is the outside layer of the planet Earth.

There are mountains on Earth's **crust**.

culture

(**kul**-chur) *noun*

Culture is the way of life of a group of people. It includes their arts, beliefs, and traditions.

This dance is part of the Mexican **culture**.

declare

(di-**klair**) *verb*

When you **declare** something, you tell people about it.

The judge **declares** Tara the winner of the contest.

delegate

(**del**-u-git) *noun*

People choose a **delegate** to speak and act for them.

Each class sends a **delegate** to this school meeting.

descendant

(di-**sen**-dunt) *noun*

You are a **descendant** of your parents, grandparents, great-grandparents, and so on.

These are my great-great grandparents. I am their **descendant**.

determined

(di-**tur**-mind) *adjective*

When you are **determined**, you keep doing something until you reach your goal.

These **determined** climbers got to the top of the mountain.

discover

(dis-**kuv**-ur) *verb*

When you find out something new, you **discover** it.

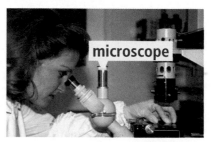

microscope

Will this scientist **discover** a cure for a disease?

distant relative

(**dis**-tunt **rel**-u-tiv) *noun*

Anyone who is part of your family but is not a brother, sister, parent, grandparent, cousin, aunt, or uncle is a **distant relative**.

I'm a **distant relative** of people who came to America long ago.

dune
(dūn) noun

A **dune** is a hill of sand.

*The wind blows the sand into this **dune**.*

E

earthquake
(**urth**-kwāk) noun

An **earthquake** is when the ground shakes or moves.

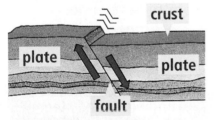

*When two of Earth's plates move against each other, **earthquakes** happen.*

electron
(i-**lek**-tron) noun

An **electron** is part of an atom.

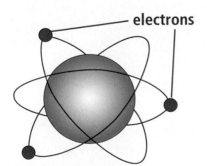

Electrons move around the center of an atom.

encourage
(en-**kur**-ij) verb

When you **encourage** someone, you tell them that they can and should do something.

*Dad **encourages** Kim to cook.*

energy
(**en**-ur-jē) noun

Energy is the power to do work.

*It takes a lot of **energy** to dance.*

*The lights of the city use **energy** from electricity.*

enormous
(i-**nor**-mus) adjective

Something that is **enormous** is very, very big.

*Look at these **enormous** trees!*

exhibit
(eg-**zib**-it) noun

An **exhibit** is a display of art or other things.

*The vases in this **exhibit** are very old.*

experiment
(eks-**per**-u-munt) noun

You do an **experiment** to test an idea and see what happens.

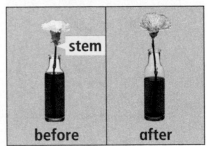

*Our **experiment** shows that water moves through a stem.*

explorer

(eks-**plor**-ur) *noun*

An **explorer** is a person who goes to different places and learns about them.

*John Cabot was an **explorer** for England. He sailed to North America in 1497.*

expression

(eks-**presh**-un) *noun*

Dancers show feelings when they move. They use their bodies for **expression**.

*The movements of this dancer are full of **expression**.*

F

fault

(fawlt) *noun*

A **fault** is a crack in the crust of the Earth.

*Many earthquakes happen along the San Andreas **fault** in California.*

favorite

(**fā**-vur-it) *adjective*

A **favorite** thing is something that you like best of all.

*Alma's **favorite** kind of ice cream is cherry.*

frontier

(frun-**tēr**) *noun*

A **frontier** is the area of land where people are just beginning to go.

▲ *Montana, 1870*

▲ *Washington, 1895*

*In America, the **frontier** moved slowly to the west as settlers crossed the land.*

G

gargantuan

(gar-**gan**-chū-un) *adjective*

Something that is **gargantuan** is very large.

ship

boat

*How many people can sail on this **gargantuan** ship?*

geyser

(**gī**-zur) *noun*

A **geyser** is a natural fountain of hot water that goes up in the air from time to time.

hot water and steam

*The state of Wyoming has over 200 **geysers**.*

gigantic
(jī-**gan**-tik) *adjective*

If something is **gigantic**, it is very big.

*This **gigantic** balloon is in a parade.*

government
(**guv**-urn-munt) *noun*

The **government** is the group of people who lead a country, a state, or a city.

*These members of a city **government** vote on a new law.*

gravity
(**grav**-u-tē) *noun*

Gravity is a force that pulls things down toward the center of Earth.

*When you toss a ball into the air, **gravity** pulls it down.*

handiwork
(**han**-dē-**wurk**) *noun*

When you make something with your hands, you create **handiwork**.

*Grandma makes quilts. Her **handiwork** is very colorful.*

harvest
(**har**-vist) *verb*

Harvest means to pick a crop when it is ripe or ready to eat.

worker ➤

*These workers **harvest** a crop of strawberries.*

heart
(hart) *noun*

Your **heart** is the organ that pumps blood through your body.

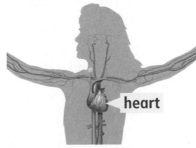

heart

*Your **heart** pumps blood each time it beats.*

heritage
(**her**-i-tij) *noun*

Your **heritage** includes the traditions, ideas, and language you get from your family.

*Drumming is part of their Vietnamese **heritage**.*

*Playing a qeej is part of his Hmong **heritage**.*

huge
(hyūj) *adjective*

Something that is **huge** is very big.

Great Dane

*A Great Dane is a **huge** dog.*

I

immigrant
(**im**-u-grunt) *noun*

An **immigrant** is someone who moves to a new country to live.

Between 1981 and 1993, about 313,000 Salvadoran immigrants came to the United States to escape a war in El Salvador.

improve
(im-**prūv**) *verb*

You **improve** something when you make it better.

She practices every day to improve her dancing.

independent
(**in**-di-**pen**-dunt) *adjective*

An **independent** country is not controlled by any other country. It is free.

George Washington fought for the colonies to become independent and free from Great Britain.

inspire
(in-**spīr**) *verb*

When something **inspires** you, it gives you a good feeling and makes you want to do something.

The beautiful sunset inspires Mia to write a poem.

invent
(in-**vent**) *verb*

To **invent** means to make something new.

wood stove

Benjamin Franklin had the idea to invent this stove.

J

joint
(joint) *noun*

A **joint** is the place where two or more bones meet.

elbow joint

shoulder joint

hip joint

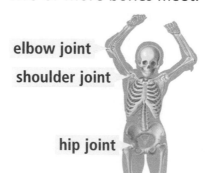

Joints let you bend, turn, and twist your body.

L

landform
(**land**-form) *noun*

A **landform** is the way a piece of land is shaped.

▲ *Rocky Mountains*

▲ *Great Plains*

Mountains and plains are two kinds of landforms.

lightning
(**līt**-ning) *noun*

Lightning is electricity passing between clouds or between a cloud and the ground.

Lightning flashes during a storm.

M

magnet
(**mag**-nit) *noun*

A **magnet** is a piece of metal that attracts another piece of metal.

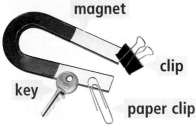

*This **magnet** pulls, or attracts, these things to it.*

make a difference
(**māk** u **dif**-runs)

When you **make a difference**, you do something to make things better.

*Paco and Rosa **make a difference** when they clean up the park.*

mammoth
(**mam**-uth) *adjective*

Something that is **mammoth** is very large.

*Dinosaurs were **mammoth** creatures that lived long ago.*

mantle
(**man**-tul) *noun*

Inside the Earth, the **mantle** is the layer under the surface layer.

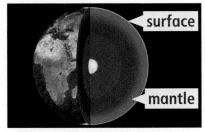

*The **mantle** of the Earth is about 1,800 miles thick.*

material
(mu-**tir**-ē-ul) *noun*

Material is cloth that you can use to make clothes.

*Lily uses pretty **material** to make a dress.*

mighty
(**mī**-tē) *adjective*

When a person or a thing is **mighty**, it is large and has great power.

*The **mighty** Mississippi River is about 2,300 miles long.*

migrant
(**mī**-grunt) *adjective*

A **migrant** farmworker travels from farm to farm to work in the fields.

*These **migrant** farmworkers came to Salinas, California, to pick broccoli.*

mountain range
(**mown**-tun rānj) *noun*

A **mountain range** is a row of connected mountains.

*This **mountain range** is hundreds of miles long.*

move on
(**mūv** on) *verb*

When you **move on**, you leave one place to travel to another.

*These people are leaving. They **move on** to another farm.*

movement

(**mūv**-munt) *noun*

When you make a **movement**, you move parts of your body.

*The **movements** of this ballerina are graceful.*

muscle

(**mus**-ul) *noun*

A **muscle** is under your skin and attached to your bones. Muscles help you move your body.

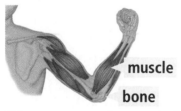

muscle
bone

*When you exercise, you build strong **muscles**.*

nerves

(nurvz) *noun*

Nerves carry messages between the brain and other parts of the body.

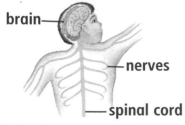

brain
nerves
spinal cord

*The brain, spinal cord, and **nerves** work together to tell the body what to do.*

oxygen

(**ok**-su-jin) *noun*

Oxygen is a gas in the air that living things need to stay alive.

lung

*When you breathe in, **oxygen** goes into your lungs.*

pack

(pak) *verb*

When you **pack**, you put things in a container so you can take them with you.

suitcase

*This girl **packs** her suitcase for a trip.*

partnership

(**part**-nur-**ship**) *noun*

When two or more people work together, they have a **partnership**.

*These two skaters have a special **partnership**.*

patriot

(**pā**-tre-ūt) *noun*

A **patriot** loves and supports his or her country.

*These **patriots** wave flags to show they support the U.S.*

performance

(pur-**for**-muns) *noun*

A **performance** is a show presented by actors, musicians, or dancers.

actor
audience

*The audience claps after the **performance**.*

pioneer

(**pī**-u-**nir**) *noun*

A **pioneer** is one of the first people to explore and settle an area.

*In the 19th century, **pioneers** headed west in covered wagons.*

plate
(plāt) *noun*

The crust of the Earth is broken into large pieces called **plates**.

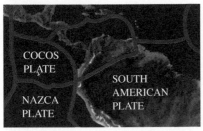

COCOS PLATE

NAZCA PLATE

SOUTH AMERICAN PLATE

*The Earth's crust is split into many **plates**.*

play
(plā) *verb*

When you **play** music, you make music on an instrument or make music come out of a radio or stereo.

*We **play** music on a guitar and drums.*

politics
(**pol**-i-tiks) *noun*

Politics is the way a government is managed or run.

*These Presidential candidates talk about **politics**.*

presence
(**prez**-uns) *noun*

Sometimes people are not with you, but they feel near to you. You feel their **presence**.

*When Hoshin looks at this photo, she feels the **presence** of her family.*

protection
(pru-**tek**-shun) *noun*

Protection is something that keeps you safe from danger or harm.

helmet

elbow pad

knee pad

*These girls could fall. They wear helmets and pads for **protection**.*

proud
(prowd) *adjective*

When you are **proud**, you feel happy about something you did.

*Chen won the spelling contest! He is **proud** of himself.*

prove
(prūv) *verb*

When you **prove** something, you show that it is correct or true.

*Tim wins the race. He **proves** that he is the fastest runner.*

public
(**pub**-lik) *adjective*

If something is **public**, it is for all the people.

*Anyone can go to this **public** park.*

R

record
(**rek**-urd) *noun*

A **record** is a disk with music on it.

record player

record

*What **record** does she put on her record player?*

503

representative

(**rep**-ri-**zen**-tu-tiv) *noun*

A **representative** is a person who speaks or acts for others.

The people of each state elect representatives to speak for them in Congress.

respect

(ri-**spekt**) *noun*

When you have **respect** for someone, you care about what that person thinks and feels.

My parents have respect for each other. They talk about their thoughts and feelings.

scenic

(**sē**-nik) *adjective*

If a part of nature is **scenic**, it is beautiful to see.

Big Sur is a scenic area of California.

settle down

(**set**-ul down) *verb*

You **settle down** when you choose a place to live and stay there.

The Jones family has settled down in this neighborhood.

settler

(**set**-lur) *noun*

A **settler** is a person who moves to a new region to live.

These settlers had to grow their own food or hunt for it. They had to build their own houses.

skeleton

(**skel**-u-tun) *noun*

A **skeleton** is the set of bones that support the body of a person or animal. Muscles and skin cover the skeleton.

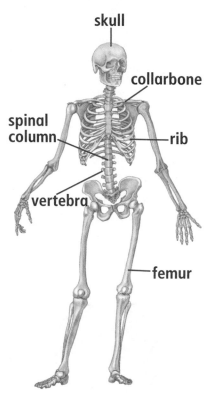

skull

collarbone

spinal column

rib

vertebra

femur

The human skeleton has 206 bones.

slavery

(**slā**-vu-rē) *noun*

When a person lives in **slavery**, he or she is owned by another person and is forced to work without pay.

Americans fought a war to end slavery. After the Civil War, these slaves were free.

soldier

(**sōl**-jur) *noun*

A **soldier** is a person who fights to protect his or her country.

*These **soldiers** learn how to protect their country.*

special

(**spesh**-ul) *adjective*

Something **special** is nicer or more important than other things.

*Mom uses the **special** dishes when our grandparents visit.*

spinal cord

(**spī**-nul kord) *noun*

A **spinal cord** is a bundle of nerves in your back that connects your brain with all the parts of your body.

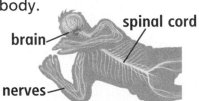

brain

spinal cord

nerves

*The **spinal cord** carries messages to and from your brain.*

stitching

(**stich**-ing) *noun*

Stitching is the work you do when you sew cloth.

pillow

pillow cover

*The **stitching** on this pillow cover is very fancy.*

superior

(su-**pēr**-ē-ur) *adjective*

Something is **superior** when it is better than something else.

*Which of these is **superior** handiwork?*

T

task

(task) *noun*

A **task** is a job you must do.

igloo

*Their **task** is to build an igloo.*

tax

(taks) *noun*

A **tax** is money people pay to their government.

RECEIPT

Rollerblades	$159.98
Subtotal	$159.98
Sales Tax	$7.99
Sales Total	$167.97

Thank you for shopping at The Sports Place!

*The government uses money from a sales **tax** to help pay for services.*

traitor

(**trā**-tur) *noun*

A **traitor** is a person who does something to hurt his or her country or group.

*This **traitor** gives secret information to an enemy soldier.*

trust

(trust) *verb*

When you **trust** someone, you believe that the person will do what he or she promises to do.

*Would you **trust** someone to catch you?*

volcano

(vol-**kā**-nō) *noun*

A **volcano** is a mountain made by hot melted rock from inside the Earth.

lava

*When a **volcano** erupts, it shoots out hot lava and ash.*

waterfall

(**waw**-tur-**fawl**) *noun*

A **waterfall** is a stream of water that falls from a higher place to a lower place.

*Niagara Falls is one of the most beautiful **waterfalls** in the world.*

welcoming

(**wel**-kum-ing) *adjective*

A place is **welcoming** when it makes you feel as if you belong there.

*My grandparents' house is a warm and **welcoming** place.*

Acknowledgments, continued

HarperCollins Publishers: "Joining the Boston Tea Party" adapted from Joining the Boston Tea Party by Diane Stanley. Text copyright © 2001 by Diane Stanley. Illustrations copyright © 2001 by Holly Berry. "Planet Earth/Inside Out". "Pride" from Gathering the Sun by Alma Flor Ada. Text copyright © 1997 by Alma Flor Ada. Illustrations copyright © 1997 by Simon Silva. "Switch On, Switch Off". "Traveler's Song" by Minfong Ho. Text copyright © 1996 by Minfong Ho. Illustrations copyright © 1996 by Jean and Mousien Tseng. All used by used by permission of HarperCollins Publishers.

Harriet Rohmer: "Honoring Our Ancestors" Overall book project copyright © 1999 by Harriet Rohmer. Individual artwork copyright © 1999 by Carl Angel; copyright © 1999 by Hung Liu; copyright © 1999 by JoeSam.; copyright © 1999 by Patssi Valdez.

Houghton Mifflin Company: "Dancing Wheels" from Dancing Wheels by Patricia McMahon and illustrated by photographs by John Godt. Text copyright © 2000 by Patricia McMahon. Photographs copyright © 2000 by John Godt. All rights reserved. Reprinted by permission of Houghton Mifflin Company. "Light" from Flicker Flash by Joan Bransfield Graham. Text copyright © 1999 by Joan Bransfield Graham. Reprinted by permission of Houghton Mifflin Company. All rights reserved. All used by permission of Houghton Mifflin Company.

Jim Marshall: "1776 Hand Jive" by Jim Marshall. Used by permission of author.

Los Angeles County Museum of Art: "A Picture of Freedom" cover (#2 request) for "Detail from Cotton Pickers" by Homer. For reprint of detail (The Cotton Pickers, 1876 by Winslow Homer) from cover of Patricia C. McKissack, A Picture of Freedom; The Diary of Clotee, A Slave Girl. (New York: Scholastic Inc., 1997). Los Angeles County Museum of Art, Acquisition made possible through Museum Trustees: Robert O. Anderson, R. Stanton Avery, B. Gerald Cantor, Edward W. Carter, Justin Dart, Charles E. Ducommun, Camilla Chandler Frost, Julian Ganz, Jr., Dr. Armand Hammer, Harry Lenart, Dr. Franklin D. Murphy, Joan Palevsky, Richard E. Sherwood, Maynard J. Toll, and Hall B. Wallis. Courtesy of the Los Angeles County Museum of Art.

Ludlow Music, Inc.: "This Land Is Your Land" text. Words and Music by Woody Guthrie. TRO © Copyright 1956 (Renewed) 1958 (Renewed) 1970 (Renewed) Ludlow Music, Inc., New York, NY. Used by Permission.

Music Sales Corporation (ASCAP): "In My Old San Juan" (English translation of En mi viejo San Juan) adapted from En Mi Viejo San Juan words and Music by Noel Estrada. Copyright © 1965 (Renewed) by Onyx Music Sales Corporation. All rights administered by Music Sales Corporation (ASCAP). International Copyright Secured. All Rights Reserved. Reprinted by Permission.

Patricia C. McKissack: "Paul Laurence Dunbar" cover art. Used by permission. Penguin Putnam Inc.: "Flossie and the Fox" illustration from Flossie and the Fox by Patricia C. McKissack and pictures by Rachel Isadora. Pictures copyright © 1986 Rachel Isadora. All rights reserved. Used by permission of Dial Books for Young Readers, an imprint of Penguin Putnam Books for Young Readers, a division of Penguin Putnam Inc.

Random House, Inc.: "The Dark-Thirty" cover illustration from The Dark-Thirty by Patricia McKissack and illustrated by Brian Pinkney. Cover copyright © 1992 by Brian Pinkney. Used by permission of Alfred A. Knopf, an imprint of Random House Children's Books, a division of Random House, Inc. "Mirandy and Brother Wind" from Mirandy and Brother Wind by Patricia C. McKissack and illustrated by Jerry Pinkney. Cover illustration by Jerry Pinkney. Cover copyright © 1988 by Jerry Pinkney. Illustrations copyright © 1988 by Jerry Pinkney. Used by permission of Alfred A.

Knopf, an imprint of Random House Children's Books, a division of Random House, Inc. "My People" from The Collection Poems of Langston Hughes by Langston Hughes. Copyright © 1994 by The Estate of Langston Hughes. Used by permission of Alfred A. Knoph, a division of Random House, Inc.

Richard C. Owen Publishers, Inc.: Patricia McKissack Photo from Can You Imagine by Patricia McKissack. Used by permission.

Scholastic Inc.: "Ben Franklin..." adapted from Famous Americans: 22 Short Plays for the Classroom compiled and edited by Liza Schafer. Copyright © 1994 by Scholastic Inc. Published by Scholastic Professional Books, a division of Scholastic Inc. "The Bunyans" adapted from The Bunyans by Audrey Wood. Copyright © 1996 by Audrey Wood. Published by the Blue Sky Press, an imprint of Scholastic Inc. Reproduced with permission. "Coming to America" adapted from Coming to America by Betsy Maestro. Copyright © 1996 by Betsy Maestro. Reproduced by permission of Scholastic Inc. "George Washington..." adapted from George Washington: A Picture Book Biography by James Cross Giblin and illustrated by Michael Dooling. Text copyright © 1992 by James Cross Giblin. Illustrations copyright © 1992 by Michael Dooling. Reprinted by permission of Scholastic Inc. "A Picture of Freedom" cover (#1 request). All used by permission of Scholastic Inc.

Shen's Books: "Piecing Earth and Sky Together" Copyright © 2001. Used by permission of Shen's Books, Fremont, California.

Simon & Schuster Children's Publishing Division: "Goin' Someplace Special" from "Goin' Someplace Special." Text copyright © 2001 by Patricia C. McKissack. Illustrations copyright © 2001 by Jerry Pinkney. Reprinted with permission of Atheneum Books for Young Readers, Simon & Schuster Children's Publishing Division. All rights reserved.

Walker & Co.: "Grandma's Records" by Eric Velasquez. Copyright © 2001 by Eric Velasquez.

The Watts Publishing Group Limited: "Moving" from First Starts: Moving. First published in the UK by Franklin Watts in 1994, a division of The Watts Publishing Group Limited, 96 Leonard Street, London EC2A 4XD.

Photographs:

Affordable Stock: p274 (arch).

Alexander Farquharson: p 498 (John Cabot).

AllSport: p123 (Mullins, Phil Cole), p168 (Cobisi & De Pra, Clive Brunskill/Getty Images).

Carl Angel: p45 (Angel family).

AP/Wide World Photos: p478 (Chinatown), p481 (Albright, Estefan and Pei).

Artville: p 494 (garden), p497 (city lights).

Art Resource: p469 ("Plantation on the Mississippi", Scala/Art Resource, NY).

Batista Moon Studio: p493 (ancestor).

BearClover: p281 (El Capitan, JR Dunster/BearClover.net).

Ka Botzis: p502 (nervous system diagram)

Brad Perks PC Image Network: p280 (Rodeo Beach, Brad Perks).

Sue Carlson: p495 (map).

The State Historical Society Library of Colorado: p504 (settlers)

Corbis: p5 (erupting, James A. Sugar), p6 (shadow, Richard Smith), p7 (Washington & Lafayette, Bettmann), p7 (Declaration of Independence, Joseph Sohm), p11 (family, Lewis Wickes Hines), p14 (couple; R, Paul Barton), p14 (grandfather, Lindsay Hebberd), p14, (grandmother, Jack Fields), p14 (grandfather, Catherine Karnow) p14 (grandfather, Jack Fields), p14 (grandfather,

Michael S. Yamashita), p15 (ceremony, Catherine Karnow), p19 (brownstones, Lee Snider), p41 (aunt, Wally McNamee), p41 (parents, Michael Keller), p62 (erupting, James A. Sugar), p64 (newspapers, Philip Bailey), p65 (road, B.S.P.I.), p65 (road, Roger Ressmeyer), p92 (San Andreas fault, Lloyd Cluff), p116 (damage, Roger Ressmeyer), p120 (shadow, Richard Smith), p159 (girl, Duomo), p182 (Washington and Lafayette, Bettmann), p182 (Declaration of Independence, Joseph Sohm), p184 (candle making, Wolfgang Kaehler), p184 (spinning yarn, Catherine Karnow), p184 (cooking, Bettmann), p184 (furniture making, Raymond Gehman), p184 (minutemen, Wally McNamee), p185 (all), p189 (Old South Meeting House, Kevin Fleming), p260 (west coast, Jan Butchofsky-Houser), p260 (waterfall, Stuart Westmorland), p261 and p277 (Aspen, Craig Aurness), p261 (Manhattan, Joseph Sohm; ChromoSohm Inc.), p264 (stalagmites, David Muench), p265 (Mammoth Cave, David Muench), p267 (postcard, Bill Rosco), p269 (postcard, Bob Winsett), p272 (Thor's Hammer, Darrell Gulin), p277 (kayaking, Paul A. Souders), p277 (dunes, Bill Ross), p278, p281 (west coast, Jan Butchofsky-Houser), p278, p279, p280, and p281 (people hiking, Bob Winsett), p278, p279, p280, and p281 (Mammoth Cave), p370 (all, Bettmann), p371 (Rosa Parks, Bettmann), p371and p429 (Martin Luther King, Jr., Bettmann), p371 (President Johnson, Bettmann), p384 (Martin Luther King, Jr., Flip Schulke), p385 (Freedom Hall, David Houser), p416 (Paul Lawrence Dunbar), p418 (Boone Hall, Joseph Sohm), p437 (Mariachi band, David Seawell), p437 (Guatemalan fabric, Dave G Houser), p437 (church, Richard Cummings), p437 (lion dancer, Phil Schermiester), p437 (tango dancers, Terry Vine), p464, p480, and p482 (Ellis Island, Felix Zaska) p465 (family, Lewis Wicke Hines), p470 (New York, Bettmann), p470 (immigrants, Bettmann), p471 (Oregon Trail, Bettmann), p472 (workers, Bettmann), p473 (plowing, Michael Maslan Historic Photograph), p473 and p484 (child worker), p473 (workers), p474 (immigrants), p475 (Statue of Liberty by Francis Hopkinson, Christie's Images), p476 (examination, Bettmann), p477 (immigrants, Bettmann), p477 and p484 (immigrants), p479 (ferry boat), p481 (Sosa, Duomo), p484, p485, and p490 (family, Lewis Wickes Hine), p484, p485 (flag, Felix Zaska), p484 (immigrants, Bettmann), p488 (girl, Brian A. Vikander), p504 (slaves), p 493 (concert, David Turnley), p494 (migrant camp, Stephanie Maze), p494 (canyon, David Muench), p494 (party, Tom & Dee Ann McCarthy), p497 (dune), p498 (fault, Craig Aurness), p497 (pottery, Wolfgang Kaehler), p498 (settlers, Museum of History & Industry), p500 (Salvadoran immigrants), p500 (crossing the Delaware), p504 (U.S. Congress, Bettmann), p500 (ballerina, Tom Stewart), p502 (ballerina, Dennis Degnan), p502 (patriots, Ariel Skelley); p501 (picking up trash, Mug Shots), p501(harvest, Morton Beebe); p504 (Big Sur, Owaki-Kulla), p506 (Niagra Falls, Joseph Sohm, ChromoSohm Inc.), p505 (soldiers, Kevin Fleming).

Corbis Royalty Free: p15 (Hanukkah), p15 (family), p166 (discus thrower), p437 (Mosque/fabric), p437 (pueblo), p488 (girl).

Corel: p4 and p13 (sunflowers), p14 (girl & couple), p15 (parent & child, playing instrument), p89 (tiger), p64 (dam, coal mine, farm, & well), p93 (magnifying glass, rock & dirt), p106 (eruption), p108 (glacier), p123 (doctor), p160 (athlete), p250 (Washington), p256 (parks, p257 (cave, glacier, river, sandbar, and dune), p260 (dune, Hawaii, and cliffs), p268 (Rockies), p276 (cliffs), p278, p279, p280, and p281 (mountains), p350 (power plant), p437, (Hula dancer), p462 (field), p480 (flags), p488 (boys).

DigitalStock: p498 (geyser), p500 (lightning)

Digital Studios: p495 (U.S. Constitution).

DigitalVision: p64 (Lamp).

Doug Bekke: p494 (circuit diagram), p497 (fault diagram), p499 (gravity diagram).

Erwin Gorostiza: p217 (candle).

John Paul Endress: p503 (musical trio).

EyeWire: p15 (eye color), p64 (turbines),

508

p405 (singer, EyeWire/Getty Images).

Faith Ringgold: p12 (The American Collection 1997 #8 Cotton Fields, Sunflowers, Blackbirds & Quilting Bee, ©1997, Faith Ringgold).

Geri Engberg: p479 (mural, Geri Engberg).

Getty Images: p6 and p180 (girl, David Madison), p8 (rocks, James Randklev), p8 (lighthouse, Colin Molyneux), p9 (plug and socket, Benjamin Shearn), p13 (denim texture), p14 (couple, Barbara Penpyar), p14 (grandmother and grandfather), p15 (painting, Bill Losh), p15 (eye color/hair color), p40 (grandma, Mark Pokempner), p40 (sugar cane), p42 (family), p64 (plug in socket, light switch, wind turbines, and lamp), p64 (plastic bottles) p94 (astronaut and spacescape), p96 (background), p98 (earthscape), p109 (paper mill), p92 (notebook, Carl Glover), p104 (fault, James Balog), p105 (building, Robert Yager), p107 (Mt. St. Helens, InterNetwork Media), p109 (trash, Werner Otto), p110 (recycling, David Young-Wolff), p111, p112, and p114 (galaxy and earth), p121 (soccer, Arthur Tilley), p121 (players, David Madison), p158 (park, Patti McConville), p160, p174 (gymnast, Michael Dunning), p162 (girl, Jim Cummins), p167 (girl, David Madison), p170 (athlete, Lori Adamski Peek), p172 (boy, Erin Patrice O'Brien), p172 (angry girl, Andersen Ross), p172 (eyes closed, Anne Menke), p173 (dancer, Stephen Wilkes), p250 (Washington Monument), p254 (rocks, James Randklev), p255 (lighthouse, Colin Molyneux), p260 (Niagra Falls, Cosmo Condina), p260 (Lake Sawtooth, Idaho), p260 (Iditarod, Paul Souder), p260 (cave, Demetrio Carrasco), p261 and p271 (deer, Daniel J. Cox), p262 (American Falls, PhotoDisc), p263, p278, p279, p280, and p281 (Horseshoe falls, Doug Armand), p263 (Yosemite Falls, Gerald French), p266 (dunes, Moritz Steiger), p270 (Old Faithful, Greg Probst), p271 (Mt. St. Helens, Photodisc), p272 (Grand Canyon; S. Rim, James Randklev), p274 (Big Sur, PhotoDisc), p277 (rafting, John Beatty), p310 (Yosemite Falls, Gerald French), p312 (plug and socket, Benjamin Shearn), p350 and p357 (wind turbines, Lester Lefkowitz), p405 (singer), p437 (Caribbean band, Oliver Benn, p462 (Tamiko, Tony Anderson), p498 (American flag, PhotoDisc), p493 (soccer field, Simon Bruty/Stone), p494 (coastline, Richard Price/Taxi), p496 (snowy mountains, Guido Alberto Rossi/The Image Bank), p496 (great grandparents, Fox Photos/Hulton Archive), p496 (mountain climbers, Alexander Stewart/The Image Bank), p497 (giant redwoods, V.C.L./Taxi), p499 (parade, Getty News), p499 (strawberry harvest, Bruce Forster/Stone), p502 (swimmer, Ulli Seer/Stone), p502 (ice skaters, Jake Martin/Allsport Concepts), p503 (Central Park, Patti McConville/The Image Bank); p505 (trapeze artist, David Madison/Stone).

GoodThings, Inc: p435 (postcard, Cole).

Hung Liu: p46 (Grandma Hung Liu, courtesyof Hung Liu).

Hulton Archive: p184 (King George III), p249 (Samuel Adam), p425 (Langston Hughes), p474, p476, p479, p485 (Ellis Island).

Image Bank: p172 (Surprised girl, Benelux Press/ IndexStock Imagery).

Image State: p506 (volcano).

Index Stock Imagery: p184 (growing crop, Kindra Clineff), p172 (surprised girl, Benelux Press), p478 (immigrants arrive at airport, ASAP Ltd.).

Jessie Harris: p256 (Yellowstone National Park).

JoeSam: p49 (Maids).

Dr. John Crossley: p256 (Bryce Canyon, Dr. John Crossley), p273 (Bryce Canyon, Dr. John Crossley), p278 (Bryce Canyon, Dr. John Crossley).

Jon Pascal: p269 (hiker on Cutbank Pass).

Ken Karp Photography: p7 (girl), p9 (boy at desk), p11 and p434 (kids painting), p41and p342 (boy`), p345 (all photos pp344, 349, 355, 356, 358, 359 (all photos) p366

(boy), p182 (girl), p408 (kids), p409 (girls).

Lawrence Parent: p265 (Ruins of Karnack with tourist, Lawrence Parent).

Library of Congress: p371 (Civil Rights Act of 19640, p473 (apricot packing).

Lunar Planetary: p495 (earth's core), p496 (earth's core), p501 (inspired poem).

Masterfile: p8 (Bryce Canyon), 273 (Bryce Canyon), p40 (great-grand dad, Puzant Apkai).

Paul Mirocha: p501 (Appalachian Mountains).

Monterey Museum of Art: p466 "Awaiting Montezuma" by Jules Tavernier ©1872, courtesy of Betty Hoag McGlynn).

NASA: p5 (Earth), p95(Earth).

Nashville Public Library: p413 and p426 (Nashville Public Library).

National Museum of African Art: p437 (Nigerian fabric, Franko Khoury).

National Park Service: p187 ("The Signing of the Constitution" by Rossiter, Courtesy the National Historical Park).

New Century Graphics: p497 (carnations in colored water), p505 (baskets)

North Wind Archive: p187 (fight at Concord bridge), p502 (19th century pioneers)

NREL Photographic Exchange: p350 (steam power).

Object Gear: p501 (magnet & objects)

Patricia McKissack: p10 (family photos), p368 (Patricia), p410 (teaching), p410 (as a child), p411 (Fred and Patricia), p412 (teaching), p415 (Fred), p426 (Fred), p415 and p426 (Patricia), p416 (house), p419 (at table), p420 (as a child), p421 (house), p422 (showing book), p427 (with book).

Photo Researchers, Inc.: p123 (penicillin, Scott Camazine), p256 (Mammoth Cave, Jeff Greenberg), p265 (Frozen Niagra, Jeff Greenberg), p496 (winner, Gerard Vandystadt), p505 (igloo, George Holton).

PhotoDisc: p15 (Parent and child), p40 (sugar cane field, PhotoDisc), p42 (family), p64 (socket, PhotoDisc), p250 (Washington Monument), p262 (Niagra Falls/ American Falls/NY State side, PhotoDisc), p274 (Big Sur, Photodisc), p436 (Statue of Liberty), p493 (album cover), p493 (family), p496 (scientist), p498 (eating), p499 (grandma and quilt), p500 (Great Plains), p504 (Caucasian family).

PhotoEdit: p493 (camping, Nancy Sheehan), p494 (flat tire, Michelle Bridwell), p496 (Mexican dancers), p501 (sewing, David Young-Wolff), p496 (meeting, Dana White), p496 (relative, John Neubauer), p497 (girl and dad), p503 (skaters, Myrleen Ferguson), p498 (ship, Deborah Davis), p499 (government, Gary Spencer), p499 (band, Jonathan Nourok), p500 (stove, Jeff Greenberg), p501 (river, Cathy Melloan), p503 (race, Dennis MacDonald).

PhotoSpin: p33 (American Flag, PhotoSpin), p498 (American Flag, PhotoSpin).

PictureQuest: p8 and p254 (seagul, Stockbyte), p13 (silk, Philip Coblentz/Brand X), p123 (immunizing, Image Source/ electraVision), p275 (Big Sur post card, Craig Lovell/Stock Connection), p308 (El Capitan Yosemite, Galen Rowell/ Mountain Light/ Stock Connection), p463 (Shante, SWP, Inc./ Brand X Pictures), p503 (debate, Rob Nelson Black Star Publishing).

Roni Shepherd: p493 (jazz band), p494 (ball in tree) p495 (mother), p495 (compromise), p495 (frog contest), p500 (Washington), p501 (skeleton), p501 (moving on), p502 (packing), p503 (playing records), p505 (dishes), p505 (stitching), p505 (traitor), p506 (welcoming).

Sandra T. Sevigny: p494 (hand bones), p502 (arm muscle), p504 (skeleton).

Sentinel & Enterprise: p499 (qccj, Amanda Bicknell).

Stockbyte: p505 (roller blade).

Tony Stone: p500 (mountains, Paul Chesley).

SuperStock, Inc.: p276 (sunrise, GoodSoot), p437 (band, Anggelo Caavalli/SuperStock).

Uniphoto: p495 (U.S. Congress, Mark Reinstein), p495 (teachers, Frank Siteman), p496 (mountain climber, James Kay).

United States Geological Society: p65 (before and after, Harry Gliken/ USGS).

W.L. McCoy: p265 (pit, W.L. McCoy).

Wild Planet Toys: pp28, 364 (Shahid Minapara, Courtesy Wild Planet Toys; SF, CA), pp28, 364 (light hand, Courtesy Wild Planet Toys; SF, CA).

Liz Garza Williams: p498 (dancer), p496 (relative today), p502 (performance), p503 (looking at photo), p503 (winner).

Whatcom Museum of History and Art: p504 (settlers/log cabin).

Wonderfile: p171 (muscles), p256 (dunes, Mike Dobel), p256 (Big Sur, Bill Brooks), p257 (Monument Valley and beach, Bill Brooks).

Yoshi Miyake: p499 (dogs), p504 (respect).

Author and Illustrator Photos:

p46 (Mitchell Kearny), p49 (Michael Jang), p49 (Vern Evans), p111 (Gail Gibbons), p151(John Godt), p211 (Diane Stanley), p245 (James Cross Giblin), p303 (Audrey Wood), p335 (Joan Bransfield Graham), p357 (Ken Karp), p401 (Myles C. Pinkney), p455 (Randy Vaughn-Dotta), p482 (Gale Zucker).

Illustrations:

JoLynn Alcorn: p160 (center), pp162 (heart and lungs), p163, p164–165, p166 (left), p167 (right), p169, p171, p173 (circulatory system); **Norman Bendell:** pp258–259, BSS: p436, p479; **Annie Bissett:** p186, p260 (center, detail), p256, p263, p265, p267, pp268–269, p271, p273, p275, p287, p375, p441, p464, p475; **Nan Brooks:** p58; **Neverne Covington:** p430; **Mike Dammer:** p315, pp342–343, p344 (center), pp348–349, pp350–351, pp352–353, p354, p357, p360 (border); **Julie Dowling:** pp124–125; **Byron Gin:** pp334–335; **Scott Goto:** p9, pp220–221, pp318–333, pp336–337, pp338–339 (background); **S&J Harris:** p122, p159 (skeletal system); **Philip Howe:** pp342–343 (background); **Katya Kregnina:** pp66–67; **Dennis Lyatt:** pp212–213; **Geoffrey McCormack:** p426 (map), p414; **Kathleen McKeehan:** p267; **John Patrick:** pp284–285; **Rodica Prato:** p468, p471; **Sebastian Quigley:** p96; **Jesse Reisch:** pp16–17; **Suling Wang:** pp438–439; **Sally Wern Comport:** pp316–317; **Fred Willingham:** p372; **Elizabeth Wolf:** p443 (map).

The Avenues Development Team

Hampton-Brown extends special thanks to those who contributed so much to the creation of the Grade 3, 4, and 5 Pupil Editions.

Editorial: Janine Boylan, Julie Cason, Lisa Cittadino, Shirleyann Costigan, Phyllis Edwards, Roseann Erwin, Nadine Guarrera, Margot Hanis, Fredrick Ignacio, Cynthia Keith, Phillip Kennedy, Tiina Kurvi, Sheron Long, S. Michele McFadden, Amy Ostenso, Heather Peacock, Sharon Ursino, and Cullen Wojcik.

Design and Production: Renae Arcinas, Katherine A. Butler, Christy Caldwell, Jen Coppens, Sherry Corley , Jeri Gibson , Terry Harmon, Rick Holcomb, Connie McPhedran, Michael Moore, Robert Myles, Russ Nemec, Marian O'Neal, Anthony Paular, Cathy Revers, Augustine Rivera, Debbie Saxton, DJ Simison, Curtis Spitler, Jonni Stains, Debbie Swisher, Vicki Vandeventer, Elvin (JR) Walker, and Bill Smith Studios

Permissions: Barbara Mathewson